JAPANESE HORROR CINEMA

Traditions in World Cinema

General Editor
Steven Jay Schneider (New York University)

Associate Editors
Linda Badley (Middle Tennessee State University)
R. Barton Palmer (Clemson University)

Titles in the series include:

Traditions in World Cinema
by Linda Badley, R. Barton Palmer and Steven Jay Schneider (eds)
0 7486 1862 7 (hardback)
0 7486 1863 5 (paperback)

Japanese Horror Cinema
by Jay McRoy (ed.)
0 7486 1994 1 (hardback)
0 7486 1995 X (paperback)

Forthcoming titles include:

New-Punk Cinema
by Nicholas Rombes (ed.)
0 7486 2034 6 (hardback)
0 7486 2035 4 (paperback)

Italian Neorealist Cinema
by Peter Bondanella
0 7486 1978 X (hardback)
0 7486 1979 8 (paperback)

African Filmmaking: North and South of the Sahara
by Roy Armes
0 7486 2123 7 (hardback)
0 7486 2124 5 (paperback)

The Italian Sword-and-Sandal Film
by Frank Burke
0 7486 1983 6 (hardback)
0 7486 1984 4 (paperback)

Czech and Slovak Cinema: Theme and Tradition
by Peter Hames
0 7486 2081 8 (hardback)
0 7486 2082 6 (paperback)

JAPANESE HORROR CINEMA

Edited by
Jay McRoy

EDINBURGH UNIVERSITY PRESS

© in this edition Edinburgh University Press, 2005
© in the individual contributions is retained by the authors

Edinburgh University Press Ltd
22 George Square, Edinburgh

Reprinted 2006

Typeset in Sabon by
Hewer Text Ltd, Edinburgh, and
printed and bound in Great Britain by
The Cromwell Press, Trowbridge

A CIP record for this book is available from the British Library

ISBN 0 7486 1994 1 (hardback)
ISBN 0 7486 1995 X (paperback)

The right of the contributors
to be identified as authors of this work
has been asserted in accordance with
the Copyright, Designs and Patents Act 1988.

CONTENTS

ACKNOWLEDGEMENTS

This volume would not exist without the dedication, encouragement and enthusiasm of many people. I am particularly indebted to the book's contributors, whose critical and passionate engagements with Japanese horror cinema fill these pages. I likewise extend my gratitude to Sarah Edwards at Edinburgh University Press for her thoughtful guidance and support throughout the production of this text, and to Steven Jay Schneider, the Traditions in World Cinema series editor, for believing in this project from its inception and providing generous guidance, feedback and friendship. Special thanks also go to the following individuals for their criticism, advice and support: Mikita Brottman, Jyotsna Kapur, Mikel Koven, Linda Badley, R. Barton Palmer, Ira Livingston, Harmony Wu, the editors and staff at *Spectator: The University of California Journal of Film and Television Criticism*, my colleagues and students at the University of Wisconsin – Parkside, my friends and my wonderful family. Finally, following the example set by my heart, my deepest thanks go out to Amy Kushner: my partner, editor, muse, collaborator and dove.

PREFACE: JAPANESE HORROR CINEMA

Christopher Sharrett

The golden age of the American and British horror cinema faded, with many of the best political aspirations of commercial film, during the Reagan/Thatcher era, a not coincidental occurrence considering the many radical challenges the horror film's impulses made to dominant culture. Long considered a low-brow genre by the mainstream press and sectors of academe, the designation might be read today as a consequence of the adversarial relationship the horror film tended to have to the assumptions of western patriarchal capitalist civilisation. Since its glorious inception first in the Weimar cinema, then at Universal Studios, few genres have been as blunt in questioning notions of the monstrous Other, the nature of the family and other elements of received social wisdom as the horror film. As if a prelude to the activism of the 1960s, landmark films such as Hitchcock's *Psycho* (1960) and *The Birds* (1963) very consciously deconstructed the more suffocating features of bourgeois life, and society's tendency to find pleasure in the sacrificial scapegoating of so-called monsters who, at various levels of their being, raised the proposition that under current social and economic assumptions we are all monsters, and our civilisation a madhouse. All of this has sadly gone by. Distinguished works such as George Romero's zombie films, Tobe Hooper's *The Texas Chainsaw Massacre* (1974), Larry Cohen's *God Told Me To* (1976) and Wes Craven's *The Hills Have Eyes* (1977) have been replaced by hi-tech rollercoaster rides enforcing the old refrain that the horror film is merely a clever device for saying 'boo!' Important horror films of the past, such as Robert Wise's remarkable *The Haunting* (1963), have been subjected to indulgent, insulting remakes that strip away the original work's radical or contentious ideas, a fate, of course, not unique to horror cinema.

As so often happens in cultural history, a tradition's legacy has been inherited and amplified by another society. At this writing, Japan is without question producing works that are the legitimate heirs to *I Walked with a Zombie* (1943), *Night of the Demon* (1957), *The Crazies* (1973) and *Videodrome* (1983). Although I cannot pretend to have in any way mastered all developments of Japanese horror, I think I have sufficient knowledge to sense that, in its essential features, it has a relationship to its society similar to that of American horror in the post-Vietnam 1970s. The dominant tone of Japanese horror seems to be hysteria, propelled chiefly by Japan's mastery with a vengeance of industrial and post-industrial capitalism. This hysteria seems a legitimate response to the social environment the genre traces, especially given the absence, in the age of transnational capital, of effective forms of political resistance. Forbidden to rearm after the Allied victory in The Second World War, Japan instead seriously challenged the US at its own economic game, only to see the chickens come home to roost. Japan's ferocious capitalism created for it a spectre almost as large as the memory of the A-bomb, which now seems as half-suppressed in the nation's mainstream culture as the reality of capitalist life. That such knowledge is not totally suppressed is evident enough in the nation's genre films. Apocalypse waits at the margins of (or is integral to) so much Japanese horror.

Images of out-of-control madness, bloodshed and mass destruction are often connected quite blatantly by Japanese horror with corporate capitalism's assault on the very institutions and values its superstructure says it holds dear: the home, the family, the community, the sanctity of the individual life. While there is nothing especially ironic about the phenomenon, Japanese horror cinema's graphic portrayal of patriarchal capitalism's rampage is especially compelling within a society that has held sacred some positive, now rather residual, traditions.

Nakata's popular *Ringu* (1998), which owes a great deal to earlier phases of the Japanese *fantastique*, portrays the collision of traditional cultural myths (many centred on an exaggerated and hypocritical veneration of the female) with their perverse realisation in the post-industrial landscape. Tsukamoto's *Tetsuo* films, perhaps the most manic and hysterical of all Japanese horror, suggest humanity's physical and psychological inability to compete with the corporatised, hypertechnological present. These films, and Miike's *Audition* (2000) and *Visitor Q* (2001), are especially compelling for their implication that an older world, the one depicted in Ozu, can exist today only in vaguest memory, a situation that *Tokyo Story* (1953) so presciently foretold. Yet the real integrity of Miike and Tsukamoto is their sense that current horrors of Japanese mainstream life are rooted in the very traditions that the society so doggedly extolled, especially the veneration of the family and ancestry. Fukasaku Kinji's *Battle Royale* (2000), the genre's most uncompromised bloodbath, may be the Japanese cinema's postmodern equivalent of Goya's *Cronos Devouring His Children*. The film is an extraordinarily cunning remark on present 'survivor' culture, with its debased 'reality TV' and similar horrendous and commonplace cultural features extolling predatory values as the most laudable. The reactionary political situation of the new millennium, which is worldwide in scope and consequence, attempts to inculcate in young people the cruellest 'only the strong survive' values, a practice not seen since the late nineteenth century, but fully in play under neoliberal economics. *Battle Royale* is among the very few films of *any* current cinema to examine clearheadedly these assumptions, and in particular Japan's gruelling, earn-more-learn-more educational system that places schooling fully in service of the corporate world. The model owes a great deal to the business-driven US, a society that insists on 'practical' education for 'today's marketplace'. The Columbine High School shootings in the US, along with other acts of youth violence, while treated as monstrous aberrations by the US media, find profound and uncompromised understanding in Fukasaku's film. Fukasaku's sequel, *Battle Royale II: Requiem*, is an even more extraordinary (and very expansive) indictment of the current civilisation, both East and West, with a particular focus on the monstrous US-driven 'war on terrorism'. Coura-geously simulating the collapse of a World Trade Center-like pair of office towers in its prelude, *Battle Royale II* (2003) associates the young people of the first film with the 'terrorists' (that is, displaced and disaffected people) of the planet, as the discarded, regimented children of the first film declare war on the adult world. The rather amazing inclusion of footage of contemporary Afghanistan makes the association explicit. The film's send-up of popular action cinema drivel, especially *Saving Private Ryan* (1998), makes *Battle Royale II* a distinguished latter-day exemplar of the fantastic cinema as social and cultural commentary.

For all of its fascinations and challenges, Japanese horror must, of course, be approached critically. Some of it, including a few of its outstanding works, seem to project nihilism, a view that is a rejection of social transformation long embodied in the western horror film, the point being that this attitude has too long substituted for genuine radicalism. At its worst, Japanese horror offers a critique of dominant culture from the right, a recurrent, tired, and dangerous perspective all too common in postwar Hollywood cinema from *The Searchers* (1956) to *Fight Club* (1999). There also appears to be a neoconservative fear of the body in some Japanese horror similar to the *Hellraiser* (1987 et al.) series and likeminded films, whose frisson (passing, it seems, for a form of resistance) comes from a bizarre synthesis of urban neoprimitive cults with religious myth.

Jay McRoy's anthology seems to me comprehensive, covering the main concerns of Japanese horror so effectively that the book's centrality may constitute a difficult challenge for future critics. Herein is an indispensable introduction both to Japanese horror and the debate about its circumscribing culture that the genre has so thoughtfully joined.

January 2004

CONTRIBUTORS

Christopher Bolton is an Assistant Professor of Japanese language and literature in the Asian Studies Department at Williams College. His research interests centre on the modern period, particularly postwar and contemporary Japanese fiction and Japanese anime.

Philip Brophy is a film director (*Salt Saliva Sperm & Sweat* (1988) and *Body Melt* (1993)) and composer/sound-designer. He has published articles on horror, sound, anime and the body in international journals, including *The Wire*, *Screen*, *Real Time* and *Film Comment*, and he is director of the Cinesonic International Conference on Film Scores and Sound Design. Philip Brophy also lectures in Audio Visual Concepts and Soundtrack at RMIT Media Arts, Melbourne.

Ian Conrich is Senior Lecturer in Film Studies at the University of Surrey Roehampton, an Editor of *Journal of Popular British Cinema*, Chair of the New Zealand Studies Association, and Regional Coordinator for England for the Asian Cinema Studies Society. He writes for the BBC and *Sight and Sound*, is Guest Editor of a forthcoming special issue of *Post Script* on Australian and New Zealand cinema, and is co-editor of seven books, including *New Zealand – A Pastoral Paradise?* (Kakapo Books, 2000), *New Zealand Fictions: Literature and Film* (Kakapo Books, 2004), *The Technique of Terror: The Films of John Carpenter* (Flix Books, 2004) and the forthcoming *Horror Zone: The Cultural Experience of Contemporary Horror Cinema*. He has written extensively on the horror genre, with his work appearing in *A Handbook to Gothic Literature* (Macmillan, 1998), *The Modern Fantastic: The Films of David Cronenberg* (Flix Books, 2000), *The Horror Film Reader* (Limelight, 2001), *British Horror Cinema* (Routledge, 2001), *Cauchemars Americains: Fantastique et Horreur dans le Cinéma Moderne* (*Les Editions du CEFAL*, 2003), *The Horror Film* (Rutgers University Press, 2004) and *Horror International: World Horror Cinema* (forthcoming from Wayne State University Press).

Gareth Evans received his MA degree in Scriptwriting at the University of Glamorgan, UK. He has directed several short films and runs the website *JPREVIEW: Reviews and News of Japanese Cinema* (www.jpreview.com), an excellent resource for fans of Japanese horror cinema.

Ruth Goldberg is a member of the faculty at SUNY – Empire State College, where she teaches film history with an emphasis on the subjects of horror film and Latin American film. She also teaches adult education courses at New York University School of Continuing and Professional Studies. She has conducted workshops at the Escuela Internacional de Cine e TV, San Antonio de los Banos, Cuba, and at El Taller Latino Americano/The Latin American Workshop in New York City. She is working on a book on the subject of disembodied hands in film.

Richard J. Hand has directed numerous plays while teaching theatre and the history of drama at the University of Glamorgan. He has written extensively on theatre, and his book, *Grand-Guignol: The French Theatre of Horror* was recently published by the University of Exeter Press.

Steffen Hantke has published essays on contemporary literature, popular culture and film. He serves on the editorial board of *Paradoxa* and as area chair for the Southwest/Texas Popular Culture and American Culture Association. He is the editor of an issue of *Paradoxa* on horror and of the anthology *Horror Film: Creating and Marketing Fear* (University Press of Mississippi, 2004). He currently teaches in the Cultural Studies programme at Sogang University, Seoul.

Matt Hills is the author of *Fan Cultures* (Routledge, 2002) and *The Pleasures of Horror* (Continuum, 2003), and is writing on the British horror-thriller writer Stephen Gallagher entitled, *Stephen Gallagher: From Dark Fantasy to Telefantasy* (forthcoming from Manchester University Press). Matt is co-editor of *Intensities: The Journal of Cult Media* (www.cult-media.com) and has recently contributed to the edited collections *Freud's Worst Nightmares* (ed. Steven J. Schneider, Cambridge University Press, 2004) and *Red Noise: Buffy the Vampire Slayer and Critical Television Studies* (eds Elana Levine and Lisa Parks, forthcoming from Duke University Press, 2004). He has also written for journals such as *Foundation – The International Review of Science Fiction, New Media and Society* and *The Velvet Light Trap*.

Frank Lafond is completing his doctorate in aesthetics at Lille University, France. The author of numerous essays on the horror genre and film noir, he is currently editing a book on the modern American horror film, as well as an annual journal entitled *Rendezvous avec la peur* (both for *les Editions du CEFAL*, Belgium).

Graham Lewis earned an MFA from the University of Arkansas in 1993. His fiction, criticism and cartoons have appeared in numerous publications, including *Asian Cult Cinema, The Quarterly, New American Writing* and *The New York Quarterly*. His first book of poems, *Forever Came Today*, was published in 2004 by Water Press and Media. He currently teaches composition and literature at Eastern Illinois University in Charleston, Illinois.

Jay McRoy is an Assistant Professor of English and Coordinator of the Film Studies Certificate Program at the University of Wisconsin – Parkside. He has written extensively on horror literature and film, appearing in numerous journals and edited collections, including *Kino Eye, The Journal of the Fantastic in the Arts, Paradoxa, Spectator, Traditions in World Cinema* (Edinburgh University Press, 2004) and *Post-Punk Cinema* (forthcoming from Edinburgh University Press, 2005), *Horror Film: Creating and Marketing Film* (University of Mississippi Press, 2004) and *Horror Zone: The Cultural Experience of Contemporary Horror Cinema* (forthcoming).

Christopher Sharrett is Professor of Communication and Film Studies at Seton Hall University. He is editor of *Crisis Cinema: The Apocalyptic Idea in Postmodern Narrative Film* (Maisonneuve Press, 1992) and *Mythologies of Violence in Postmodern Media* (Wayne State University Press, 1999). He has recently co-edited, with Barry Keith Grant, the second edition of *Planks of Reason: Essays on the Horror Film* (Scarecrow Press, 2004). He has written for *Cineaste, Persistence of Vision, Cineaction, Film Quarterly, Kino Eye* and numerous anthologies.

Eric White is Associate Professor of English, Comparative Literature and Humanities at the University of Colorado at Boulder. He is currently completing a book on the concept of metamorphosis in contemporary literature, science and the arts.

Tony Williams received his PhD from the University of Manchester in 1974. His research interests include: representations of Vietnam in literature and cinema; film and literature; classical Hollywood cinema; the writings of Jack London and James Jones; Hong Kong cinema; film genres; and naturalism and cinema. Professor of English and Area Head of Film Studies at Southern Illinois University at Carbondale, Williams is the author of numerous articles on film and cinematic horror. His book, *My Body and Soul: The Cinematic Vision of Robert Aldrich*, was published in 2004 by Scarecrow Press.

INTRODUCTION

Jay McRoy

Nightmare Japan

Horror cinema has long been a vital component of the Japanese film industry. During the politically and socially turbulent decades following the end of the US military occupation of Japan, directors like Honda Ishirô (*Gojira*, 1954; *Attack of the Mushroom People*, 1963), Shindo Keneto (*Onibaba*, 1964) and Tanaka Tokuzo (*Kwaidan*, 1964) created compelling cinematic visions that met with assorted critical and financial success both domestically and in foreign markets. Often informed by folklore and frequently indebted to the aesthetics of Japanese Noh and Kabuki theatre, these films engage a myriad of complex political, social and ecological anxieties, including – but by no means limited to – apprehensions over the impact of western cultural and military imperialism, and the struggle to establish a coherent and distinctly Japanese national identity. Over the last two decades, however, Japanese horror cinema has reached new levels of popularity, with representatives of the genre appearing everywhere from the programmes of prestigious international film festivals to the shelves of even the most overtly commercial video stores. Such visionary directors as Kurosawa Kiyoshi, Miike Takashi, Tsukamoto Shinya and Nakata Hideo have produced some of the world's most innovative, thought-provoking and visually arresting works of cinematic horror.

In 2003 alone, Japanese horror films not only reached increasingly wider audiences through satellite and cable television services like The Sundance Channel, but also received remarkably expansive critical and theoretical consideration in venues as diverse as academic journals dedicated to film and cultural studies, internationally distributed periodicals such as *Film*

Comment and *Asian Cult Cinema*, and a plethora of Internet sites committed to everything from informed cultural investigations of the genre to enthusiastic fan-based appreciation of the films and directors most frequently associated with this new 'new wave' of Japanese cinema. If one factors in the success of Gore Verbinski's *The Ring* (2002) and the recent Hollywood remake of Nakata's extraordinarily successful 1998 supernatural thriller *Ringu*, the influence of Japanese horror cinema becomes even more apparent. Indeed, with US remakes of Kurosawa's *Kaïro* (or *Pulse*, 2001) and Shimizu Takashi's *Ju-on* (2002), and a British remake of Nakata's *Chaos* (2001) looming on the horizon, it is quite likely that Japan's latest renaissance in filmic terror will continue to shape the direction of Japanese and world cinema for years to come.

SOME CURRENT TRENDS IN JAPANESE HORROR CINEMA

The essays that comprise this book examine the current national and international appeal of Japanese horror cinema, locating this 'explosion of [Japanese] horror films'[1] within what Jeffrey Jerome Cohen would describe as an 'intricate matrix of relations (social, cultural, and literary-historical)'[2] – a socio-political cauldron from which emerge constructions of monstrosity and horror, both progressive and reactionary. Of course, categorising films by genre (for instance, 'horror', 'science fiction', 'romance') is a perilous exercise, as is any attempt at providing an even remotely 'exhaustive' introduction to a cinematic genre or tradition, be it the Japanese horror film or the American western. In this sense, what many scholars understand as 'generic conventions' are, like the 'monstrous' embodiments that often populate those texts traditionally designated as 'horror' films, resistant to easy classification. Genres and subgenres, then, are slippery and frequently hybrid constructions that bleed through and across both related and seemingly unrelated filmic categories in a perpetual process of cross-pollenation.

In the case of Japanese horror cinema, representations of fear, horror and monstrosity can be evidenced in texts commonly assigned to such established, yet by no means impermeable, film traditions as *pinku eiga* (the 'pink' or 'softcore' film), *chanbara eiga* (the samurai film) and *yakuza eiga* (the Yakuza or 'gangster' film).[3] Similarly, prominent conventions from these established film cycles appear within the plots of Japanese horror films, though usually to a degree that renders them subordinate to the development of terror. A film like Kitamura Ryuhei's *Versus* (2000), for example, features dead Yakuza rising – zombie-like – to pursue the film's hero and love interest through a magical, albeit blood-drenched, forest. In addition, a horror film that contains elements of the *kaidan* or 'ghost story' tradition may also include features that audiences usually associate with apocalypse narratives or works of postmodern body horror. Hence the following outline of major trends in Japanese horror cinema offers a provisional (and always already conditional) guide to some of the genre's more common motifs. As such, it is my hope that it will not only reveal something of the breadth and diversity of the Japanese horror film over the last half decade, but also show how cinematic horror, in the words of Harmony Wu, 'offers a highly charged and usefully pliable framework for articulating diffuse, intangible and various anxieties'.[4]

The *kaidan/*'avenging spirit' film

Representative texts include: the *Ghost Cat* (*kaibyo*) films (Arai Ryohei et al., 1953–68); *Onibaba* (Shindo Keneto, 1964); *Kwaidan* (Tanaka Tokuzo, 1964); Kurosawa Kiyoshi's *Sweet Home* (1989); Nakata Hideo's *Ghost Actress* (1996), *Ringu* (1998) and *Dark Water* (2001); *Audition* (Miike Takashi, 1999); *Freeze Me* (Ishii Takashi, 2000).

Although a broader interpretation of the 'avenging spirit' motif incorporates films that rely less on the spiritual and the uncanny to unsettle viewers (for example, Miike's *Audition* or Ishii's *Freeze Me*), most cinematic texts designated as *kaidan* depict the incursion of supernatural forces into the realm of the ordinary, largely for the purposes of exacting revenge. To relate the tale of a 'wronged', primarily female entity returning to avenge herself upon those who harmed her, films like *Onibaba*, *Kwaidan* and *Ringu*, to name only a select few, draw on a multiplicity of religious traditions (Shintoism, Christianity, etc.), as well as the plot devices from traditional literature and theatre (including Noh theatre's *shunen-* [revenge-] and *shura-mono* [ghost-plays], and Kabuki theatre's tales of the supernatural [or *kaidan*]). Prominent features associated with the woman as 'avenging spirit' include long black hair and wide staring eyes (or, in some instances, just a single eye), as long black hair is often symbolic of feminine beauty and sensuality, and the image of the gazing female eye (or eyes) is frequently associated with vaginal imagery.[5] Furthermore, while valid arguments can be advanced that the haunted house occupies its own generic category, linking depictions of haunted houses (see, for example, Ohbayashi Nobuhiko's *House* (1982) and Kurosawa's *Sweet Home* (1989)) with the trope of the 'avenging spirit' seems particularly appropriate when one considers the dominant societal coding of the domestic realm as feminine.

Similarly, recent films such as *Audition* and *Freeze Me*, in a manner reminiscent of both *kaidan* and western rape-revenge films like *I Spit on Your Grave* (Meir Zarchi, 1978) and *Ms. 45* (Abel Ferrara, 1981), recall and, in the case of more contemporary offerings, articulate the complex, paradoxical and increasingly protean role of women within Japanese culture.

Depicted as 'both a source of danger to the norm and the very means of perpetuating that norm', such texts frequently position women as 'both symbolically dangerous . . . as well as the source of all that is Japanese';[6] through their vengeance, they simultaneously balance the scales of a perceived sense of justice, evoke fears of social change or the return of a 'monstrous past'[7] and expose the inequities inherent within a largely patriarchal culture. With recent transformations in the national economy begetting an influx of women in the workforce, as well as radical changes in both family dynamics and the conceptualisation of domestic labour, the 'avenging spirit' motif remains profoundly popular. As Susan Napier and Ann Allison posit, in a transforming national and international landscape informed by increasingly reimagined gender roles, Japanese men have 'apparently suffered their own form of identity crisis',[8] resulting in a panicked cultural reassessment in which contemporary manifestations of the 'avenging spirit' motif can be understood as symptomatic.

The *daikaiju eiga* (the giant monster film)

Representative texts include: Honda Ishirô's *Gojira* (1954) and its over twenty sequels, *Rodan* (1956), *Mothra* (1961), *Dogora the Space Monster* (1965); *Gamera* (Yuasa Noriaki, 1965) and its sequels; *Majin: Monster of Terror* (Yasuda Kimiyoshi, 1966) and its sequels.

Among the most immediately recognisable films in Japanese cinema, *daikaiju eiga* provide the perfect arena for the mobilisation of numerous social anxieties, not the least of which constellate about the dread of mass destruction, mutation and the environmental impact of pollution resulting from rapid industrialisation. As Japan remains the only nation to have suffered a direct atomic attack followed by decades of exposure to US military exercises (including atomic tests) in the Pacific, the aquatic and heavenward origin of these mutated creatures seems only appropriate, as does their intentional, and sometimes unintentional, annihilation of major urban centres. Tokyo in particular endures repeated destruction in these narratives, a motif that has received notable critical attention in texts ranging from Darrell William Davis's *Picturing Japaneseness – Monumental Style, National Identity, Japanese Films* to Mick Broderick's recent anthology, *Hibakusha Cinema: Hiroshima, Nagasaki and the Nuclear Image in Japanese Film*.

Additionally, the recurring portrayal of friction between scientists and the military – conflicts that often delay the monster's vanquishing – seems an ideal plot device for a cinematic tradition arising from a nation that is at once 'ground zero' for wide-scale industrial, technological and economic development, and the victim of perhaps history's most deadly union of science and warfare. In this simultaneous dread of atomic disaster and rapid industrialisation, *daikaiju eiga* resemble American giant monster films of the 1950s, like Gorden Douglas's *Them!* (1954) and Bert I. Gordon's *The Beginning of the End* (1957), in that both cinematic traditions depict a socio-cultural dread over what Mark Jancovich, in his book *Rational Fears: American Horror in the 1950s*, describes as 'processes of social development and [scientific, technological, and cultural] modernization'.[9] Additionally, even when openly marketed towards children and characterised as friendly protectors of the Japanese islands (a tropological shift suggestive of the notion that, despite their origins, monsters like Gojira and Gamera are profoundly products of Japanese popular culture), *daikaiju eiga* remain creative forums where very human fears over very human threats are projected onto fantastical physiognomies, battled, but, in the majority of cases, never fully destroyed.

The apocalyptic film

Representative texts include: *Last War* (Matsubayashi Sekai, 1961); Fukasaku Kinji's *Virus* (1980) and *Battle Royale* (2001); *Burst City* (Toshi Bakuretsu, 1982); *Uzumaki* (Higuchinsky, 2000); *Kaïro* (a.k.a. *Pulse*, Kurosawa Kiyoshi, 2001).

Akin to *daikaiju eiga* in their depiction of contemporary civilisation under assault or in ruins, these 'ominous yet captivating'[10] films recall a history of destruction and reconstruction that has resulted, both nationally and internationally, in the correlation of the Japanese social body with 'not only apocalypse, but the fact of its transcendence: the finite and, through it, the infinite'.[11] The events that bring about the 'end of the world as we know it' can be secular (for example, ushered in through technological means), religious (informed by any, or even a combination, of the multiple religions practised in Japan), or both. Fukasaku's dystopian bloodbath *Battle Royale*, for instance, places a class of students on a remote and heavily secured island, where they are compelled by the government to fight to the death in a highly publicised annual spectacle. But as Tony Williams notes in his contribution to this volume, the film is far more than a cross between *Lord of the Flies* (Peter Brook, 1963) and the American 'reality'-TV series, *Survivor* (2001–), and the physical and philosophical struggle between the students becomes a frightening and starkly pessimistic metaphor for Japanese social and political concerns at the dawn of the new century.

With its final injunction to 'run', *Battle Royale* does offer a razor-thin sliver of hope as the film comes to a close; however, most apocalyptic narratives offer a somewhat more explicit implication that 'the end' is, perhaps, only a new beginning. The anime series *Neon Genesis: Evangelion* (1995–6), for example, merges the destructive power of technology with a multi-faceted composite of concepts harvested from numerous faiths in its futuristic account of global death and regeneration. Likewise, Kurosawa's *Kaïro* combines the technological and paranormal to craft a narrative with an eerily cataclysmic finale infused with threat and promise. Of the theme of apocalypse in his work, the director notes: 'In . . . my films . . . you see cities destroyed, and perhaps even hints that the end of civilization is near. Many people construe those images and ideas as negative and despairing, but I actually see them as just the opposite – as the possibility of starting again with nothing; as the beginning of hope.'[12]

The techno-/body-horror film

Representative texts include: *Attack of the Mushroom People* (Honda Ishiro, 1963); *Horror of a Malformed Man* (Ishii Teruo, 1972); *Death Powder* (Izumiya Shigeru, 1986); Fukui Shozin's *Pinnochio 964* (1992) and *Rubber's Lover* (1997); Tsukamoto Shinya's *Tetsuo: The Iron Man* (1990), *Tetsuo II: Body Hammer* (1991) and *Adventures of Electric Rod Boy* (1995).

Like the many texts that comprise the apocalypse genre and *kaiju eiga*, 'techno-/body-horror' films literalise the darker side of a process of nation-wide industrialisation largely orchestrated as a result of, and in direct response to, western military and cultural imperialism. As horror films, they contribute to a discourse of boundary violation and body invasion, graphically enacting, in the process, perhaps the most dreadful apocalypse of all – the perpetual intimate apocalypse of the human body revealed not as a consolidated and impregnable citadel, but as a flexible assemblage that disallows for illusions of corporeal integrity or of the sovereignty of the human form. In their focus on issues of 'biological privation, technological instrumentality, and the loss of biological control',[13] these works closely resemble what Eugene Thacker describes as 'biohorror', a union of 'futuristic dystopia produced through science and technology' and 'the violent monstrosities that manifest themselves within the human body'.[14]

As scholars like Andrew Tudor, Philip Brophy, and Kelly Hurley have illustrated, works of postmodern body horror – with their representations of 'the human body defamiliarized, rendered other'[15] – constitute a significant amount of contemporary horror cinema. Given that these themes of corporeal disintegration and the fusion of the organic with the mechanical within pervade some of the most influential works of Western horror cinema by maverick directors like David Cronenberg, David Lynch and Clive Barker, it should come as little surprise that works like Tsukamoto's *Tetsuo: The Iron Man* and *Tetsuo II: Body Hammer* have found avid and devout audiences worldwide. No matter how well these texts seem to travel, however, one should not lose sight of the films' cultural specificity. As Sharalyn Orbaugh reminds us, the Japanese cyborg differs from its western counterpart in that the 'other'-ing of the Japanese corporeal and social body by 'Western hegemonic discourse allows for an exploration of the hybrid, monstrous, cyborg subject from a sympathetic, interior point of view rarely found' in North American and European 'cultural products'.[16] Thus accompanying the horror of the physical body rendered/revealed as indiscrete in its multifarious hybridy is the notion of the Japanese social body as 'monstrous' both to itself and to an orientalist western imagination.

The torture film

Representative texts include: Ishii Teruo's *Joys of Torture* (1965), *Hell's Tattooers* (1969) and *Oxen Split Torture* (1969); *Beautiful Girl Hunter* (Suzuki Norifumi, 1979); *Guts of a Beauty* (Sato Toshio, 1986); *Bloody Fragments on a White Wall* (Hashimoto Izo, 1989); *Legend of the Overfiend* (*Urotsukidoji*, Takayama Tokugawa Onna, 1989); the *Guinea Pig* series (eight episodes, Satoru Ogura et al., 1985–93).

Often cited as some of world cinema's most notorious motion pictures, the torture genre, long popular in Japan, has become increasingly attractive to an ever-wider array of western horror fans hungry for films that push the portrayal of violence and gore to new extremes. Influenced by *chanbara eiga* (samurai film) and *pinku eiga* (soft-core erotic film), the scenes of rape and ritualised brutality that infuse many of these narratives convey multiple aesthetic traditions and social concerns. The often deliberate and almost ceremonial evisceration of the (often eroticised) female body, for instance, is reminiscent of Japanese rituals like *hara-kiri*, 'an ancient act in which female votives would offer up the "flower" of their entrails and blood by a self-inflicted knife wound',[17] while the apportioning of gender roles addresses concerns about the stability of traditional sex- and, by extension, class-based divisions of labour.

This latter point is particularly evidenced when one recognises that it is primarily the men in these productions that do the abusing; correspondingly, it is largely women who prove the recipients of phallic assault via rape and other assorted forms of corporeal violation. Far and away the most infamous torture films, however, are those that comprise the *Guinea Pig* series. Primarily shot on video, and with unknown – and often disguised – actors cast in major roles, these texts, at times, resemble documentaries. As remarkable exercises in special effects technology, guerilla-style editing and gut-wrenching *mise-en-scène*, the look and feel of these films differ radically from virtually any work of western horror cinema, an aesthetic that prompted the American actor Charlie Sheen to mistake an episode of the series (Hino Hideshi's *The Flower of Flesh and Blood*, 1985) for an actual snuff film.[18] Merging the aesthetics of *cinema vérité* and *cinema vomitif*,[19] these films are by turns sadistic and contemplative, gruesome and elegiac. Each text is its own 'flower of flesh and blood', sprouting forth and blooming its bloodiest shade of red where traditional conceptions and emerging notions of gender, class and nation intersect.

Serial killers and doves

Two final noteworthy (but comparatively minor) subgenres within Japanese horror cinema include, on the one hand, a collection of bleak, nihilistic films that depict what Thomas Weisser and Yuko Mihara Weisser describe as '*dove style violence*',[20] and on the other, the serial killer film. The former, a filmic phenomenon best illustrated by Matsumura Katsuya's dark and controversial *All Night Long* trilogy (*All Night Long*, 1992; *All Night Long 2: Atrocity*, 1995; *All Night Long 3: The Final Chapter*, 1996), are studies in postmodern alienation taken to its direst terminus: the affect-less, almost Darwinian destruction of the weak by the strong. The term 'dove style violence' stems directly from this expression of detached cruelty and refers to the practice of 'certain species of bird; when a flock member is *different* or weaker, the others peck at it dispassionately until it's dead'.[21] Focusing primarily on the lives of desperate, often jaded young people who perpetrate acts of deliberate cruelty upon those whose very isolation, timidity and frail physiques render them least capable of marshalling a defence, these films present viewers with protagonists that seemingly embody the most destructive and extreme consequences of scholastic competition, economic recession and recent shifts in gender dynamics.

Although a careful viewer can locate antecedents within the gory torture film tradition, the serial killer subgenre – as represented by suspenseful and complex narratives like Kurosawa's *Cure* (1999), Iida George's *Another Heaven* (2000) and Iishi Sogo's *Angel Dust* (2002) – is a relatively late development in Japanese horror cinema. Generally focusing on the complex relationship between a detective/law officer and her/his psychotic yet disquietingly comparable adversary, these films not only resemble American thrillers like *Manhunter* (Michael Mann, 1986), *Silence of the Lambs* (Jonathan Demme, 1991) and *Se7en* (David Fincher, 1995), but also provide, through the figure of the serial killer, a distinctly human body upon which Japanese film-makers, like their North American and European counterparts, may 'encode, deliberately or otherwise, many . . . cultural phobias in their polysemous narrative representation in . . . film'.[22] Curiously, in a trend that seemingly separates Japanese serial murder films from their western cousins, several of the genre's more prominent texts interweave the themes of murder and mesmerism (for example, *Cure*, *Saimin* (Ochiai Masayuki, 1999), *Suicide Circle* (Sono Shion, 2002)), or depict the force behind the slayings as a body-hopping supernatural entity (*Another Heaven*).[23] Such narrative devices render serial murder as a phenomenon that, arising within a modernised capitalist culture, perpetuates itself in an almost viral manner. Virtually no one is immune from the allure of violence and anybody is a potential killer.

CINEMA VISCERA

In the years to come, how Japanese horror cinema continues to develop will be interesting to watch, and thanks to the increasing availability of Japanese horror films through both commercial 'bricks-and-mortar' venues and Internet sites like www.asiancult.com, www.hkflix.com and www.pokerindustries.com (to name but a scant few), western audiences should only have greater access to future titles and emerging trends. At present, one fact remains certain: Japanese horror films exert a powerful influence upon world cinema, and if the current international prestige enjoyed by directors like Kurosawa Kiyoshi, Nakata Hideo and Miike Takashi is any indicator, the impact of these influential texts will surely be felt well into the twenty-first century.

The diverse and insightful essays that fill the pages to follow offer an important initial – but by no means exhaustive – foray into what are at once the darkest and, in some ways, the most enlightening regions of this vital cinematic and cultural tradition. In various and exciting ways, the following critical explorations and detailed case studies combine sophisticated cultural analyses with close readings of 'key' works of Japanese cinematic horror. Consequently, this book's chapters are both thought-provoking and accessible. Proceeding from a plurality of aesthetic and theoretical approaches, the authors in this volume map the shifting historical and cultural climates from which, and against which, some of the most influential and best known works of Japanese horror cinema emerge. Dedicating considerable attention to the impact of transforming notions of gender identity, economic security, (inter)-nationalism and emerging technologies upon Japanese culture, the contributors to this book aim not only to provide students, scholars and fans alike with a valuable critical overview of one of world cinema's most creative, provocative and visceral traditions, but also to assemble a vital collection of foundational studies to which future students of horror film in general, and Japanese horror cinema in particular, may turn as they embark upon further investigations of this unique cinematic phenomenon.

NOTES

1. Lu, Alvin (2002) 'Horror: Japanese-Style', *Film Comment*, January and February, p. 38.
2. Cohen, Jeffrey Jerome (1996) 'Monster Culture (Seven Theses)', in Jeffrey Jerome Cohen (ed.), *Monster Theory: Reading Culture*, Minneapolis: University of Minnesota Press, pp. 2–3.
3. Even these traditions are not mutually exclusive. For instance, in Komizu Kazuo's exploitation film, *Guts of a Beauty* (1986), a young girl is brutally raped and tortured by members of the Yakuza, only to have her psychiatrist exact a gruesome revenge.
4. Wu, Harmony (2002) 'Tracking the Horrific', *Spectator: The University of Southern California Journal of Film and Television Criticism*, 22:2, Fall, p. 3.
5. See Barrett, Gregory (1989) *Archetypes in Japanese Film: The Sociopolitical and Religious Significance of the Principle Heroes and Heroines*, Selinsgrove, PA: Susquehanna University Press. For a detailed study of hair in Japanese culture, see Batchelor, John (2000) *Ainu of Japan: The Religion, Superstitions and General History of the Hair*, Mansfield Centre, CN: Martino Publishing.
6. Martinez, D. P. (1998) 'Gender, Shifting Boundaries, and Global Cultures', in D. P. Martinez (ed.), *The Worlds of Japanese Popular Culture: Gender, Shifting Boundaries and Global Cultures*, Cambridge and New York: Cambridge University Press, p. 7.
7. Tateishi Ramie (2003) 'The Japanese Horror Film Series: *Ring* and *Eko Eko Azarak*', in Steven Jay Schneider (ed.), *Fear Without Frontiers: Horror Cinema Across the Globe*, Guildford: FAB Press, p. 296.
8. Napier, Susan J. (2001) *Anime from* Akira *to* Princess Mononoke: *Experiencing Contemporary Japanese Animation*, New York: Palgrave, p. 80. See also Allison, Ann (2000) *Permitted and Prohibited Desires: Mothers, Comics, and Censorship in Japan*, Berkeley and Los Angeles: University of California Press. This is not to suggest that the collapse of the culturally erected partitions separating social spheres traditionally occupied by men or women is imminent. On the contrary, as Martinez reminds us, 'these sharp divisions between the male and female domains in Japan ... are held to be complementary and necessary for the construction of the social' (p. 7).
9. Jancovich, Mark (1996) *Rational Fears: American Horror in the 1950s*, Manchester and New York: Manchester University Press, p. 2.
10. Brophy, Philip (1994) 'Introduction', *Kaboom! Explosive Animation from America and Japan*, Sydney: Museum of Contemporary Art, p. 9.
11. La Bare, Joshua (2000) 'The Future: "Wrapped ... in that mysterious Japanese way"', *Science Fiction Studies*, 80: 27, Pt 1, March, p. 43.
12. Stephens, Chuck (2002) 'High and Low Japanese Cinema Now: A User's Guide', *Film Comment*, January/February, p. 36.
13. Thacker, Eugene (2002) 'Biohorror/Biotech', *Paradoxa: Studies in World Literary Genres*, 17, p. 111.
14. Ibid., p. 112.
15. Hurley, Kelly (1995) 'Reading Like an Alien', in Judith Halberstam and Ira Livingston (eds), *PostHuman Bodies*, Bloomington and Indianapolis: Indiana University Press, p. 203.
16. Orbaugh, Sharalyn (2002) 'Sex and the Single Cyborg: Japanese Popular Culture Experiments in Subjectivity', *Science Fiction Studies*, 88: 29, Pt 3, November, p. 440.
17. Hunter, Jack (1998) *Eros in Hell: Sex, Blood and Madness in Japanese Cinema*, London: Creation Books International, pp. 159–60.

18. See Biro, Stephen (2003) *The Guinea Pig History Page*, http://www.guineapigfilms.com/History.html.
19. See Brottman, Mikita (1997) *Offensive Films: Towards an Anthropology of* Cinema Vomitif, Westport, CT: Greenwood.
20. Weisser, Thomas and Yuko Mihara Weisser (1998c), *Japanese Cinema Encyclopedia: Horror, Fantasy, Science Fiction*, Miami, FL: Vital Books, p. 21; emphasis added.
21. Ibid., p. 21.
22. Simpson, Philip L. (2000) *Psycho Paths: Tracking the Serial Killer through Contemporary American Film and Fiction*, Carbondale, IL: Southern Illinois University Press, p. 2.
23. Gregory Hoblit's 1998 film, *Fallen,* stands out as a notable exception here.

PART I

HISTORY, TRADITION AND JAPANESE HORROR CINEMA

INTRODUCTION

As critics like Andrew Tudor and Jeffrey Jerome Cohen note, 'horror' narratives are 'the products of the interaction between specific textual features and distinct social circumstances'.[1] In fact, analysing representations of horror and 'monstrous embodiment' in oral, literary and cinematic texts has long provided one of the most compelling avenues for understanding the cultural impact of social and political change. Critics who focus upon these particular modes of aesthetic production, however, must resist the reductive inertia of imposing an all-encompassing 'theory of horror' or 'monstrosity' by maintaining 'sensitivity to cultural variations'.[2] Certain themes and images that emerge and re-emerge throughout Japanese horror cinema, for instance, can be traced back to Japanese folklore, as well as the performative traditions of Noh and Kabuki theatre. This does not mean that these tropes and motifs remain static in their social significance or ideological resonance. Nor am I suggesting that Japanese horror cinema evades the influences of other cultures' literary and cinematic productions. In keeping with many of the chapters to follow, what this brief introduction proposes is that, although horror texts may retain the ability to evoke fear in audiences across multiple generations and cultural boundaries, a fuller comprehension of the extent to which works of Japanese horror cinema engage with historically specific social anxieties may offer scholars a crucial barometer for measuring the impact of economic, philosophical and political continuities and discontinuities upon a nation and its populace's various, and often conflicting, notions of national, class and gender identity.

Through insightful explorations of both 'classic' and more recent Japanese horror films, the three chapters that open *Japanese Horror Cinema* lay crucial groundwork for understanding the historically and ideologically coded matrices from which contemporary Japanese horror films emerge, and against which they frequently define themselves. Richard Hand's 'Aesthetics of Cruelty: Traditional Japanese Theatre and the Horror Film', for example, maps the complex relations between postwar Japanese cinematic horror and 'the apogees of traditional Japanese culture – Noh and Kabuki theatre'. Focusing his critical lens on dramatic formulae that date back as far as the fourteenth century, Hand mines the fertile intersection of contemporary film and traditional Japanese theatre, locating within Noh and Kabuki practices vital precursors for some of Japanese horror cinema's most prevalent narrative trajectories and iconographic images. Included among these is the trope of the 'demonic woman' (the *kyojo-mono* or *shunen-mono* in Noh theatre, or 'the *akuba*' or *akujo* [evil woman] in Kabuki plays), and the graphic, yet often highly stylised, presentations of blood and gore, for which Hand finds antecedents in the practice of *keren*, Kabuki 'stage tricks' designed to 'startle the audience with moments of irrational display' akin to contemporary special effects. Importantly, this chapter refuses to define a direct, causal relationship between traditional theatrical tropes and contemporary cinematic practices. Throughout this book's initial chapter, Hand astutely notes that extensive 'cultural cross-fertilisation', as well as modernist and postmodernist modes of intertextuality, may ultimately render the very quest for origins futile.

In her reading of romantic passion as monstrous nightmare in Nakagawa Nobuo's *Jigoku* (*Hell*) (1960), Masumura Yasuzo's *Moju* (*Blind Beast*) (1969), and Mizoguchi Kenji's *Ugetsu Monogatari* (*Tales of Ugetsu*) (1953), Ruth Goldberg likewise considers the transnational appeal of Japanese horror films, though she does so through an examination of fears of commitment and erotic obsession that 'resonate across cultures even if they manifest in culturally specific ways'. Through an examination of Nakagawa's, Masumura's and Mizoguchi's respective cinematic visions as 'meditations on impermanence and desire' that both reveal the perils of 'dualistic thinking' (the blind adherence to the illusion that one exists apart from the rest of the universe) and expose misogynist fears of female desire, Goldberg's chapter interrogates how these films depict 'the nightmarish potential of romantic passion from three different moments in the life cycle of a man – or from, perhaps, three different paths that a man might travel in relating to women – and the horror implicit in each one'. In part, it is the extension and reworking of this theme, Goldberg posits, that informs much of the appeal of recent works of Japanese horror cinema (most notably Miike Takashi's notorious *Audition*, 2000) that conflate images of 'sex and death' and, consequently, provoke 'extreme visceral reactions' from audiences around the globe.

A case study of Nakata Hideo's *Ringu* films (*Ringu,* 1998; *Ringu 2,* 1999), the first of which is most frequently credited with propelling Japanese horror films to their present status as one of the world's most intense and influential filmic traditions, at once concludes 'Part 1' of *Japanese Horror Cinema* and functions as a pivotal bridge to the essays in 'Part 2', which focus on contemporary manifestations of gender 'difference', terror and the 'avenging spirit' motif. In his close reading of Nakata's films, Eric White argues that although these seminal texts mobilise the 'traditional motif of the vengeful ghost longing for eternal rest', it would be shortsighted to read them merely as tales of 'the uncanny'. Instead, White advocates Nakata's unsettling narratives as films that expose the emergence, both within Japan and internationally, of a culture of simulation in keeping with the postmodern theories of late capitalist culture advanced by Jean Baudrillard and Gilles Deleuze.[3] In particular, White locates Nakata's *Ringu* films as works that foreground societal shifts towards a posthuman economy marked by a 'ubiquitous technological mediation', an historical (and an always ahistorical) moment that renders notions of a consolidated individual, 'human' and national identity obsolete.

NOTES

1. Tudor, Andrew [1997] (2002) 'Why Horror?', in Mark Jancovich (ed.), *Horror: The Film Reader*, London and New York: Routledge, p. 53.
2. Wu, Harmony (2002) 'Tracking the Horrific', *Spectator: The University of Southern California Journal of Film and Television Criticism*, 22:2 Fall, p. 8.
3. See Baudrillard, Jean (1988) 'Simulacra and Simulations', in Mark Poster (ed.), *Selected Writings*, Stanford, CA: Stanford University Press, pp. 166–84; and Deleuze, Gilles (1990) 'Plato and the Simulacrum', *The Logic of Sense*, New York: Columbia University Press, pp. 253–66.

I. AESTHETICS OF CRUELTY: TRADITIONAL JAPANESE THEATRE AND THE HORROR FILM

Richard J. Hand

INTRODUCTION

A dominant concern when non-western culture is analysed by western eyes is the issue of international cultural exchange. Kurosawa Akira, for example, takes Shakespeare's *Macbeth* (1600) and creates *Throne of Blood* (1957), while Gore Verbinski adapts Nakata Hideo's *Ringu* (1998) to create *The Ring* (2002). These examples immediately divide opinion. Many spectators see in Kurosawa's Shakespeare the film director as theatre director legitimately 're-versioning' an existing work. Kurosawa's 'production' turns the Scottish play into what is often called the 'Kabuki *Macbeth*' if not 'the finest Shakespearean adaptation ever committed to the screen'.[1] In contrast, many would see *The Ring* as symptomatic of an over-cautious Hollywood plundering the successes of 'foreign' cinema. In short, the adaptive process is neither unproblematic nor uncontroversial. Adaptation is, nonetheless, at the heart of cultural practice and is closely linked to intertextuality. It is also a cross-generic practice. For example, the contemporary Japanese horror film, as much as it may build on the achievement of earlier cinema, makes frequent reference to other popular culture. This phenomenon may be foregrounded, as in the film adaptations of the Manga horror writer, Ito Junji's *Uzumaki* (books, 1998; film, Higuchins-ky, 2000) and *Tomie* (books, 1997; film, Oikawa Ataru, 1999). There are also examples of the intertextual use of computer games, e.g. the scenes of Ichi playing/watching the Playstation fight game *Tekken 3* in *Ichi the Killer* (Miike Takashi, 2001), while films such as *Versus* (Kitamura Ryuhei, 2001) use not simply the scenario and violence of the 'beat 'em up' genre, but, arguably, the form's narrative structure (a series of small fights culminating in 'boss fights').

For the sake of this essay, however, we will concentrate not on contemporary popular culture, but rather look at the apogees of traditional Japanese culture – Noh and Kabuki theatre – and assess their ramifications in the horror film. Japanese cinema often foregrounds traditional theatre, such as in Ichikawa Kon's *An Actor's Revenge* (1963), a tale of human vengeance in a Kabuki theatre environment, or his *Noh Mask Murders* (1991), about the curse of an evil theatre mask. But the use of traditional theatre is not always so blatant; in many examples, there are latent stylistic and thematic influences from the classical theatres. It is indeed apposite that we began this study with reference to *Throne of Blood*. As well as using Shakespeare to create his Kabuki *Macbeth*, Kurosawa also had to use features of Kabuki theatre. Such a statement sounds obvious, but it is worth emphasising because Kabuki is a traditional form of theatre that is itself contemporaneous with the theatre of the English renaissance. In other words, Kurosawa consciously has to import the style of Kabuki as well as Shakespeare's story. Moreover, the manifestation of traditional theatre in Japanese cinema has proved somewhat confusing to critics. While *Throne of Blood* has been called the Kabuki *Macbeth*, it has also been described as the Noh *Macbeth* as though the terms were interchangeable. Although Noh and Kabuki are linked, they are expressly different.

NOH THEATRE

Noh is a dramatic form established since the fourteenth century. It is characterised by its use of masks and stylisation, and is more strictly a fusion of song, dance and music than its status as a theatrical form implies. Nevertheless, the place of narrative is all-important. There are over two hundred plays in the Noh repertoire, which has grown over the centuries just as performance practice has evolved and been fine-tuned. All Noh plays hinge around two actors: the *shite* and the *waki*. The *shite* is the principal actor at the heart of the performance and narrative. The *shite* is nearly always masked, and his roles may include women, old men, animals, gods, ghosts and demons. The *waki*, in contrast, is never masked and only portrays one of three distinctly 'earthly' categories: officials (*daijin-waki*), priests (*so-waki*) and common men (*otoko-waki*) such as warriors or villagers. The function of the *waki* is to call 'the *shite* to the stage, to question him, and to provide the incentive for him to dance'.[2] Once this has been achieved, the *waki* will withdraw so that everything is focused on the performance of the *shite*.

The subjects covered in the Noh repertoire include 'filial piety, love, jealousy, revenge, and *samurai* spirit'.[3] A performance of Noh drama presents a sequence of five plays, selected from the five categories of the repertoire respectively:

1. Group I: *Waki-noh* ('celebratory plays') or *kami-mono* ('god plays'). In these two-scene plays, the *shite* appears in human form in the first scene and recounts a story, and in the second scene he reappears as a god.
2. Group II: *Shura-mono* ('battle plays' or 'ghost plays'). In these plays the *shite* is the ghost of a dead warrior who recounts, to a priest (*waki*), his final battle and his present sufferings in hell. The ghost begs the priest to pray for his soul. The ghost warriors are usually men, although the eponymous *Tomoe* is a female warrior.
3. Group III: *Katsura-mono* ('wig plays') or *onna-mono* ('woman plays'). These plays are the centre point of the five-play structure and attempt to be the zenith of spectacle. The plays focus on women as protagonists and the emphasis is on beauty and grace, embodied in costume and dance.
4. Group IV: *Kyojo-mono* ('mad woman plays') or *kurui-mono* ('frenzy plays'). This group includes subcategories such as *shunen-mono* ('revenge plays') and *kyoran-mono* ('insanity plays') and centre on heightened emotion, whether in the form of hatred or ecstasy. Many plays focus on an archetypal mother figure driven insane through bereavement. The category also strays into the domain of the *shura-mono* ghost plays, as the *shunen-mono* revenge subcategory features ghosts who seek vengeance on those that wronged them in life.
5. Group V: *Kirino-mono* ('concluding plays') also known as *kichiku-mono* ('demon plays'). This group echoes the *waki-noh* plays. Frequently, the *shite* once again appears in human form in the first scene and then reveals his true identity in the second scene. However, in these plays the *shite*'s true identity is not that of a god, but rather a demon, *tengu* (hobgoblin), or other such monster. Closure is given to these plays – and hence to a complete Noh performance – with the human triumphing over the supernatural.

KABUKI THEATRE

Kabuki has thrived since the seventeenth century, and just as it has drawn on traditions of Noh for its stories and aspects of style, it continues to evolve and still exerts a strong influence on contemporary theatre. Kabuki is renowned for its theatricality: elaborate costumes, remarkable stage effects, virtuoso performers. The sum result is a style of theatre that is 'a spectacle, colourful and intoxicating'.[4] Ironically, although Kabuki was created by women, in 1629 female performers were outlawed and, to this day, men play the female roles (known as *onnagatta*). The word Kabuki derives from the three words *ka* (music), *bu* (dance) and *ki* (acting), and the form is an amalgamation of the performing arts.

Although not classified like Noh, Kabuki presents a variety of genres and styles, including the *aragoto* (literally 'rough business') performance style, which is larger than life, often dealing in the supernatural and using mask-like make-up. In contrast, the *wagoto* ('gentle business') style is, to some extent, akin to realism and uses gentle humour in plays largely concerned with social issues. This is not to say, however, that the two styles do not mix: Samuel L. Leiter argues that the '*aragoto/wagoto* contrast is the core of the drama'.[5] Other genres include *jidaimono*, historical dramas set in samurai society, and *sewamono*, dramas concerned with the life of the common people. The genre of plays performed on the Kabuki stage is dictated by the seasons of the year: celebratory plays in early spring follow plays set in palaces or pleasure quarters; in the summer and early autumn, ghost and violent plays are popular, following the logic that the hot weather can be tempered with plays that 'send chills down the backbones of the audience'.[6]

Kabuki is a highly stylised form: it is 'an unrealistic art; it is an art of bold outlines'[7] in which its distinctiveness 'consists not in making the real look real, but in making the unreal look real (and by working on) principles of symbolism and impressionism'.[8] By the same token, like much contemporary horror, Kabuki has a heightened register in which technically straightforward narratives are embellished with the uncanny. To this end, Kabuki developed many *keren*, which Keiko I. McDonald defines as 'the practice of unorthodox acting and staging technique aimed at achieving novel effects'.[9] These impressive stage effects include *hayagawari* (quick costume change), *honmizu* (real water on stage) and countless other play-specific effects. Kabuki drama also has a range of sequences and stylistic features in its plots and performance practice. One significant example is the *mie*, in which an actor will strike a dramatic pose and hold it, rather like a freeze frame. Characteristic sequences in the more brutal Kabuki plays include scenes of torture, as well as *korishiba* (violent/murder scenes), self-mutilation and *seppuku* (suicide), and *tachiwara* (elaborate fight sequences). These aspects of the form establish a distinct quality in Kabuki that is known as *zankoku no bi* ('aesthetic of cruelty'), which Samuel L. Leiter defines as 'a highly aestheticized, even fantastical world where the inherent sadism is muted by artistic techniques'.[10]

NOH, KABUKI AND HORROR CINEMA

Clearly, Noh and Kabuki contain the uncanny and the horrific as recurrent motifs. Sometimes this is in the supernatural domain of gods, demons and ghosts, or the emphatically earthbound world of killers, bandits and their victims (deserving or otherwise). An argument can be advanced that the Japanese horror film draws on the storylines, structure, performance practice and iconography of traditional theatre as much as on the traditions and mechanisms of western horror.

In terms of western influence, we might cite Nakata's *Ringu* (1998), which in its opening 'teenager at home' death sequence, technophobia and female investigative journalist as central character, seemingly alludes to *Scream* (Wes Craven, 1996). It should be stated, however, that Reiko (Matsushima Nanako), the protagonist of *Ringu*, finds a precursor in the even earlier Japanese horror movie *Evil Dead Trap* (Toshiharu Ikeda, 1988), the protagonist of which is Nami (Ono Miyuki), a female investigative journalist. By extension, Ikeda openly acknowledges the influence of Tobe Hooper, Dario Argento and David Cronenberg on his work.[11] The process of cinematic cross-fertilisation is not merely complex, but perpetual, for as Julia Kristeva's theory of intertextuality makes clear, no text can ever be 'unravelled back to some primordial moment of "origin"'.[12] Be this as it may, it is nonetheless possible to identify topoi in many horror films that predate cinema itself and are theatrical in origin.

The most paradigmatic Kabuki ghost play is *Yotsuya Kaidan* (*The Yotsuya Ghost Story,* 1824) by Tsuruya Nanboku. It is also the most frequently adapted horror play. Thomas and Yuko Mihara Weisser cite eleven different versions between 1928 and 1994,[13] all of which recount the same tale but variously shift emphasis from the cerebral to the violent or the sexual to the farcical. The most celebrated adaptation is the 1959 version by Nakagawa Nubuo ('the Nippon Hitchcock'[14]), often regarded as a masterpiece of the horror genre. The Weissers do not discuss the silent versions of the story, and since their book was published, there has been the video release of an updated stage version (Ninagawa Yukio, 2002). The plot concerns Iemon, an unscrupulous *ronin* (and archetypal antihero or *iroaku*) who kills a man and marries the victim's daughter. His wife, Oiwa, becomes ill, and rather than caring for her, Iemon embarks on an affair with a rich mistress. Iemon's mistress, Oume, arranges for Oiwa to be given poison in the guise of medicine. Oiwa dies, but not without becoming hideously scarred and disfigured in the process. Oiwa returns as a ghost and drives Iemon insane, causing him to kill Oume and much of her family on their wedding night until he himself is slain by Oiwa's brother-in-law. The play makes impressive use of the *mawari butai* (revolving stage). This mid-eighteenth-century Kabuki innovation allow for quick scene changes that, in the case of *Yotsuya Kaidan*, create a fast pace and allows an ironic montage sequence (in horror movie style) to be established between Oiwa's doom and Iemon's proposal. *Yotsuya Kaidan* also makes extensive use of *keren*: in the poisoning scene Oiwa's hair comes off in bloody clumps, her skin turns purple, one of her eyes distends and a sword pierces her throat. When she returns as a ghost, *keren* enable her to float in midair and appear inside a lantern; in a garden scene, eggplants transform into a representation of her face.

We might liken traditional theatrical *keren* to contemporary cinema special effects. Certainly these stage tricks startle the audience with moments of irrational display, which find modern-day equivalents in the spectacle of Sadako (Inou Rie) crawling out of the television set in *Ringu*, or the fantastic horrors besetting the benighted community of *Uzumaki* where everything – eyes, hair, bodies – contorts into spirals. In contrast, some *keren* are used in order to provide verisimilitude to *korishiba*, especially those that make use of stage blood. The protracted death of Oiwa could be likened to the realist murder in *Guinea Pig: Devil's Experiment* (1988) and other examples of Japanese exploitica. Indeed, if we return to the idea of the Kabuki aesthetic of cruelty, we find that scenes involving the torture of women are recurrent in Kabuki, with characters using grotesquely ingenious methods to inflict pain, from the use of snow to musical instruments,[15] to oil in *Onna Koroshi Abura Jigoku* (*Murder of a Woman in a Hell of Oil*). *Guinea Pig: Devil's Experiment* is similarly inventive in its range of torture implements, including boiling oil, carpenter's tools and a swivel chair. We have already seen that Kabuki 'consists not in making the real look real, but in making the unreal look real', and certainly the verisimilitude in *Guinea Pig: Devil's Experiment* and *Guinea Pig 2: The Flowers of Flesh and Blood* (1985) could be seen as evidence of a contemporary success at that endeavour. However, although Kabuki might foreground the detail of verisimilitude, such moments are built into an overarching highly-stylised presentation so that it becomes, as Leiter says, 'aestheticized torture'.[16] This phrase seems extremely apt in relation to the *Guinea Pig* films: although 'Hollywood moron Charlie Sheen'[17] may have thought he had stumbled across a snuff movie when he viewed *Guinea Pig 2*, for most viewers the *Guinea Pig* films are a disturbing yet obviously aestheticised spectacle, despite the deliberate 'found footage' feel.

Aside from the *Guinea Pig* series, Oiwa's demise can be pertinently related to the gruesome yet unreal horrors of Sato Hisayasu's *Naked Blood* (1995), where although the sequences of self-mutilation and self-cannibalism may be realistic, they are nonetheless as irrational as the action(s) in the Noh play *Ama*, in which a woman hides a jewel by slicing open her breast and placing it inside. The extraordinary horrors on display in *Naked Blood* also owe something to Kabuki as they are elaborate takes on the traditional self-mutilation/*seppuku* sequence: in *Natsu Matsuri* (*Summer Festival*, 1745) a woman willingly places a red-hot iron onto her face to destroy her beauty, while in *Kirare Otomi* (*Scarface Otomi*, 1864) and *Yoshibei Ume no Yoshibei* (*Plum Blossom Yoshibei*, 1796) women cut off their fingers. The interplay of the real and the unreal also finds a special place in *Ichi the Killer*, which incorporates explicit but impossible murder sequences ironically juxtaposed with moments of realistic violence. In contrast to individual suffering, the set pieces of the Kabuki *tachiwara* anticipate the stylised excesses of *Versus*, which although seeming like a 'beat 'em up' videogame, finds a precedent in the battle between dead and living warriors in the Noh play *Funa-Benkei*.

THE DRAMATIC WOMAN

The perfect woman throughout Japanese theatre is dignified, graceful and demure, but her female antithesis is unruly and hideous. Examples of the monstrous-feminine – the *femme castratice* or the abject woman (*à la* Kristevan analysis by Barbara Creed) – abound in classical Japanese theatre, and the demonic women in the Noh *kyojo-mono* or *shunen-mono* subcategories, or the *akuba* or *akujo* (evil women) or *dokufo* (poison ladies) in Kabuki, are great icons of their respective forms. The monstrous women who permeate Noh and Kabuki are motivated through revenge or grief, or are, especially in the case of the supernatural female, inherently evil. As Samuel L. Leiter explains:

> One of the chief ways in which women who have been trampled on become empowered is to turn into vengeful spirits after they have died. The entire world of selfish, unfaithful husbands and lovers must take cover when one of these women comes back from the other world to seek revenge on those who have wronged her.[18]

Oiwa in *Yotsuya Kaidan* is one such nemesis. She is a woman so tragically wronged that her return from beyond the grave is obviously motivated by a ferocious desire for revenge rather than merely as a manifestation of Iemon's guilt. Japanese horror films have provided many fine examples to join this panoply of traditional earthbound or supernatural demonic women. Shindo Kaneto presents demonic cat-women in *Kuroneko* (1968), while in his *Onibaba* (1964), the Mother (Otowa Nobuko), in a spiteful rage of sexual jealousy, steals a demon mask to frighten her daughter-in-law and her lover; ironically, the mask proves irremovable and, ultimately, her rotting face makes her the incarnation of a demon. In *Ghost Story of Sex* (Nishihara Giichi, 1972), a rape victim bites off her tongue and returns from the grave to haunt her attacker. Yamazaki Asami (Shiina Eihi) in *Audition* (Miike Takeshi,

1999) is a quasi-supernatural incarnation with a vendetta against men, while the eponymous *Tomie* uses her power to bewitch for destructive purposes against humankind in general. Similarly misanthropic is Sadako in the *Ringu* cycle, a tragic young woman whose irreconcilable childhood pain turns into a ruthless curse against all humanity. Leiter emphasises the 'sharp streak of sentimentality'[19] in Kabuki that accounts for the evil nature of these women, frequently betrayed or forsaken by love, but Sadako's childhood unhappiness is not entirely sentimental. Nevertheless, her pathetic death in a well is also prefigured in Kabuki, with a play like *Bancho Sarayashiki* (*The Chamberlain and the China Mansion*, 1916) in which a woman is thrown down a well to her death by her husband.

The power of transformation and mutation has a special place in horror in general, but is a central motif in Japanese horror theatre and film. In Noh, a humble old woman may prove to be a demon (*Yamanba*), while in Kabuki a mysterious monk may really be a gigantic spider (*Tsuchigumo*). Such examples permeate the traditional theatres, and are motifs that continue in contemporary films such as *Tetsuo: The Iron Man* (Tsukamoto Shinya, 1988) and *Tetsuo II: Body Hammer* (Tsukamoto Shinya, 1992), both of which are masterpieces of mutation. In her analysis of Japanese pornographic animation, Susan J. Napier argues that the genre presents a 'frenzy of metamorphosis'[20] of the female body that is not simply misogynistic, but in some ways empowering. Sometimes transformation takes place steadily through a narrative. *Ai No Corrida* (Oshima Nagisa, 1976), for example, is an erotic tale that becomes aestheticised pornography and culminates in horror: Sada (Eiko Matsuda) is indeed a 'demon woman', but as Leger Grindon asserts, she is a remarkable example because 'she is presented with sympathy'.[21] The fact that Tomie is no ordinary schoolgirl (just as Tomoe is really the ghost of a dead female warrior) draws from the same fascination in Noh theatre that informs the transformation of *Audition*'s Yamazaki Asami (the narrative gradually reveals her as demonic) or *Ringu*'s Sadako (gifted child becomes evil spirit).

In *Dojijo*, a priest tells his servant the legend of a rejected lover who transformed into a serpent and destroyed the man who refused her by incinerating him inside a giant temple bell. This aspect of the play is equivalent to the establishment of the videotape urban legend in *Ringu*. In *Dojijo*, the servant waits outside the legendary temple and encounters a beautiful woman who enraptures him with her dance. The *rambyoshi* dance is peculiar to this play and is famous for its transition from gentleness to frenzy. We could liken this to Sadako's own dance of death: the frail crawling, the contorted body movements as she moves into an upright position, and the frenzied culmination in the evil eye. In *Dojijo*, after hiding in the bell, the woman reappears as a raving demon. The servant and the priest are only saved through a ritual of fervent prayer. Similarly, Reiko's redemption in *Ringu* is the discovery of another kind of ritual: the dubbing of the videotape. Moreover, the invocation of Sadako through the contemporary 'ritual' of viewing the video is comparable to moments of ritualised summoning in Noh. In *Uneme*, for example, a prayer invokes the ghost of a drowned woman to stand on the water, while in *Eguchi*, the recitation of a poem over the grave of a dead prostitute causes the prostitute's ghost to rise from the earth.

Many demonic women in Japanese theatre have long, black hair. Contemporary Japanese horror cinema's reiteration of this motif can be evidenced through the unkempt hair obscuring Sadako's face in *Ringu* or the spiralling tresses in *Uzumaki*. In *Kakashi* (Tsuruta Norio, 2001), the uncanny scarecrows are all characterised by long, black hair, whether they are 'male' or 'female'. 'Black Hair' ('*Kurokami*'), the first episode in *Kwaidan* (Kobayashi Masaki, 1964), presents a samurai (Mikuni Rentaro) who cruelly abandons his wife (Aratama Michiyo) to marry into nobility. His guilt makes him return to her, and they enjoy a night of passion and reconciliation. In the morning, beneath his wife's lustrous black hair he discovers a skeleton. The finale of the tale is a virtuoso display of performance in which the samurai tries to escape the black hair and his face gradually transforms into the blue-white hue of terror and death.

The place of masks in Noh performance practice is all-important: 'The actor is taught that he is not to put the mask on, but that he must put his whole self, body and soul, into the mask.'[22] This statement pertains to the art of the *shite* performer, but can be applied to a film like *Onibaba*, where the fury of the Mother means that she does not merely wear a mask but *becomes* it. There are many hundreds of Noh masks, each with a clearly defined role. Masks such as *Kawazu* (the drowned man mask), *Deigan* (the jealous woman mask) and *Aku-jo* (the sorrowful ghost mask) all have a human frailty to their horror, like the dead faces in *Ringu*. Other masks explore dehumanisation for the purposes of horror. These include the horned female demon *Hannya*, the fanged male mask *Shushi-Guchi* and countless other monsters.

CONCLUSION

This chapter has located points of allusion and intersection between Noh, Kabuki and postwar Japanese horror cinema. This should not be understood as implying that in the beginning there was Noh, then Kabuki and now there is cinema. Such a progressive narrative would be illusory. As intertextuality shows us, there is perhaps no point of origin. Certainly many motifs in classical theatre emerge from traditional religion and folklore. However, the endeavour to draw comparisons between theatre and film is enlightening. Certainly it is possible to find specific or generic examples that are the same across time and strike a peculiar chord in Japanese culture. But similar chords are struck throughout horror. Although much is made of Greek or Elizabethan-Jacobean tragedy as precursors to modern horror, it is clear that classical Japanese theatre boasts the most developed template for contemporary horror cinema. Time and again in Noh and Kabuki theatre we see the iconography of demonic women and other horrors in worlds that oscillate between the real and the supernatural in a manipulated structure of suspense. Similarly, the Kabuki's invention of *keren* demonstrates the development of technology for gruesome or uncanny effect, while the performance practice of the Kabuki actor requires stylised intensity to capture the moments of terror, fury or demise so familiar in horror performance. Moreover, while classical western drama uses horror as part of the ennobling process of catharsis, the Kabuki stage has no qualms in claiming that it is going for the 'goosebumps' effect to take the sting out of summer's heat. As demonstrated, one of the most striking features of Kabuki is its aesthetic of cruelty, whereby the taboos of sadism or *Todesangst* are explored through the high-stylisation of art. The contemporary horror film plays the same game, often juxtaposing the arcane with the contemporary or the mundane with the extraordinary in carefully developed structures. A videotape or a PC, for example, become like an ancient curse in *Ringu* and Kurosawa Kiyoshi's *Kairo* (2001) respectively. As Laurence R. Kominz argues, the appeal of Kabuki lies in its 'vivid contrasts and startling juxtapositions',[23] and it is fair to say that we find the same mechanisms at work in the Japanese horror movie, a broad film genre that could not exist without its theatrical antecedents. The director Toshiharu Ikeda complains: 'When I was young there were no horror films in Japan.'[24] It may have felt so, but consciously or otherwise, traditional Japanese theatre provides an incomparable legacy upon which horror directors continue to draw.

NOTES

1. *The Guardian* (2001) quoted on *Throne of Blood*, DVD, British Film Institute.
2. Maruoka Daiji and Yoshikoshi Tatsuo (1969) *Noh*, Osaka: Hoikusha, p. 109.
3. Ibid., p. 98.
4. Miyake Shutaro (1948) *Kabuki Drama*, Tokyo: JTB, pp. 61–2.
5. Leiter, Samuel L. (2002b) 'Introduction', in Samuel L. Leiter (ed.), *A Kabuki Reader: History and Performance*, New York: Sharpe, p. 16.
6. Miyake, p. 105.
7. Ibid., p. 25.
8. Ibid., p. 70.
9. McDonald, Keikio I. (1994) *Japanese Classical Theater in Films*, Cranbury, NJ: Associated University Presses, p. 91.
10. Leiter, Samuel L. (2002a) 'From Gay to *Gei*: The *Onnagata* and the Creation of *Kabuki*'s Female Characters', in Samuel L. Leiter (ed.), *A Kabuki Reader: History and Performance*, New York: Sharpe, p. 221.
11. See Ikeda biography (2002) *Evil Dead Trap*, DVD, Artsmagic.

12. Terry Eagleton, quoted in Susan Bassnett-McGuire (1991) *Translation Studies*, London: Routledge, p. 104.
13. Weisser, Thomas and Yuko Mihara Weisser (1998c) *Japanese Cinema Encyclopedia: Horror, Fantasy, Science Fiction*, Miami, FL: Vital Books, p. 105.
14. Ibid., p. 105
15. Leiter, p. 221.
16. Ibid., p. 221.
17. Hunter, Jack (1998) *Eros in Hell: Sex, Blood and Madness in Japanese Cinema*, London: Creation Books International, p. 158.
18. Leiter, p. 225.
19. Ibid., p. 226.
20. Napier, Susan J. (2001a) 'The Frenzy of Metamorphosis: The Body in Japanese Pornographic Animation', in Dennis Washburn and Carole Cavanaugh (eds), *Word and Image in Japanese Cinema*, Cambridge: Cambridge University Press, p. 361.
21. Grindon, Leger (2001) 'In the Realm of the Censors: Cultural Boundaries and the Poetics of the Forbidden', in Dennis Washburn and Carole Cavanaugh (eds), *Word and Image in Japanese Cinema*, Cambridge: Cambridge University Press, p. 305.
22. Maruoka and Yoshikoshi, p. 118.
23. Kominz, Laurence R. (2002) 'Origins of *Kabuki* Acting in Medieval Japanese Drama', in Samuel L. Leiter (ed.), *A Kabuki Reader: History and Performance*, New York: Sharpe, p. 16.
24. Toshiharu Ikeda (2000) 'Director's Commentary', *Evil Dead Trap*, DVD, Image.

2. THE NIGHTMARE OF ROMANTIC PASSION IN THREE CLASSIC JAPANESE HORROR FILMS

Ruth Goldberg

Why is it that even the most clear-eyed monk cannot sever the red thread of passion between his legs? (Zen koan attributed to Sung-yuan[1])

On the screen a stunningly beautiful young woman arrives home. She keeps a man imprisoned in a sack in her apartment. As he emerges, moaning incoherently, we see that she has previously cut off both of his feet, an ear, three fingers and his tongue. She feeds him on her own vomit, making him eat from a bowl on the floor like an animal. He is no longer fully human. Later in the film, she dismembers another man whose only offence was not loving her 'enough'.

During each of these brutal scenes, more than a dozen people run out of the theatre, but in spite of this, the film's run is extended, with more and more people coming every night to watch this 'unwatchable' film: a grisly meditation on romantic love.

The woman on the screen is the heroine of Miike Takashi's *Audition* (2000). *Audition*, along with Nakata Hideo's *Ringu* (1998), is arguably one of the films most directly responsible for the recent wave of interest in Japanese horror cinema, due in no small part to its powerful reworking of a previously established trope – that of the nightmare of romantic passion. In looking at the recent success of Japanese horror films and the power they have in provoking audiences to experience extreme visceral reactions, it is impossible to avoid looking carefully at this trope and at the conflation of sex and death which gives many of these films their unique and particular character.

In his book *Eros in Hell: Sex, Blood and Madness in Japanese Cinema*, Jack Hunter makes the illuminating claim that one tendency in Japanese film is to present a vision of sex as hell on earth.[2] Beyond, or perhaps *behind*, this assertion is a set of larger ideas rooted in and unique to their cultural context. One could argue that in the Japanese horror film, it is often not the sex act itself that is at the centre of the horror, but rather the larger concepts of passion and romantic attachment which are represented as being monstrous.

This chapter examines Nakagawa Nobuo's *Jigoku* [*Hell*] (1960), Masumura Yasuzo's *Moju* [*Blind Beast*] (1969) and Mizoguchi Kenji's *Ugetsu Monogatari* [*Tales of Ugetsu*] (1953), three early modern Japanese films about death and desire. Each film indicates preoccupations which would remain central to the horror film in Japan, and which would ultimately lead to new explorations of these themes in later films like *Audition* and *Chaos*. Over the course of repeated viewings, what emerges is the sense that the way these thematic preoccupations are reflected in this set of films may be inextricable from the context of Buddhist philosophy and the world-view generated within this framework. This is not to say that these are 'Buddhist' films (since they are not), but rather that seeing the films in the context of Buddhist philosophy may serve to further illuminate an exploration of the ideas that recur in this set of films. The cultural presence of Buddhism and Buddhist teachings are explicitly addressed in the narratives of *Jigoku* and *Ugetsu*, and are echoed, if not overtly referenced, in *Moju*. Dismissing this understanding potentially ignores a great source of resonance and integrity in these works.[3]

Each of these films, in its own way, addresses the *price* of passion, a vision of romantic longing as a cause of loss and suffering. In this way the films mirror Zen teachings on recognising the nature of desire as a pathological craving; the grasping and clinging to sensory experience consigns us to suffering as long as we remain ignorant of its true nature. The dynamics of desire and attachment, craving and suffering in the three films under examination are illuminated when understood within this larger context of Buddhist philosophy. Seen in this light, the films can be understood as meditations on impermanence and desire, and as thematic forerunners of the Japanese horror films that are setting new trends today.

Each of these films explores male fantasies about and fears of women and romantic attachment. This particular range of films represents the nightmarish potential of romantic passion from three different moments in the life cycle of a man – or from, perhaps, three different paths that a man might travel in relating to women – and the horror implicit in each one.

SEX AND THE RED THREAD OF PASSION:
THE BUDDHIST PHILOSOPHICAL CONTEXT

As religious scholar Bernard Faure describes in his work on *The Red Thread: Buddhist Approaches to Sexuality*, in awakening to enlightenment the Buddha realised the nature of 'the world of samsara, the cycle of transmigration through birth-and-death . . . [He] came to understand the nature of sexual desire, which ties humans to their earthly body, to the circle of rebirths'.[4] Faure goes on to explain that 'sexual desire belongs to the realm of the senses and these senses are deluding us . . . Only the mind, a sixth sense according to Buddhists, can reveal things as they really are – provided that it can detach itself from sense perceptions. Buddhist soteriology teaches that there are three obstacles to deliverance: passions, acts and their retribution.'[5]

Within this system of thought, it is dualistic thinking, or the delusion of imagining oneself as separate from anything else, which fates beings of all kinds to endure endless cycles of rebirth and suffering. At every moment, with each new sensation, sentient beings have the opportunity to either react/attach (often imagined as the actions of grasping and clinging, craving or aversion), or detach and wake up from the dream of duality. Grasping, clinging and aversion are all predicated on dualistic thinking and serve merely to create new karma – another go-round on the flaming wheel of life. Conversely, detachment from desire frees one from the endless cycle of karma and allows for progress towards enlightenment – the fully experienced realisation of the interconnectedness of all things.

The conflict is inherent in the schema: desire is responsible for suffering, but sexual desire, the force that drives human existence, is also unavoidable. Buddhist scholar John Stevens elaborates on this conflict at length in his book *Lust for Enlightenment: Buddhism and Sex*:

> Sex, 'the blaze of passion', is the primary element of the will to live and the chief expression of craving, the 'thirst' that creates the chaos, unease, and suffering that plagues the world. More than anything else it is the chords of sensuous desire that bind us tighter and tighter to the wheel of life.[6]

In the Zen Buddhist tradition these ideas are most famously reflected in the concept of the 'red thread of passion', which comes from the teaching of Zen Master Sung-yuan:

> Master Sung-yuan, addressing the assembly, said, 'In order to know the Way in perfect clarity, there is one essential point you must penetrate and not avoid: the red thread of passion that cannot be severed. Few face

the problem, and it is not at all easy to settle. Attack it directly without hesitation, for how else can liberation come?'[7]

Ultimately, the teaching of the red thread, while 'not at all easy to settle', is also extremely clear. Craving is delusion and leads straight back to rebirth and, within the Buddhist cosmology, into the hell realms. The red thread cannot be severed, so the problem must be attacked directly on the battlefield of the human body, which is at once an illusion and the only possible vehicle for awakening.

A Funny Thing Happened on the Way to the Altar: *Jigoku* and the Fear of Commitment

Of the three films, Nakagawa Nobuo's *Jigoku* is the one that most overtly addresses Buddhist teachings on desire and impermanence. *Jigoku* tells the story of Shirô (Shigeru Amachi), a young man on the threshold of commitment to his fiancée Yukiko, who is the daughter of Shirô's religion professor, Professor Yajima. As the film opens, Professor Yajima is lecturing on the Eight Great Hells of the Buddhist sutras. Shirô is riveted to the lecture out of guilt and anxiety over the events of the previous evening, during which he inadvertently ran over a drunken yakuza mobster in his car and then fled from the scene. Shirô is wracked with guilt, even though he was only in the passenger seat during the time of the hit-and-run. The actual driver was the mysterious and sinister Tamura (Numata Yoichi), Shirô's uncanny double who haunts him as an ever-present reminder of his guilt, and who dissuades him from going to the police to confess to the murder.

When Shirô is involved in a second car crash resulting in the death of his fiancée Yukiko, he drowns his sorrows in a bar, ending the night in the arms of the gun moll Yoko who, unbeknown to him, is the lover of the dead yakuza, and who has sworn to avenge his death. The next day, he receives the news that his mother is dying and heads out to visit her at the Tenjoen Senior Citizens Facility. There, he encounters another ghostly double: a young girl named Sachiko, who is an exact replica of his dead fiancée. Meanwhile, the domestic scene that Shirô encounters at the Tenjoen is relentlessly surreal, with his mother dying in one room while his father lives with his young mistress in the adjoining chambers.

Shirô hides out among the shady and eccentric inhabitants of the Tenjoen, but he cannot hide for long. Soon enough his past catches up with him as his double, Tamura, suddenly materialises, Professor Yajima and his wife happen by and, later, the vengeful Yoko sniffs him out as well. As the celebrations for the senior citizens centre's tenth anniversary degenerate into a frenzied bacchanal, Tamura recounts the past sins of all present ('everyone here has killed'), time suddenly stands still and the characters are all plunged into hell. As Jasper Sharp so eloquently describes:

> ... After the eye-popping descent into the Abyss via a pit of flames, Shirô's subsequent voyage through the netherworld is ceaselessly spectacular. Alongside designer Kurosawa Haruyasu, Nakagawa stunningly evokes a Dante-esque vision of hell using little more than dry ice and coloured spotlighting and the fruits of an extremely vivid imagination. From Shirô's convergence with Tamura on the banks of the Sanzu no Kawa, the River that acts as the border between life and death, the narrative flows with a dreamlike fluidity through a succession of encounters that alternate between the grotesque and the tragically poetic.
>
> A scene in which Shirô dangles upside down with a spike thrust gruesomely through his neck as he is judged by the Lord of the Eight Hells of Fire and Ice blurs into a reunion with his dead lover Yukiko. Lured on by the ghostly cry of their daughter Harumi, conceived days before Yukiko's death, he floats through a nightmarish landscape with sword blades protruding from the ground and inhabited by a chanting procession of corpses, by turns haunted with visions of carnality and the burning symbol of the Buddhist Wheel of Life.[8]

Every conceivable taboo desire that might have been latent in Shirô's actions is realised in the hell realms. The film reveals a kind of dark, interior dialogue about the weight of societal pressure to marry a 'nice' girl and lead a respectable life. In the face of this impending reality, Shirô conjures up the hell of 'wrong action', in which his fears and ambivalences are made manifest and he is punished for them. The irony, of course, is that even in hell he still doesn't have to face marrying the girl. Hell, for Shirô, is quite possibly a way out.

The repeated theme of 'I was all set to get married when I suddenly turned into/encountered a monster' is not unique to Japanese horror, but rather is critical to the canon of international horror cinema as a whole. It is on the verge of marriage, after all, that the Baron von Frankenstein unleashes a monster, Jonathan Harker is suddenly called away to Transylvania, and Dr Jekyll starts mucking about in his lab. As always in these tales about the horrors of intimacy, ambivalence is fatal. It takes form and agency, with foreseeably deadly results.

Within this broad trope *Jigoku* would find its closest western counterpart in Hitchcock's *Strangers on a Train* (1951), which is a particular variation on the 'I can't go through with the wedding' theme that introduces the figure of a demonic and uncannily prescient doppelganger who haunts the protagonist, acting on his ambivalent desires to kill/flee and then reminding him of his guilt at every turn. In *Jigoku*, the Buddhist cultural context is obviously of paramount importance, but the source of the horror is not culturally specific. As in *Strangers on a Train*, *Jigoku* explores fears of commitment that resonate across cultures, even if they manifest in culturally specific ways. [9]

The film's dividing and doubling motif is consistent throughout, with the main characters all divided into pairs representing tensions and conflicts within the narrative. These divisions are also played out in the visuals and sound of the film, with the modern, jazz-infused aesthetic characteristic of the Japanese New Wave contrasting with the film's representation of ancient Buddhist teachings.

MOJU: FEAR AND LOATHING IN THE FLOATING WORLD

Where *Jigoku* envisions hell in the ambivalent avoidance of intimacy, Masumura Yasuzo's *Moju* is a descent *into* the imagined hell of intimacy. It is perhaps the most searing vision of what people both secretly want and also fear in the idea of an all-consuming passion since Buñuel's *El* (or, *This Strange Passion* (1952)). *Moju* plays on the classical Japanese idea of the ephemeral 'floating world' of pleasure and entertainment in which the proprieties and rigid constraints of the real world are suspended. *Moju* is a dark twist on this idea, creating instead a private, liminal world in which the underside of passion is revealed in all of its most hideous depravity and pathology.

Michio (Funakoshi Eiji) is a psychopathic blind sculptor who, disguised as a masseur and aided by his equally deranged mother (Sengoku Noriko), abducts a young model named Aki (Midori Mako). Michio needs Aki to model for him so that he can realise his obsessive desire to construct the perfect sensual sculpture of the female form. In reviewing the film, Jasper Sharp explains:

> The rest of the action takes place in one location, the artist's cavernous studio in the basement of a secluded house, each wall covered in biomorphic swells representing parts of the female anatomy – breasts, eyes, lips. The studio is dominated by two recumbent sculptures of male and female nudes. Masumura depicts this claustrophobic milieu with an edgy, hallucinogenic intensity that borders on hyper-realism to explore the cloying, all-encompassing relationship between the artist and his art and the obsessive closed world that the artist inhabits. As Michio maps out the curves of his subject in his attempt to reproduce her in clay, the two engage in a continuous stream of dialogue, and as Aki's fear for her captor turns to respect, she eventually reciprocates to his intense tactile fixation on her body. [10]

After some competitive back-and-forth between Aki and Michio's mother, the mother is accidentally killed in a struggle, and Aki and Michio are left alone to consummate endlessly their desire, never leaving the dark basement and gradually turning to increasingly brutal sex play as they degenerate into pure madness. Such a passion can only lead to the total annihilation of all parties involved, and Aki and Michio end up dismembered and eviscerated by the end of the film after their incessant exploration of physical sensation turns deadly.

Moju imagines what might happen if the fantasy of the floating world were fulfilled. It is a world without commitments or societal pressures for Michio: no marriage or children, no responsibility, no possessive mother – just unlimited time to indulge in sexual pleasures with a beautiful woman who cannot seem to get enough. Of course, *Moju* turns this ultimate hedonistic fantasy on its head, merging it with the fear of intimacy as a destructive, devouring force that consumes everything in its path. It posits an apocalyptic vision of desire, true to the Buddhist world-view described above, and, of the three films under examination, *Moju* is the most indicative of the direction Japanese horror cinema would ultimately take. One can see Aki and Michio's obsessive passion and also the use of graphically sexualised violence replayed in more recent horror films from Japan (*Audition* chief among them), in which couples and romantic love are situated at the root of the horror.

Both the New Wave visual aesthetic and the action of the film are dizzyingly hallucinatory, and they combine to give a true sense of the horrors of obsession. To borrow from a different Buddhist tradition, *Moju* unfolds like an encounter in the Bardo,[11] a disorienting test of how one will face fear and desire, craving and impermanence when the time comes to do so.

'I WOULDN'T CARE IF YOU *WERE* A DEMON': FORBIDDEN PASSION IN *UGETSU*

Set during the civil wars of feudal Japan, Mizoguchi Kenji's *Ugetsu Mono-gatari* tells the story of two peasants who abandon their families out of misguided ambition for fame and fortune. Tobei (Ozara Eitaro), a poor farmer, dreams only of becoming a samurai warrior, while Genjuro (Ma-sayuki Mori), a potter, longs to be wealthy so that he can give his wife Miyagi (Tanaka Kinuyo) and their young son the life they deserve. When their village is destroyed by marauding armies, the two couples head for the city, but are soon separated along the way, as Genjuro sends Miyagi back home with their son, promising to return to her soon, and Tobei, in his passion to become a samurai, abandons his wife Ohama (Mito Mitsuko).

Genjuro quickly forgets his promise to return to his wife and son when he is bewitched by the mysterious Lady Wakasa, who lures him to her estate after buying his pots and praising his talent as an artist. She pampers and beguiles

Genjuro in her mansion and, in an eerie sequence, he awakens to find that he has become Lady Wakasa's husband and lord of the estate. They spend the following days cavorting in endless delight. He can sense that something is amiss – why would this beautiful, wealthy woman want *him*, after all? But his desires ultimately get the better of him and he dismisses his fears, declaring 'I wouldn't care if you *were* a demon', as Lady Wakasa, who is indeed a restless ghost from the spirit world, binds him to her ever tighter.

Soon, Genjuro has forgotten his family entirely, and it is only through the intervention of a wandering priest that Genjuro is made to see that he is being held prisoner by supernatural forces. He escapes and returns home where, to his profound relief and comfort, his son is asleep and Miyagi is waiting for him. In the morning, Miyagi has disappeared, and Genjuro is told that she died long ago. Genjuro realises that it was only her ghost who welcomed him home; all that remains of Miyagi is the memory of her voice, which he hears as he returns, grief-stricken, to his lonely routine. He is now without his wife, and their son is seen putting an offering of food by his mother's grave.

Set against the desolate backdrop of war-torn feudal Japan, *Ugetsu* is a lyrical, erotic meditation on the price of ambition and the illusory nature of happiness. Genjuro's story is just one small part of the larger drama, but it contains an instructive and moral lesson. The Lady Wakasa sequence explores the idea of being tempted away from the path – in this case, a happy marriage – and the fantasy of magically realising all of one's ideals and ambitions in the blink of an eye. What allows this to work, both within the individual psychology of the film and also within the Buddhist context, is the lie that Genjuro tells himself – that he longs to be wealthy so that he can provide for his family. At the first temptation, it is revealed that his ambition is actually self-serving and based on his own hungers. True to the Buddhist understanding of causality, it is at this very moment that the appropriate demon appears to teach Genjuro the exact lesson he needs to learn about himself, just as his desires bring tragedy upon his family.

There is a false ending in *Ugetsu*; it occurs when Genjuro returns home and briefly imagines that he can escape repercussions for having abandoned Miyagi. He has learned the lesson, that fulfilment was right there at home all along, but he has learned it too late. *Ugetsu* is a masterpiece; it is one of the most beautiful and haunting films in the history of cinema, and it would be a mistake and a disservice to distil this work of art down to a simple moral teaching. Indeed, in doing so we would perhaps miss what Mizoguchi is able to do to us with the wrenching and elegant visuals of the film. In this one strand of the narrative, however, *Ugetsu* further illustrates the potential horrors of commitment – that one might be weak, blind, unworthy, that in falling into temptation, one might be culpable for the suffering of loved ones, only learning too late what is of true importance.

As I have discussed, within a Buddhist cultural context craving and desire can be understood as manifestations of dualistic thinking. It is then all the more poignant that one of the final images of *Ugetsu* is that of Genjuro and Miyagi's young son bowing before the grave and making '*gasho*', bringing his hands together in the Buddhist gesture which affirms that there is 'no gap' between the worlds. As if in silent entreaty for an end to the illusory divisions that keep us thirsting and craving and clinging to the wheel of life, Mizoguchi ends his masterpiece with an embodied gesture, a reminder that there is only 'this very body' and 'this very life' in which to navigate desire, echoing the Zen teaching 'this very body is the lotus of the true law, linking human beings to birth and death by the red thread of passion'.[12]

NOTES

1. Stevens, John (1990) *Lust for Enlightenment: Buddhism and Sex*, Boston: Shambala Press, p. 91.
2. Hunter, Jack (1998) *Eros in Hell: Sex, Blood and Madness in Japanese Cinema*, London: Creation Books International, p. 3.
3. As Bernard Faure points out in his work on the Red Thread, it is both somewhat misleading and also possibly unavoidable to talk about 'Buddhism' or even 'Zen Buddhism' as a unified philosophy, when the history of these ideas is so complex. See Faure, Bernard (1998) *The Red Thread: Buddhist Approaches to Sexuality*, Princeton, NJ: Princeton University Press, p. 11.
4. Ibid., p. 15.
5. Ibid., p. 17.
6. Stevens, p. 22. The evolution of Buddhist ideas about sexuality and desire has been the subject of numerous works of scholarship and it would be impossible to do more than address these ideas in a cursory way here.
7. Loori, John Daido (1996) *The Heart of Being: Moral and Ethical Teachings of Zen Buddhism*, Rutland, VT: Charles E. Tuttle, p. 173.
8. Sharp, Jasper (2001b) 'Jigoku Review', in *Midnight Eye: The Latest and Best in Japanese Cinema*, 25 June, http://www.midnighteye.com/reviews/jigoku.shtml.
9. This is not meant to imply that there are no horror films in which women undergo monstrous transformations on the threshold of commitment, although there seem to be far fewer. Jacques Tourneur's *Cat People* (1942) is a good example of the shoe on the other foot.
10. Sharp, Jasper (2001a) 'Moju Review', in *Midnight Eye: The Latest and Best in Japanese Cinema*, 20 March, http://www.midnighteye.com/reviews/moju.shtml.
11. Bardo is the Tibetan word for gap or interval. In Tibetan Buddhism there are a series of intervals that all beings pass through over the cycle of rebirths. The Bardo of Suffering is experienced at the moment of death and one's karma determines whether the transition will be peaceful or nightmarish.
12. Barzaghi, Subhana (1993) *Red Thread Zen: The Tao of Love, Passion, and Sex*, given at Spring Sesshin, Gorricks Run Zendo, NSW, Australia. http://www.buddhistinformation.com/red_thread_zen.htm.

3. CASE STUDY: NAKATA HIDEO'S *RINGU* AND *RINGU 2*

Eric White

At the beginning of Nakata Hideo's recent horror film *Ringu* (1998), an urban legend has begun to spread among the teenage population of Tokyo during the late summer of 1997. The legend concerns a mysterious videocassette, the mere playing of which dooms the viewer to certain death. Those unlucky enough to watch the video immediately thereafter receive a telephone call informing them that they have but one week to live. Events soon reveal the death-dealing video to be no mere legend; a group of teenagers who had seen it while on holiday at a resort on the Izu peninsula southwest of Tokyo all die under unexplained circumstances. In each case, the immediate cause of death can readily be inferred from the terror-stricken expressions on their dead faces: their hearts have stopped beating from sheer fright. Asakawa Reiko, a journalist preparing a feature piece on the legend of the video curse, is horrified to learn that her own niece, who was among those on the Izu trip, has now been frightened to death. After examining a disturbing photograph of the deceased teenagers taken while they were on their weekend trip, a photograph in which the teenagers' faces are strangely blurred and distorted almost beyond recognition, Reiko travels to the resort herself to try to discover some explanation for the curse that will prevent a further round of similarly tragic events.

Once at the resort, Reiko quickly locates the videotape and proceeds to watch it herself in the very cabin to which the teenagers had sojourned. The curse video unfolds as an oneiric montage of enigmatic images: night-time clouds scud across the face of the moon as we gaze upward from what we will later realise is the bottom of a well to see someone looking down at us from above; a mirror jumps back and forth across the wall on which it hangs, revealing first a woman brushing her hair and then a small figure in a white gown; what the screenplay for the film describes as a 'twitching, undulating, impenetrable sea of characters' appears in the midst of which only one word – 'eruption' – can be made out clearly; a crowd of people are seen crawling and shuffling forward apparently with some difficulty, while a host of voices murmur monotonously and indistinctly; a human figure, its head covered with a cloth, gestures in the direction of a backdrop of moving water; and finally, after a close-up image of a staring eye in whose lens floats the mirror-image of a single character, 'sada', there is an outdoor expanse in the middle of which can be discerned a low-lying, flat-topped, evidently circular structure that, once again, will later be recognisable as a well.[1] As soon as the video ends, the stunned Reiko turns off the television set. At that moment, as she stares at the now blank screen, she glimpses herself and, ever so briefly over her shoulder, another form reflected in the glass of the television screen, but when she turns around, she sees nothing. Then the telephone rings, and she begins to fear that she too will die in seven days.

Returning to Tokyo, Reiko studies the videotape closely with the assistance of her ex-husband, a mathematics professor at a nearby university. The pair seek to decipher the meaning of the unsettling images they believe must somehow be connected to the curse visited upon anyone who watches them. Eventually, they piece together a tragic history going back some four decades concerning a woman from Oshima island (located just to the east of the Izu peninsula) whose telepathic prediction of a volcanic eruption brought her to the attention of a scientific researcher specialising in the study of extrasensory perception. After becoming romantically involved with the scientist, the telepathic woman gave birth to a child named Sadako, whose psychic powers surpassed even her own. One fateful day, when her mother was reduced to tears by a crowd of hectoring journalists, the child telepathically willed the death of one of their number. The intimidating journalist died on the spot from sheer fright; shortly thereafter the child's mother committed suicide and the scientist, before disappearing himself, threw the child down a well, where her bones have lain undiscovered ever since. It is thus the ghost of the child who seeks revenge upon a cruel world by means of the video curse.

Reiko and her ex-husband hope that the curse will lift once this tragic tale has been made public and the bones of the dead child given a proper burial. Accordingly, they return to the resort in Izu and uncover the well, which, it turns out, lies under the cabin earlier visited by both the dead teenagers and the investigative journalist, precisely beneath the spot where the ghostly reflection she glimpsed in the television screen had been standing. But immediately after the retrieval of Sadako's remains, the ex-husband's seemingly offhand speculation that the child's real father may not have been the scientist after all but a god or demon from the sea, signals a sudden, catastrophic turn of events. In a terrifying scene, the ghost of the dead child emerges from the television set in the ex-husband's living room. Like so many before him, he dies of fright. The public revelation of the child's tragic end has in no way assuaged this vengeful, tormented spirit or prevented the continued propagation of its curse upon humankind. The curse never could have been lifted by restoring Sadako symbolically to the human community by means of a proper burial, because she was not herself 'human' to begin with, and her ultimate motivation was never, therefore, humanly intelligible.

Sadako's terrifying eruption from the television set thus dramatically alters our understanding of the nature of the tale told in *Ringu*, and in so doing retrospectively clarifies the meaning of a series of hitherto puzzling details in the story. We can now appreciate why the eyeball glimpsed in the video is described in the film screenplay as 'inhuman' and 'alien-looking', why the noise heard over the telephone line when Sadako calls her victims sounds like 'metallic, insectoid screeching', and why the manner of her emergence from the television set when we finally see her in the flesh is 'more insect-like than human'.[2] We can also grasp the significance of the revelation that Sadako's mother had long ago spent many hours sitting by the sea, where she would address the ocean in a non-human language. We also understand why the indistinct murmuring voices heard on the videotape, when properly amplified, can be perceived as chanting 'frolic in brine, goblins be thine' (or, in another translation, 'play in the water and a monster will come for you'), and why, too, the hooded figure seen in the curse video itself may have been directing our attention to the waves. Sadako is the supernatural offspring of a human being and a sea monster. Although *Ringu* employs the traditional motif of the vengeful ghost longing for eternal rest, this narrative should not be understood, at least in the most familiar sense, as a tale of the uncanny. Sadako's emergence from a well of forgetting cannot finally be explained as the return of the repressed in the sense of an unresolved trauma that has endured in the unconscious, waiting to be exorcised by means of a therapeutic catharsis.[3]

But if the import of *Ringu*'s narrative is not conventionally uncanny, neither can the tale be taken at face value as merely a series of bizarre supernatural occurrences. When the journalist, standing in the living room of her former husband's flat, wonders aloud to herself why she was the only one saved, she has another vision of the mysterious figure with the cloth draped over its head pointing this time not at the ocean, that traditional symbol of the chaos of threatening otherness, but at the overnight bag containing her own copy of the curse video. As she retrieves her copy of the curse video and compares it with the videocassette she gave to her ex-husband – on the spine of which the word 'copy' is marked clearly in English – she realises that her recent experience has differed from her ex-husband's in one respect only: while she duplicated the video and gave the copy to him, he never made a copy for anyone else. We thus learn that while the curse cannot permanently be dispelled, its fulfilment can be postponed indefinitely by means of a simple technological expedient: one has merely to pass a copy of the videotape to a third party who, upon viewing it, passes a further copy to someone else, and so on *ad infinitum.*

This introduction of the motif of the simulacrum – understood as the copy of a copy – is of considerable interpretive consequence. It turns out that Sadako's revenge upon a cruel world entails the inauguration of a new cultural logic, a logic of the simulacrum according to which copies of copies vary continually from an always already lost original.[4] At the moment of their deaths, the horrified faces of Sadako's victims instantaneously change from bodily flesh-and-blood into the black-and-white reverse imagery of photographic negatives. They thus cross over to the other side of everyday life as simulacral images that copy, but do not identically reproduce, their former selves. As Reiko's ex-husband concludes with reference to Reiko's dead niece, whose ghost places their young son, Yoichi, at risk by enticing him to view the curse video, she is no longer herself. Similarly, even those lucky ones who survive their encounter with the video curse by passing on a copy to someone else are ineluctably transformed by the experience of having viewed Sadako's enigmatic message from beyond. As we learn in Nakata's second *Ringu* film, *Ringu 2* (1999), even after the curse has ostensibly been lifted, the living continue to be haunted by Sadako's irrecuperable otherness. One might therefore speculate that their faces will continue to shape-shift should anyone try to photograph them, such that successive photos will vaguely resemble, but never perfectly coincide, with one another. In other words, the survivors fall victim to a logic of the simulacrum as well: they will never again quite be themselves. The film thus associates ubiquitous technological mediation – that is, the cameras, television sets, videocassette recorders, telephones and other such hardware foregrounded throughout the film – with the intrusion of 'posthuman' otherness into contemporary cultural life. As the imagery at the very beginning of the film suggests – where a nocturnal scene of watery turbulence fades into the electronic static or noise of a television screen seen in extreme close-up – the unpredictable mutability of the ocean, a traditional metaphor for threatening alterity, can also be understood to figure a cultural upheaval brought about by the simulacral proliferation of information in a media-saturated social sphere. In other words, the cloth that covers the head of the enigmatic figure who gestures now at the ocean, now at the videocassette, may conceal from view a face that is no longer human.

What the advent of a 'posthuman' culture might literally entail only becomes clear, however, in *Ringu 2*, whose storyline commences just a week or so after the discovery of Sadako's mortal remains at the bottom of the well.

As *Ringu 2* opens, a police detective at the morgue where the body has just been autopsied questions the sole surviving relative who knew Sadako in life, an elderly man who long ago first introduced Sadako's mother to the psychic researcher in the hope, it seems, of profiting from her telepathic abilities.[5] The detective informs the old man that the police are attempting to ascertain the connection between Sadako's tragic end, the death of the mathematics professor and the apparent disappearance of his ex-wife, Reiko, and their son, Yoichi. At the same time, across town, a graduate research assistant who was romantically involved with the professor launches her own unofficial investigation into the death of her lover. Joining forces with one of Reiko's newsroom colleagues, the pair search Reiko's apartment, discovering a variety of clues including a television set smashed to pieces in the living room, a videocassette burned in the bathtub and, in a bureau drawer, the disturbingly out-of-focus photographs of the four teenagers who died mysteriously of fright following their fateful sojourn at the Izu peninsula resort. While they are searching the flat, the police telephone with the news that Reiko's father has become Sadako's latest victim. It seems he saved the life of his grandson by watching the curse video but, failing to understand the necessity of passing on a copy of the tape to someone else, perished.

All paths soon converge on a hospital psychiatric ward, where a schoolmate of Reiko's dead niece has recently been confined. The schoolmate, who witnessed the horrifying demise of her friend and subsequently suffered a nervous breakdown, is now herself haunted by the vengeful spirit of Sadako. As we see her brought by a nurse along a hallway, with her head lowered and her face covered by her long hair, she in fact resembles Sadako. Although she is afraid of television sets, when she passes a TV in a patient lounge, she turns to watch in spite of herself. The curse transmission immediately appears on the television screen. As Sadako climbs out of the well and begins her terrifying progress toward her viewers, the other patients in the psychiatric ward writhe on the floor and emit incomprehensible cries in a frightening scene of collective panic.

A psychiatrist interested in paranormal phenomena attempts to explain the previous events by showing the assembled investigators examples of what he calls 'spirit photography'.[6] Some of these are photographs of the schoolmate, in which the ghostly form of the cloth-shrouded figure from the curse video can indistinctly be discerned. In other photographs, which were made by asking the haunted teenager to touch unexposed photographic film, the character 'Sada' is clearly legible. The psychiatrist theorises that the various haunted survivors of Sadako's wrath remain suffused with 'some kind of energy'. This mysterious energy is responsible for the eerie apparitions that populate his collection of spirit photographs. Evidently confident that a cure can be effected by draining the energy from those who harbour it, he then proceeds to conduct an experiment on the hospitalised schoolmate. Seated amid sundry scientific equipment, her head covered with electrodes and the like, the schoolmate begins to transmit the images associated with Sadako's curse on the living. The psychiatrist, his aide, the detective, the research assistant and the journalist colleague all begin to watch the fateful sequence of images. According to the scientist, they have nothing to worry about. Even if they get that video on tape, he reasons, videos don't kill: fear kills. Prove that, he posits, and its energy dissipates and frees the schoolmate. The research assistant is not, however, persuaded of the validity of his theory. When the schoolmate suddenly falls unconscious – and we sense something catastrophic is about to occur – the research assistant destroys the video monitor and the videotape on which the psychiatrist is recording the curse images.

Shortly thereafter, Reiko and her young son, Yoichi, are taken into police custody. Both remain haunted, Yoichi says, by 'the woman with long hair'. Yoichi in particular is shadowed by the supernatural. As is the case with the schoolmate who witnessed the death of her friend, television sets in close proximity to him mysteriously switch on. When the police seize Reiko and Yoichi, the research assistant telepathically warns Yoichi that they must flee. As Yoichi runs down a hallway pursued by the police detective, Yoichi's own powers are revealed in a psychic assault that leaves the detective gasping desperately for air. Like Sadako, it would appear that Yoichi can will the death of those who oppress or oppose him. He may in fact now be possessed by Sadako's spirit; when the ghost of Reiko's father appears to her in a vision, he tells her that her child isn't himself anymore.

Following Reiko's tragic death (she is struck and killed by a lorry in the course of their escape attempt), Yoichi becomes the de facto ward of the research assistant. In the hope of bringing the haunting to an end by tracing it to its source, they make the journey to Oshima island and rent a room at an inn owned by the son and daughter-in-law of Sadako's elderly relative. The psychiatrist surmises where the pair have gone and soon follows. As he arrives at the inn, the lights flicker and dim, suggesting the influence of some supernatural energy source whose presence is shortly thereafter confirmed when the psychiatrist and the research assistant are shocked to witness the ghosts of Sadako and her mother materialising before their horrified eyes. The psychiatrist then performs a test on Yoichi to ascertain the extent to which he has become a vessel for Sadako's malign psychic energy. In a scene recalling the psychiatrist's earlier experiment with the haunted teenager, Yoichi is asked to concentrate his attention upon a glass of water. The water apparently absorbs a portion of the psychic energy. Thus acquiring supernaturally kinetic properties, it flows across a table top in a manner reminiscent of the way Reiko's blood flowed across the pavement toward Yoichi when she was struck by the lorry. The psychiatrist announces that it is the boy's anger that summons Sadako. 'He can't control it . . . He channels the energy. He's the best medium . . . There are no ghosts, no "next world,"' he continues, 'only a vast invisible reservoir of psychic energy.' All that remains to be done is to 'conduct the energy [the little boy] generates into the water where it will dissolve. And Sadako will disappear.' He says they'll need a very large quantity of water indeed to absorb Sadako's terrible wrath.

Night falls as the scene shifts to an indoor swimming pool, alongside which Yoichi and the research assistant are hooked up to an array of scientific instruments. As Yoichi begins channelling, we glimpse the faces of both of his now deceased parents – beneficent imagos that evidently reside in his unconscious – telepathically broadcast on a television monitor. In order to anger him so that he will then powerfully project the psychic energy for which he is the medium, the psychiatrist tells Yoichi that the research assistant is responsible for his mother's death. The pool of water begins to churn and froth as images from the curse video appear on the monitor. The water also shimmers with a throng of spectral apparitions as multifarious psychic impulses become turbulently concentrated in the pool. As the research assistant cries out, 'I can see into the next world,' Sadako's coffin appears and the lid begins to slide off. The old man enters the pool, crying, '[t]ake me and put an end to this.' At the same moment, the psychiatrist, as if hypnotised, falls into the pool, where he apparently drowns.

Meanwhile, the research assistant and Yoichi both faint. When they regain consciousness, they find themselves clinging to the side of the well in which Sadako met her end. As we hear the refrain 'Frolic in brine, goblins be thine,' Yoichi says, 'let me fall.' He then plummets to the water below, followed by the research assistant. Yoichi's father now appears and tells his son to 'give your fear to me.' As Yoichi and his guardian begin climbing to safety, Sadako pursues them, asking the research assistant, 'Why are you the only one saved?' before tumbling to the water below. Though no direct answer is given to her question, the viewer may surmise that the pair have been saved from her clutches precisely thanks to Yoichi's internalised parental imagos, in particular the father who, cold and distant in the first film, has at last intervened to support and affirm his son. In a stunningly hallucinatory moment, the pair then erupt from the surface of the water in the swimming pool at the Oshima island inn. It is daylight. The bodies of the psychiatrist and the elderly relative float in the water; the psychiatrist's aide lies dead by the side of the pool.

The allegorical significance of the two films may now be ventured. In the first film, the oscillating reflection of Sadako and her mother in the mirror alludes to the foundational role traditionally played by the internalisation of familial images in the formation of individual identity. But the *Ringu* films depict a social milieu in which the family matrix no longer provides the exclusive basis for psychological structure. Instead, omnipresent information technology functions as a vast psychic apparatus, or better, a psychotronic apparatus randomly propagating affective dispositions, libidinal intensities, decontextualised personae and partial selves across the social sphere.[7] The two films propose that information technology induces a shape-shifting fluidity of identity by installing a culture of simulacral proliferation in which contagious shards of personality infect anyone who comes into contact with them, reconstituting those thus touched as no longer quite themselves.[8] Although a therapeutic catharsis of family trauma does take place in the second film when the ghost of the father tells Yoichi to 'give me your fear', the fact that the research assistant and the child subsequently ascend from the well of traumatic forgetting to surface in what we know to be an enormous pool of turbulent psychic energy suggests that conventionally 'human' psychological formations will henceforth comprise only a subset of the veritable sea of possibilities that I have been referring to as the 'posthuman'.

Support for this interpretation may be adduced from the conclusion to the second film. At the very end of *Ringu 2*, we learn that the journalist colleague who participated in the research assistant's investigation at the beginning of the film has now been hospitalised in the psychiatric ward. It seems he accepted a copy of the curse video from a helpful teenager, promising to view the video himself and then pass on a copy to a third party. But when he loses his nerve and decides not to view the tape, the teenager becomes Sadako's latest victim and begins to haunt him. From the horror-stricken expression of his nurse as she regards a portrait photograph, we may assume that the colleague's face has begun to shape-shift in response to an infusion of psychic energy from beyond, or, more precisely, from the ghost of the teenager who appears over his shoulder in the film's closing shot, laughing softly, but with unnerving intensity. The denouement by the side of the swimming pool at the Oshima island inn notwithstanding, no final catharsis has been achieved. Instead, psychic energy continues its incessant propagation, displaced from one individual to another in a theoretically endless chain or 'ring'. Individual personality must therefore remain in a state of perpetual flux. Subjected to ceaseless modification, the self consequently becomes a contingent assemblage, a bundle of provisional identifications rather than a cohesive unity, a composite copy of randomly encountered psychic dispositions and fragments of personality.

I'll close now with this observation: the aleatoric metamorphosis of self looming on the cultural horizon in the *Ringu* films does not provoke horror as the sole response to this advent of the posthuman. In the novel by Suzuki Koji upon which the first film is based, the journalist believes that the enigmatic stream of images on the curse video must emanate from the Id, which could here be seen 'squirming, worrying, finding an exit . . . maybe it was the throb of life. Thought had energy . . . Strangely, [the journalist] felt no desire to push stop . . . this intense outpouring of energy felt good.'[9] Similarly, the children whose laughter is heard at intervals throughout the first film and who cheerfully recount the legend of the curse at the film's end appear to be undismayed by the prospect of individual identity as a revisable pastiche of drives, appetites and personality fragments. The *Ringu* films thus articulate a troubled and yet oddly expectant vision of a future in which the great collective psychotronic apparatus of contemporary information technology ceaselessly reconstitutes individual identity. As the journalist's ex-husband puts it when asked how urban legends like the tale of Sadako originate, such tales do not have a definite beginning: 'It's more like everyone's fear just takes on a life of its own . . . Or maybe it's not fear at all. Maybe it's what we were secretly hoping for all along.'

NOTES

1. A translation of the film screenplay by J. Lopez, along with much valuable information about both of Nakata's *Ringu* films, may be found at the following website: http://www.somrux.com/ringworld/

2. Sadako's appearance also recalls traditional representations of vengeful female spirits in Japanese art. In the novel upon which the film is based, her face is compared to the mask of a *hannya* or female demon; see Suzuki Koji [1991] (2003) *Ring*, trans. Robert B. Rohmer and Glynne Walley, New York: Vertical, p. 50.

3. Freud's characterisation of the uncanny as the return of the repressed can be found in his essay on the subject; see Freud, Sigmund [1925] (1958) 'The Uncanny', *On Creativity and the Unconscious: Papers on the Psychology of Art, Literature, Love, Religion*, selected with introduction and annotations by Benjamin Nelson, New York: Harper, pp. 122–61.

4. For two classic formulations of the cultural significance of the simulacrum, see Baudrillard, Jean (1988) 'Simulacra and Simulations', in Mark Poster (ed.), *Selected Writings*, Stanford, CA: Stanford University Press, pp. 166–84, and Deleuze, Gilles (1990) 'Plato and the Simulacrum', *The Logic of Sense*, New York: Columbia University Press, pp. 253–66.

5. *Ringu 2*. Directed by Nakata Hideo; screenplay by Takashi Hiroshi; produced by Hara Masato, Ichise Takashige and Ishihara Makoto; cinematography by Yamamoto Hideo; edited by Takahashi Noboyuki; production design by Saitô Iwao; music by Kawai Kinji (1999).

6. Incidentally, the respective scientists of *Ringu* and *Ringu 2* are loosely based on a controversial early twentieth-century psychic investigator, Fukurai Tomokichi, whose research into spirit photography, or 'thoughtography', resulted in his dismissal from the Imperial University of Tokyo shortly after he published an account of his experiments in 1913. For an abundantly illustrated presentation of his research, see Fukurai Tomokichi (1931) *Clairvoyance and Thoughtography*, London: Rider.

7. For a brief explanation of psychotronics as a concept positing a linkage between the psychic realm and electronic media, see Christopher Cerf's foreword to Weldon,

Michael (ed.) (1983) *The Psychotronic Encyclopedia of Film*, New York: Ballantine, p. ix.

8. In Suzuki's novel, Sadako's curse spreads precisely by viral contagion: her desire for revenge is so lethal because it has been supernaturally fused with the instinct to reproduce, like a virus on the brink of biological extinction; see Suzuki, *Ring*, p. 281.

9. See Suzuki, *Ring*, p. 76.

PART 2

GENDER, TERROR AND THE 'AVENGING SPIRIT' MOTIF IN JAPANESE HORROR CINEMA

INTRODUCTION

The representation of women in Japanese popular culture in general, and Japanese cinema in particular, has remained a consistent subject of critical inquiry for film and media scholars. This recurrent focus is due in large part to the various, and often extreme, ways in which women have been depicted on screen by generations of filmmakers, from the complex and, at times, transcendental images offered by such icons of Japanese cinema as Kurosawa Akira (*Rashomon*, 1950) and Ozu Yajahiro (*Floating Weeds*, 1959, and *Tokyo Story*, 1953), to the overtly politicised representations that inform the works of Japanese New Wave directors like Oshima Nagisa (*Cruel Story of Youth*, 1960, and *In the Realm of the Senses*, 1976), to the visions of degredation and fetishised violence that constitute a substantial amount of the *pinku eiga* released through Nikkatsu Studios. As David Desser contends in his groundbreaking *Eros Plus Massacre: An Introduction to the Japanese New Wave Cinema*, '[I]n Japanese high and popular culture one sees images of women ranging from outright worship to hatred and fear'.[1] The latter representation is certainly not uncommon in works of Japanese horror cinema. As mentioned in this book's introduction, although the *kaidan*, or 'avenging spirit' films, are a staple of the horror genre, the 'avenging spirit' narrative is by no means a recent conceit. Thus, while the story of a wronged, primarily female spirit returning from beyond the grave to avenge herself upon those who have done her an injustice informs the plots of numerous 'classic' Japanese horror films, from Arai Ryohei's *Ghost Cat* (1953) and Mizoguchi Kenji's *Ugetsu Monogatari* [*Tales of Ugetsu*] (1953) to Shindo

Keneto's *Onibaba* (1964) and Tanaka Tokuzo's *Kwaidan* (1964), narrative precursors can be found in the alleged activities of literary/historical figures like Sugawara Michizone (845–903), 'a [male] courtier aristocrat who died in exile because of court intrigues, and who came back as a ghost to wreak havoc in the imperial capital',[2] as well as in the teachings and writings of Shintoist and Christian religious traditions and the plot devices of Noh and Kabuki theatre.

The three essays that follow not only engage with the representation of women (including the 'avenging spirit' motif) in recent works of Japanese horror cinema, but also examine how contemporary audiences read these texts both within Japan and internationally. In 'Japanese Horror Under Western Eyes: Social Class and Global Culture in Miike Takashi's *Audition*', Steffen Hantke opens his essay with an in-depth consideration of Miike's controversial film of loneliness, love and revenge in light of its cross-cultural success. In the course of this chapter, Hantke's thoughtful analysis locates the film as a revenge tale that, while deviating from the traditional 'avenging spirit' conceit in important ways, nonetheless reveals the presence of restrictive social and gender codes that maintain economies of subjugation within Japanese society and against which women continue to struggle. Beginning his inquiry into the film's surprisingly wide appeal by questioning whether *Audition*'s transnational popularity results from a lack of cultural specificity within its narrative or from the existence of 'something specifically "global"', Hantke locates numerous telling intersections between late capitalist western and Japanese culture. These include the presence of similar reactionary postures frequently triggered by the perceived threat of emasculation in the home and in the workplace, and directed against feminist movements and shifting gender roles.

As Susan Napier observes, the figure of the female avenger, like the culture from which she emerges, transforms over the course of the twentieth century; no longer merely representing 'opportunities for either vengeance against the modern or escape from the modern', the feminine becomes 'increasingly other, unreachable, even demonic'.[3] As Christopher Bolton points out in 'Anime Horror and Its Audience: *3x3 Eyes* and *Vampire Princess Miyu*', such an association of the female body with monstrous alterity often informs the fantastic story lines and radical transmutations common to Japanese animated (or anime) texts variably intended to frighten viewers. Thus, like Hantke's reading of Miike's *Audition*, Bolton's chapter engages with issues of audience reception. However, unlike Hantke's expansive, transnational consideration of Miike's 'live action' text, Bolton narrows the focus of his critical eye to Japanese *otaku* (anime and manga fans), positing them as exceptionally sophisticated and savvy spectators that at once recognise the artificiality of anime bodies and violence, and respond to the genre's intended impact upon its consumers. For Bolton, then, *otaku* possess a metaphorical 'third eye' that 'allows the spectator to watch him or herself watching the text' and, consequently, ponder his or her 'own manipulation by this media'. This practice, Bolton posits, reveals anime's potential for broadening 'audience . . . perspective' and, quite possibly, increasing the viewer's ability to perceive the operant gender codes informing contemporary culture.

Frank Lafond's case study, which concludes this section of *Japanese Horror Cinema*, offers a close reading of Ishii Takashi's *Freeze Me* (2000) as a variant of the 'rape-revenge' cycle, a primarily western horror film subgenre written about at great length by scholars like Carol Clover and Jacinda Read.[4] Acknowledging the difficulties inherent in viewing Ishii's film through a western lens occluded by the contributions of, and politics surrounding, 'the rise of second-wave feminism of the 1970s', Lafond asserts that '[I]t is in the similarities or in the gaps between Ishii Takashi's film and canonical examples of the rape-revenge subgenre that we might be able to bring to the forefront the film's specific social concerns'. A variation upon the 'avenging spirit' motif in that the film's heroine, Chihiro, unleashes her fury upon an abusive system of patriarchal authority, *Freeze Me* is a harrowing and multi-faceted text that, according to Lafond's careful dissection, articulates a nihilistic feminist perspective by combining a meditation upon sexist violence in the professional, interpersonal and domestic realms of modern-day Japan, with a critical assessment of the further-reaching implications of Chihiro's desperate actions, interrogating their effectiveness in terms of advocating an activist agenda.

NOTES

1. Desser, David (1988) *Eros Plus Massacre: An Introduction to the Japanese New Wave Cinema*, Bloomington and Indianapolis: Indiana University Press, p. 108.
2. Barret, Gregory (1989) *Archetypes in Japanese Film: The Sociopolitical and Religious Significance of the Principle Heroes and Heroines*, Selinsgrove, PA: Susquehanna University Press, p. 17.
3. Napier, Susan J. (1996) *The Fantastic in Modern Japanese Literature: The Subversion of Modernity*, New York and London: Routledge, p. 57. In the following chapter, see Steffen Hantke's discussion of Miike Takashi's *Audition* for a more thorough investigation of the implications one may construe from this observation.
4. See Clover, Carol J. (1992) *Men, Women and Chainsaws: Gender in the Modern Horror Film*, London: BFI; Princeton, NJ: Princeton University Press; Read, Jacinda (2000) *The New Avengers: Feminism, Femininity and the Rape-Revenge Cycle*, Manchester and New York: Manchester University Press.

4. JAPANESE HORROR UNDER WESTERN EYES: SOCIAL CLASS AND GLOBAL CULTURE IN MIIKE TAKASHI'S *AUDITION*

Steffen Hantke

In a September 2002 article on horror film in the *Guardian*, Steve Rose states bluntly, 'US horror has had no new ideas since the slasher movies of the 1980s'.[1] In support of this indictment, he gleefully cites the titles of US horror films in the making: 'Looking forward to *Scary Movie 3: Lord of the Brooms*? Or *Halloween: Resurrection*? Or how about *Freddy VS Jason*, which doubles as *Nightmare on Elm Street Part Nine* and *Friday 13th Part 11*?'[2] Given these titles, Rose seems right when he concludes: 'formulas and franchises have been squeezed dry'.[3] The remedy for this creative attrition, according to Rose, is Hollywood's purchase of the rights to Asian horror films and their subsequent remakes. Nakata Hideo's *Ringu* (1998) has already been reincarnated as Gore Verbinski's *The Ring* in October 2002. Another Nakata film, *Chaos* (1999), is being remade by Jonathan Glazer, while Wes Craven is working on his version of Kurosawa Kiyoshi's *Kaïro* (or *Pulse,* 2001), and Tom Cruise and associates have bought the rights to Oxide and Danny Pang's *The Eye* (2002). A dose of healthy Japanese horror, the cross-fertilisation with an exotic cinematic tradition, may cure the ailing American horror film, or so Rose believes.

Another symptom of the same malaise is the Western market's increased interest in the products of Asian cinema, especially in Japanese horror films.

Kurosawa Kyoshi's *Cure* (1997), for example, had a critically and commercially successful run in US arthouse cinemas in 2001, as did Fukasaku Kinji's *Battle Royale* (2000). Similarly, the availability of Japanese horror film on video and DVD has increased as distributors market their wares via the Internet to rising numbers of fans. Although films like *Cure*, *Battle Royale* or *Ringu* obviously cannot compete with the desperately inflated advertising budgets of large US horror productions, their increasing prominence and commercial viability in American theatres are signs that there is an audience that responds favourably to niche marketing. Having done well in Japan, these films get a new lease on life in western markets. By the same token, they create a broader awareness of Japanese horror films and, hence, a larger demand for films to follow.

Of the Japanese horror films that have made inroads into the western market, Miike Takashi's *Audition* deserves special attention. Its arrival was accompanied by scandal, as audiences during the 2000 Rotterdam Film Festival walked out in record numbers and viewers during a showing in Switzerland fainted and needed to be taken to the emergency room by ambulance.[4] Incidents (or rumours) like these tend to endear a film to horror audiences, but *Audition* also did well in the mainstream. Reviewer Peter Bradshaw waxes poetically about *Audition*'s ability to morph from an 'almost Reineresque romantic comedy' into 'a horrific black butterfly emerg[ing] from the chrysalis', while a nameless web reviewer praises Miike for doing 'a wonderful job sucking us into his cinematic world'.[5] Yoram Allon admires Miike's high degree of self-awareness in negotiating the margins of genre cinema ('This works as cinema because it presents its tale in reassuring "arthouse" compositions before toying with horror-genre conventions that really explore just what it is the viewer wishes to see'[6]). Ken Eisner praises the film's 'haunting beauty',[7] its lyrical pacing, and its potential for 'arthouse play . . . especially in latenight venues'.[8]

These critical accolades, published in Western mainstream journals and newspapers like the *Guardian* and *Variety*, indicate that, though *Audition*'s notoriety may have given it a certain degree of cult leverage, it is not Miike's willingness to resort to visual and thematic extremes that makes the film unique. Rather, it is its success with a variety of different audiences, its ability to cross social and national boundaries: from popular entertainment to arthouse cinema, and from Japan to the West. One wonders whether this flexibility or adaptability is the result of generic and cultural blandness, a lack of distinguishing features, or a plethora of 'gaps' that reader-response theory postulates as the essential prerequisite of all meaningful reading engagement. Does *Audition* lack cultural specificity, or is there something specifically 'global' about the film that has allowed it to work so well transnationally?

These questions hold little interest for the film's creators – director Miike

Takashi, scriptwriter Tengan Daiske and writer Murakami Ryu, on whose short story the film is based. Miike himself dodges questions about his film's success in the West: 'I can't say I was completely surprised,' he says when asked about *Audition* turning out to be 'a hit' with western audiences. 'But I have no idea what goes on in the minds of people in the West and I don't pretend to know what their tastes are. And I don't want to start thinking about that. It's nice that they liked my movie, but I'm not going to start deliberately worrying about why or what I can do to make it happen again.'[9]

At first glance, the plot of *Audition* is simple, straightforward and familiar. The film's protagonist Aoyama, a middle-aged widower raising a teenage son, decides to get married a second time, seven years after the death of his beloved wife. Yoshikawa, a friend of his in the film industry, suggests that the two of them schedule a fake audition which would allow Aoyama to interview a group of women selected to meet his specific standards for a new wife. Among the contestants is a young woman named Asami, whose application catches Aoyama's eye and who subsequently turns out to be everything he hopes for. Despite Yoshikawa's vague sense of unease about her, Aoyama asks Asami out. She gratefully accepts his invitation, and after a short time he decides to propose to her. However, during a romantic weekend getaway, Asami vanishes from their shared bed. She leaves the hotel and disappears without a trace. Still in love, Aoyama begins investigating some of the personal information she provided during the audition. He discovers that her connection in the music industry, the director of a company for whom she supposedly was on retainer, has mysteriously disappeared. The ballet school where she trained as a child is boarded up, and the bar where she used to work has been closed after the owner was gruesomely murdered. At a dead end in his investigation, Aoyama returns to his apartment and sits down with a glass of whisky. But Asami has spiked the drink and hidden upstairs. When Aoyama falls paralysed, yet awake, to the floor, Asami appears and begins to torture and mutilate him. When his son returns home unexpectedly, a shuffle ensues between the two, which ends with Asami being fatally injured in a fall down a steep flight of stairs.

Most of this story is told in the most self-effacing manner possible. Through much of the film, Miike uses continuity editing, medium shots and naturalistic lighting, eschewing compositions that draw attention to themselves by appearing contrived or melodramatic. The pace is consistently slow, even sluggish at times. When Miike goes against the grain of the Hollywood style, as he does with small details, the stylistic idiosyncrasy is submerged in a text so low-key that most viewers will associate it with a made-for-television aesthetic rather than that of a feature film.

While reviewers complain about the lack of visual novelty and adventurousness in *Audition*, western audiences may respond with relief at seeing the cultural gap between themselves and the text bridged so conveniently. The 'invisible style', coupled with the formulaic elements of genre, its very predictability, may in fact work in the film's best interest with an audience that has no immediate access to its culturally more specific subtext. Stylistically, the lowest common denominator may ease this audience into the text, just as the foregrounding of genre serves as a kind of ethnocentric filter.

In the third and final reel, however, all of this changes. The shift is so dramatic that reviewers talk about Miike 'seducing' (Morris) and 'blind-siding' (Bartok) the viewer, committing 'a sadistic breach of contract between filmmaker and audience of which Hitchcock could only dream'.[10] Gary Morris describes how *Audition* accomplishes this feat: 'For close to an hour it has the look and feel of a classic Japanese family drama . . . Just past midpoint everything changes: the film bails on the narrative, intertwines dream sequences and reality so densely there's no telling what's real, and pushes the gore and grue to a limit rarely seen outside the cheesy cinematic bloodbaths of 1960s schlocksters like Herschell Gordon Lewis or Al Adamson.'[11]

This shift and the ensuing ambiguities translate into a complexity that makes the film deliberately 'difficult' for viewers in search of verisimilitude. Miike himself keeps suggesting that ambiguities result from shifts between Aoyama's and Asami's subjective points of view; that, in a manner of speaking, the film goes from 'he said' to 'she said'.[12] Viewers who pay close attention to the structural complexity of *Audition*, especially to the logic of thematic and visual association, may find that this reading by Miike himself falls short of the film's complexity. For them, its pleasures may derive more from accepting its difficulty than from any attempt to impose upon it a coherent 'realist' reading that resolves all ambiguities and establishes closure. Curiously enough, the reviews I have cited never admit to frustration. What is more, they embrace difficulty and make it the aesthetic linchpin of their critical assessment, endorsing it as a hallmark of the film's high modernist style. The film, in turn, accommodates them, as it constructs a position for an implied viewer cognisant of modernism as an international style recognisable across national cultural boundaries.[13]

Paradoxically, it is the film's radical modernist ambiguity that opens the door for the trivialities of the horror genre. Formulaic elements in plot (the intrusion of a radical other into the sphere of bourgeois normality), in character (the friend whose warnings about the imminent threat go unheeded until it is too late) and in theme (images of the abject body, as Asami feeds another amputated male victim with her own vomit) are undeniably derived from the horror genre. To such objections, critical discourse responds by withdrawing to that shady borderland of what Jeffrey Sconce has called 'paracinema'.[14] In her own examination of the politics of taste, Hawkins has made a strong argument that 'high culture trades on the same images, tropes, and themes that characterize low culture'.[15] The objective of these tropes, whether they are derived from one end of the social spectrum or the other, is to challenge 'the formally constructed notion of mainstream good taste'.[16] Taste, she states, 'is never class neutral . . . [Rather] it becomes the means through which class values are normalized and perpetuated within the larger society'.[17] Consumers of 'both low and high culture', Hawkins explains, 'during the postwar period, attempted to define themselves in opposition to a dominant mainstream taste aesthetic, and the interests that both mainstream and, occasionally, high culture have had in policing taste.'[18] By settling comfortably at the point where the far ends of the spectrum meet, *Audition* suggests that paracinema might succeed as a genuinely international style in a postmodern age that has abandoned the transcultural pretensions of the avant garde and high modernism.

Miike's stylistic high-wire act is reflected in his use of the film's central thematic trope. Reviewers have pointed out that he employs a rather clichéd western motif of horror film, that of the female avenger. Barbara Creed and Carol Clover have both argued for the crucial importance of this trope in horror films.[19] Clover praises *I Spit on Your Grave*, a legitimate 'entry into a thriving branch of modern horror', for 'reduc[ing] the genre to its essence'.[20] She also acknowledges that revenge dramas 'are by no means the sole property of horror: vengeance may very well be the wellspring of American popular culture, from Westerns and *Dirty Harry* to teen comedies and courtroom dramas'.[21] Clover's acknowledgment marks the point of departure for later critics. Jacinda Read objects to Clover's definition of horror because it comes across as unsystematic and strategically weighted in favour of low-budget productions.[22] Read contends that 'rape-revenge is not a genre but a narrative structure, which has been mapped over other genres',[23] including 'the western and the domestic/maternal melodrama', as well as neo-noir and the erotic thriller.[24] Its ubiquity among all these genres, combined with its uniquely revealing capacity about American culture, according to Clover, make it an immediately recognisable trope for audiences raised on film traditions other than those of Japan.

What is striking about Miike's treatment of the female avenger, however, is that he employs it purely as a generic element.[25] That is to say, he makes no noticeable attempt at endowing it with a sense of aesthetic freshness or originality. Predictably enough, reviewers complain. David Perry sees Miike 'mixing Adrian Lyne with Brian De Palma and Sam Raimi', which leads him to conclude that 'the path the movie does take . . . feels like little more than a contrivance'.[26] Peter Bradshaw is equally dissatisfied. 'Of course, the casting couch try-out is hardly a novelty,' he writes, 'and the audition scene here is shot like every audition scene in every film you've ever seen: with a jokey collage of clips of all the desperately unsuitable hopefuls.'[27] And yet another reviewer complains that we 'know the score from the outset: man falls for beautiful woman. Woman is a bit strange, but man ignores this and continues to find himself enraptured by her beauty and mystique'.[28]

Obviously, however, there are cultural subtexts unaccounted for by such mechanisms, as Peter Tombs points out in his discussion of new Japanese horror film:

> When cinema came to Japan 100 years ago, it drew on the repertoire of the popular kabuki drama. Many of these plays were ghost stories. The most famous, *Yotsuya Kaidan*, a tale of spectral revenge meted out to a treacherous husband, has been adapted for the screen more than 25 times. Its ghost is an archetypal image of Japanese horror cinema: a wronged woman, hungry for revenge.[29]

Gregory Barrett traces the image of the wronged woman, who seeks 'justice through revenge',[30] to 'Izanami, the *Kojiki* goddess who dies after giving birth to many islands and deities'.[31] The *Japanese Cinema Encyclopedia* lists fifty-two entries under the heading 'ghost', among which, judging by the brief plot summaries provided, at least twenty-six revolve around a woman who takes revenge on those who wronged her.[32] In other words, even before Miike and Tengan depict Asami as a female avenger recognisable to western audiences, the 'avenging demonic woman was [already] a popular icon in fantastic literature'.[33]

It is also important to note that Miike's handling of audience sympathy seems to place *Audition* more into a uniquely Japanese context. Revenge drama, no matter if the avenger is male or female, is often constructed to place the audience in the position of the avenger. According to Barrett, 'filmmakers aid and abet [proper identification] by painting the culprit as evil and cruel as possible, thereby filling their audiences with absolute loathing for him. In Japan, however, this is not necessary'.[34] Cultural idiosyncrasies, Barrett explains, are such that it is sufficient for the smooth working of the revenge plot if 'the ending is inevitable', that is if justice is restored.[35] A strong sense of social propriety prevails over the details of individual psychology. While a Japanese audience might derive satisfaction from seeing justice doled out even to a sympathetic character, western audiences will require more psychological justification, needing to see an individual deserving of justice rather than watching the gears of the social machine turning.

Audition manages to subvert this dictate of Japanese culture. Aoyama, though far from perfect, does nothing to deserve Asami's ferocious violence. On the contrary, Miike goes to great lengths to present him as a well-intentioned, decent man. Nonetheless, Asami's revenge, once initiated, seems inevitable, a process that, once set in motion, cannot be stopped. It is exactly in this depiction of Aoyama as a nice guy that *Audition* deviates from the formula Barrett outlines. If the object of the revenge does not, properly speaking, deserve to be punished, is it even appropriate to use the term 'revenge' in the first place? What exactly is the sense of social justice that is being reinstated by Asami's actions?

If we see Asami as a figure in the Japanese tradition of the female avenger, her capacity for violence and destruction is directed against Aoyama as a proponent of a reactionary ideology of the family. If viewers experience a sense of ambivalence about this attack, it may be because we see this family as 'often already dysfunctional' and male authority as 'often already undermined'.[36] The violence is presented as a revenge for Aoyama's breaking the promise to love 'only her', which leads Asami to extend her aggression, albeit unsuccessfully, to Aoyama's son. Aoyama's promise, it is crucial to keep in mind, is not the product of a culture in which the majority of all marriages are arranged in the best interests of two families. That is to say, his promise is not the product of premodern Japanese culture. Instead, it is coded as a form of romantic hyperbole, ritualised, and thus emptied of all meaning, by a commercially driven culture that circulates romantic love as a profitable commodity. Nonetheless, the social role into which romantic love is eventually channelled, that of the perfect wife, is still rigid and constricting; this is the role that Aoyama has scripted for Asami. It is hardly a coincidence that her manner of death – a broken neck – is foreshadowed by the way in which she kills Aoyama's and Shigehiko's family pet, a beagle. For an instant, we see the dog lying on the floor with its neck twisted backward. Asami's violence, in response to this role, is strikingly archaic – a direct attack on the body of the oppressor, or its bodily substitutes, that foregoes socially sanctioned mediation by state bureaucracies or the mobilisation of social prejudice against him. Like Glenn Close's Alex in Adrian Lyne's *Fatal Attraction* (1982), Asami's 'demands are of an atavistic absoluteness', displaying the 'voracious, pre-rational drives . . . suggestive of a devolution to the level of comparatively uncomplex life-forms, driven by tropisms'.[37] While Alex finally reveals her true self in the violent lunge for her faithless lover's throat, a dynamic act of aggressive desire, Asami's act of violence, paradoxically, consists of her lack of motion, coded positively as a traditional Japanese sign of feminine refinement.

Michel Foucault argues in *Discipline and Punish* that, in most European nations during the second half of the eighteenth century, 'a few decades saw the disappearance of the tortured, dismembered, amputated body, symbolically branded on face or shoulder, exposed alive or dead to public view'.[38] According to Foucault, the historical disappearance of this body makes room for one of the paradigms of modernity, a complex network of medical, military, educational, and bureaucratic institutions designed to categorise and control all forms of delinquency, which he calls the 'carceral archipelago'.[39] Problematic as the transfer of Foucault's concept to Japanese modernity may be, it is nonetheless striking that Asami's revenge, which is directed in all its premodern excess against the body of Aoyama, makes visible the social areas, such as the domestic incarceration of women, over which modernisation seems to have passed without leaving a trace. These social lacunae function as historical spectres haunting modern Japanese society. They have the power to disrupt the smooth functioning of a modern society by reminding it that it still depends on the social and cultural subjugation of women.

The fact that Miike can draw from a Japanese tradition of the 'female avenger' that precedes American horror films suggests that the meaning of the trope will differ depending on the audience. For those capable of perceiving Asami as a reincarnation of a specifically Japanese 'premodern archetype', the source of horror in *Audition* may be located in cultural anxieties about the success or failure of modernisation. For those less susceptible to this reading, she may appear specifically as a backlash phenomenon against late 1960s feminism. It would be reasonable to assume that western audiences, given their cultural predispositions, may lean more toward the latter interpretation.[40]

But the alignment of cultural background and interpretive preference is not as simple as that. According to Susan Napier, the trope of the female avenger does undergo changes throughout twentieth-century Japanese culture as well. For Napier, the 'postwar fantasies of male writers', of whom Murakami Ryu would be an example, 'are notable for the absence of women characters. Women are no longer part of [male] wish-fulfillment fantasies. Instead, they are part of the reality which the male protagonist longs to escape'.[41] Women are 'frequently seen as agents of entrapment, of humiliation'.[42] Unlike older writers like Tanizaki or Soseki, more contemporary Japanese writers depict women who 'do not seem to offer opportunities for either vengeance against the modern or escape from the modern. Instead, women seem to have become increasingly other, unreachable, even demonic.'[43] This means that women can now become the agents rather than the means or ends of revenge, though they are still projections of a predominantly male imagination. Napier traces this increasingly uncomfortable relationship between men and women back to 'the marked ups and downs of the Japanese economy, especially in the years since the 1973 oil shock'.[44] These market fluctuations have 'contributed to an individual sense of powerlessness, especially in men, who are still the primary breadwinners in Japan'.[45] It follows that twentieth-century socio-economic history adds a facet to the trope of the female avenger that aligns it more strongly with a western 'post-feminist backlash' interpretation.

Napier's updating of the 'premodern archetype' fits perfectly with the linkage between gender and power in *Audition*. In conversation between Aoyama and his friend Yoshikawa, the theme of Japan's economic decline in the years after the 'bubble economy' is aligned with Aoyama's inability to find a proper replacement for his late wife. In the background of the bar where the two men commiserate about the hardships of their jobs and the general malaise of modern life, a group of women, coded by their physical appearance and demeanour as mid-level professionals, is talking noisily and laughing. Their lack of inhibition triggers a misogynist comment from Yoshikawa and causes Aoyama to despair even further in his search for the perfect old-fashioned wife. Though the structure and development of the job market in the US and Japan may be uniquely different, this brief scene of male aggression, triggered by real or perceived professional emasculation, will ring a bell with western viewers. Since men must share the role of 'the primary breadwinner' with more and more women in developed nations, especially since this ratio has come to dominate more middle- and upper-middle-class households, the backlash no longer requires a specifically western feminist movement as a trigger. Viewers may cite perceived structural similarities between different late capitalist economies when they choose to ignore whatever may be uniquely Japanese about gender-related male anxieties.

In the final instance, *Audition* succeeds both stylistically and thematically in working around the disorienting experience western audiences have when they encounter a text from a non-western culture. Its success in western markets is based on mobilising neither of the two strategies Miyoshi Masao ordinarily sees at work in this situation. 'To restore the accustomed equilibrium,' Miyoshi writes, 'the reader either *domesticates* or *neutralizes* the exoticism of the text. The strategy for domestication is to exaggerate the familiar aspects of the text and thereby disperse its discreteness in the hegemonic sphere of first world literature', whereas the 'plan for neutralization . . . operates by distancing the menacing source', defusing its otherness with '[s]uch "pseudocomments" as "delicate," "lyrical," or "suggestive," if not "illogical," "impenetrable," or "incoherent"'.[46] While these strategies owe more to the old distinction between high and low culture, between modernist avant-gardes and global pop culture, Miike plays on a register of cultural competence that has been better described by Tatsumi Takayuki who calls it 'Japanoid', a 'post-eighties hyper-Creole subjectivity transgressing the boundary between the Japanese and the non-Japanese, and in so doing, naturalizing the very act of transgression'.[47] Directly relevant to *Audition*'s western audience is Tatsumi's argument that what is at stake now 'is the canonical distinctions between western identity and Japanese identity, Orientalism and Occidentalism, and Anglo-American narcissism and Japanese masochism'.[48] His notion of the 'Japanoid' would invalidate such an intercultural psychological dynamic, denying western audiences, for example, the foundation for constructing Japan as both a threatening and exotically seductive other. With the cultural boundaries demolished, there would be no longer any reason for neutralising the menacing alterity in Miike's film. Retroactively, a Japanoid perspective would also pull the carpet from under all arguments about the domesticating effects of US remakes of Japanese films since Tatsumi's ideal viewers would be capable of reading both text and subtext simultaneously.

NOTES

1. Rose, Steve (2002) 'Nightmare Scenario: Hollywood Horror is Creatively Dead, but Asian Films are Reviving the Genre', *Guardian*, Friday, 20 September, http://www.guardian.co.uk/arts/fridayreview/story/0,12102,794834,00.html.
2. Ibid.
3. Ibid.
4. For a more detailed description of this incident, see 'Three Collapse at Swiss Horror Premiere', *Guardian*, Thursday 10 January, film.guardian.co.uk/News_Story/Exclusive/0,630495,00.html, and Morris, Gary (2001) 'Gore Galore: Takashi Miike's *Audition*', *Bright Lights Film Journal*, 34, October, http://www.brightlightsfilm.com/34/audition.html.
5. *For Men* (2002) 'Audition: Takeshi Miike's Twisted Take on Modern Dating is a Warped Hitchcockian Slice of Paranoia', *Eastern Connection*, 39, 14 September, formen.ign.com/articles/098/098316p1.html?fromint=1.
6. Allon, Yoram (2002) '*Audition*', *Kamera*, kamera.co.uk/reviews_extra/audition.php.
7. Eisner, Ken (1999) '*Audition*', *Variety*, 1 November, findarticles.com/cf_0/m1312/11_376/57608502/p1/article.jhtml?term=audition.
8. Ibid.
9. Musetto, V. A. (2002) 'An Interview with Takeshi Miike', *Asian Cult Cinema*, 37, Winter, p. 60.
10. Falcon, Richard (2002), qtd in *For Men*.
11. Miike himself, in the interview with Bartok, recalls viewers coming up to him, feeling 'psychologically cheated'. Especially female viewers, he adds, 'won't accept this ending; it's as if they've been molested.' See Bartok, Dennis (2000) 'Interview with Takashi Miike', *Audition*, DVD, Ventura Distributors.
12. Miike Takashi (2002) 'Commentary Track', *Audition*, DVD, Ventura Distributors.
13. Together with such keywords as interiority, polygenericity, difficulty and ambiguity, it is self-reflexivity that characterises *Audition*. The central trope of the audition, during which identity is constructed within the field of the male gaze, announces Miike's ability to thematise the medium of film. The reification of the male gaze is complemented by Asami's attack on Aoyama, as she inserts needles under his eyes, reversing the flow of power and sadistic pleasure.
14. See Hawkins, Joan (2000) *Cutting Edge: Art-Horror and the Horrific Avant-Garde*, Minneapolis, MN: University of Minnesota Press, p. 3.
15. Ibid., p. 3.
16. Ibid., p. 30.
17. Ibid.
18. Ibid., p. 205.
19. For further discussion of the female avenger as a trope of the horror genre, see Christine Holmlund and Julianne Pidduck, cited in Read, Jacinda (2000) *The New*

Avengers: Feminism, Femininity and the Rape-Revenge Cycle, Manchester: Manchester University Press, pp. 53–4.

20. Clover, Carol J. (1992) *Men, Women, and Chainsaws: Gender in the Modern Horror Film*, London: BFI/Princeton, NJ: Princeton University Press, p. 115.
21. Ibid., p. 115.
22. Read, pp. 23–5.
23. Ibid., p. 25.
24. Ibid., p. 45.
25. This may, however, be the perception exclusively of a western audience. Jack Hunter's study *Eros in Hell: Sex, Blood and Madness in Japanese Cinema* suggests that it is the ubiquity of rape in Japanese culture, as a form of violent entertainment exclusively directed against women and often stylised in elaborately staged S/M scenarios, that distinguishes Miike's use of the female avenger from the norm. Further, the actual revenge scenes in *Audition* are free of an eroticisation of violence – there is no eroticised nudity, no masturbatory content and no (strong) masochist undertone to Aoyama's suffering at the hands of Asami. For further discussion of the rape theme in Japanese cinematic and popular culture, see Hunter, Jack (1998) *Eros in Hell: Sex, Blood and Madness in Japanese Cinema*, London: Creation Books International, pp. 67–102.
26. Perry, David (2001) 'Audition', *Xiibaro Newsletter*, 4.01, cinema-scene.com/archive/volume-4number-01.html#Audition.
27. Bradshaw, Peter (2001) 'Audition', *Guardian*, 16 March, film.guardian.co.uk/News_Story/ Critic_Review/Guardian_Film_of_the_week/0,4267,452311,00.html.
28. *For Men*.
29. Tombs, Pete (2000), 'Oh, Noh . . . Japan Has the Horrors Again', *Guardian Unlimited*, 18 August, film.guardian.co.uk/features/featurepages/0,4120,356916,00.html.
30. Barrett, Gregory (1989) *Archetypes in Japanese Film: The Sociopolitical and Religious Significance of the Principal Heroes and Heroines*, Selinsgrove, PA: Susquehanna University Press, p. 98.
31. Ibid., p. 97.
32. Weisser, Thomas and Yuko Mihara Weisser (1998c), *Japanese Cinema Encyclopedia: Horror, Fantasy, Science Fiction*. Miami, FL: Vital Books, pp. 97–108.
33. Napier, Susan J. (1996) *The Fantastic in Modern Japanese Literature: The Subversion of Modernity*, New York and London: Routledge, p. 23.
34. Barrett, p. 104.
35. Read, p. 46.
36. Ibid., p. 46.
37. Morgan, Jack (2002) *The Biology of Horror: Gothic Literature and Film*, Carbondale/Edwardsville, IL: Southern Illinois University Press, p. 103.
38. Foucault, Michel (1979) *Discipline and Punish: The Birth of the Prison*, trans. Alan Sheridan, New York: Random House, p. 8.
39. Ibid., p. 8.
40. Still, it does remain arguable whether a structural equivalent of a Japanese feminist movement in the 1960s comparable to that in many western countries exists. According to Read, the 'rape-revenge and fatal femme cycles, which both emerged during the period of second-wave feminism, can perhaps be seen as sharing more in terms of historical context. In particular, while both cycles can be partially understood in terms of backlash politics [elsewhere, Read cites Susan Faludi's work as shedding light on this phenomenon], it can also be argued that it is precisely second-wave feminism that has enabled such representations'. See Read, p. 47.
41. Napier, p. 54.
42. Ibid., p. 56.

43. Ibid., p. 57.
44. Ibid., p. 57.
45. Ibid., p. 57.
46. Miyoshi Masao (1989) 'Against the Native Grain: The Japanese Novel and the "Postmodern" West', in Miyoshi Masao and H. D. Harootunian (eds), *Postmodernism and Japan*, Durham, NC and London: Duke University Press, p. 144. Italics added.
47. Tatsumi Takayuki (2002) 'The Japanoid Manifesto: Toward a New Poetics of Invisible Culture', *Review of Contemporary Fiction*: XXII.2, Summer, p. 16.
48. Ibid.

5. ANIME HORROR AND ITS AUDIENCE: *3X3 EYES* AND *VAMPIRE PRINCESS MIYU*

Christopher Bolton

In one of the most celebrated scenes in Japan's popular visual literature, a spurned woman pursues a priest who has rejected her advances, chasing him as far as the banks of a rushing river only to find that he has escaped to the opposite shore. With no way to cross, she flings herself into the water, where her rage and passion transform her into a giant serpent that can swim the river.

The scene is from the legend of *Dôjôji*, a medieval tale that has been adapted over and over for progressively more popular visual media, from early picture scrolls to the eighteenth-century puppet theatre. No matter what the medium, the climax is always portrayed with impressive visual effects and the scene draws applause from the audience. But what are they cheering? The man's narrow escape? The woman's hidden power and frantic determination? Or the visual effects that seem to push the story momentarily into the background?

Japanese horror since classical times has revolved around these depictions of beautiful female victims who undergo monstrous transformations when betrayed or threatened. This is particularly true of animated (or anime) horror. A number of critics have suggested that in anime these figures represent the sexual fantasies and anxieties of a largely adolescent male audience – a conclusion bolstered by the snakes, demonic worms and other phallic transformations in these *Dôjôji* descendents. But the question posed above – what is the audience cheering? – should direct our attention to the complex ways these figures or performances are received by the spectator.

Elsewhere I have compared animation with the puppet theatre for the ways that both media foreground the artificiality of the bodies involved, so that violence is experienced differently.[1] This essay, too, turns on the motif of the puppet, but this time as a figure that mirrors not only the animated actors, but also the spectator or consumer, who is invited to identify with the puppet as a figure manipulated by the text. While some theorisations of anime audiences see these kinds of films as reflections of unacknowledged male anxieties, I will argue that these transforming puppet figures ultimately permit the audience to see itself, and allow the films to carry out a surprisingly layered interrogation of the way anime is received.

THE *OTAKU*'S THIRD EYE

Susan Napier argues that the transforming female bodies common to anime reflect the changing role of women in Japanese society. Napier suggests that there is something liberated or liberatory about these images, which 'depict the female body as being in touch with intense, even magical, forces capable of overwhelming male-dominated reality'.[2] But she sees the social anxiety over these changes reflected in anime as well, and notes that many animated series try to reign in these transforming figures over the course of the story.

These powerful women are often juxtaposed with weak male figures who (like the fleeing priest in *Dôjôji*) seem bewildered or overwhelmed by women's potent sexuality. Napier's readings could be invoked to support Susan Pointon's contention that these kinds of stories reflect adolescent male viewers' unease about either women or the demon of sexuality. Critics like Annalee Newitz link this unease with a widely held stereotype of anime's audience as composed of '*otaku*' – a Japanese term that suggests immature male viewers, with limited social skills, who prefer the simplicity of fictional fantasy girlfriends over relationships with real live women.[3]

Napier focuses on gender anxiety at a more abstract social level, but a scheme for these more individual neuroses is found in Barbara Creed's theory of the monstrous-feminine, which Napier cites.[4] Drawing on Lacan and Kristeva, Creed constructs her theory around the abject or castrating female figures of western horror films, figures who threaten the male privilege of language or signification by absorbing or cutting off the phallus that Lacan associates so closely with signification itself.

Creed's book, and some parts of Napier's discussion, seem caught in the same dilemma as the audience for *Dôjôji*. One is never quite sure whether or not to cheer for these monsters: they are supposedly distortions of the feminine created from subconscious male fears, but they also wreak a satisfyingly cathartic revenge on the male symbolic order. This ambivalence stems from the fact that these readings often treat the films as texts that operate undetected on an audience that consumes them uncritically. By seeing these films as expressions of conscious fantasies and subconscious anxieties, these readings tend to suggest that the films' spectators are unable to make a very sophisticated distinction between reality and representation or fantasy, and that the films do not encourage any deep examination of these fantasies, except when read by the critic.

I would argue, though, that because its mode of representation differs from so-called live-action film, anime can be particularly effective at forcing the spectator to reconsider representation itself – not just the character, as it were, but the manipulation of the 'puppet'. Some of these anime horror texts encourage the viewer to ask what it means to fantasise and to see the ways in which he or she is manipulated by the medium itself. Adapting Paul Willemen, I propose to label this perspective 'the *otaku*'s third eye', an eye that does not watch the screen, but instead allows the spectator to watch him or herself watching the text.[5]

To address this I would like to examine some motifs of manipulation and fantasy in two anime horror series, *3x3 Eyes* (*Sazan aizu*, 1991, 1995) and *Vampire Princess Miyu* (*Vanpaia Miyu*, 1988).[6] Both of these series feature teenage heroines who alternate between schoolgirl cuteness and demonic strength, as well as male characters who are alternately their victims and their saviours. And yet, alongside these wish-fulfilment fantasies, these films also feature elements that foreground representation and wish-fulfilment itself – monsters who wrap their victims in empty fantasies, for example, and demonic puppeteers. Further, the split female characters also refigure the notions of the phallic woman and the castrating woman in a way that may regain some measure of control over the signifying function for the women characters and the viewer alike.

A FIRST LOOK AT *3X3 EYES*

Based on the first several volumes of a long-running manga (comic book) series by Takada Yûzô,[7] the anime version of *3x3 Eyes* comprises two short OAV series (original animated series released directly to video). The protagonists are a teenage Japanese boy named Fujii Yakumo and a supernatural creature from Tibet named Pai. Pai resembles a typical anime schoolgirl, a sexually appealing pubescent who is innocent, naively cheerful and non-threatening. But in times of danger, a third eye opens on her forehead and she is transformed into the demon/goddess Sanjiyan. Besides a deeper, more masculine voice and fearsome psychic powers, Sanjiyan also has a scornful attitude toward Yakumo and the other humans she ends up protecting. Yakumo is transformed into Pai's 'Wu', a minion and guardian who remains almost indestructible as long as Pai lives. In this way Yakumo also gains a dual personality – bodyguard to the violent Sanjiyan, but also a normal teenager carrying on an uncertain courtship with the innocent Pai.

3x3 Eyes is associated with a variety of anime called the 'magic girlfriend' genre, and it combines a powerful female goddess with a child-like girl in just the way Napier describes. One can certainly see this combination in terms of adolescent anxiety that alternates between fantasies of empowerment and sexual uncertainty; it's an anxiety that recalls Annalee Newitz's 'representations of male sexual passivity . . . which are simultaneously seductive and terrifying', or Susan Pointon's 'graphic enactment of adolescent sexual anxiety and guilt'.[8] Furthermore, a number of details point even more specifically to Oedipal and castration anxiety. Consider, for example, Pai/Sanjiyan's ambiguous relationship with Yakumo's absent father, or Yakumo's ambivalence over his part-time job as a transvestite host in a gay bar. Pai/Sanjiyan is also depicted with the tiny fangs Barbara Creed identifies with the castrating vagina dentata, and she is menaced by phallic demons against which Yakumo must compete.

In the climax of the first series, for instance, Yakumo enters a demonic temple to rescue a girlfriend who is tied, almost naked, to a sacrificial altar and sexually molested by a demon who possesses a barbed tail, an elongated ram-like skull and a probing tongue several metres in length. Forced into Oedipal battle with this phallic father, Yakumo first cuts off its tongue and then stabs it in the skull with a spear, but the demon gains control of Yakumo's right arm and nearly forces him to eviscerate the girl with a large sword. If this represents Yakumo's (and the spectator's) anxiety over his own sexual performance, then cutting off his own demon-possessed right hand in order to stop himself is an act of self-castration. Later, however, he reclaims this phallus, using his regenerative powers to draw his severed hand across the room with the sword still in it, and then wielding the blade to kill the demon. With the Oedipal father slain and his manhood reclaimed, Yakumo rescues the girls and saves the day.

A scene like this presents an embarrassment of riches for the Freudian critic, though one might question whether such an easy reading really adds much to the text. I would ask further if there is not some irony or critical distance inevitably generated by scenes like this – if the directors, illustrators and complicit spectators are not deliberately baiting their critics. Instead of waiting for analysis to expose the neuroses at the heart of this fantasy, are viewers perhaps taking an ironic or open-eyed view of (frequently sexual) fantasy, including the way it is marketed and consumed, and the way they are constituted by it? These questions may be unanswerable in the first *3x3 Eyes* series, but in the second, the plot turns much more explicitly to questions of representation, fantasy and manipulation, while these phallic figures get a new twist.

GEEKS AND OTHER MONSTROSITIES, OR,
YOU HAVE SEEN THE *OTAKU*, AND THE *OTAKU* IS YOU

Before looking at the second *3x3 Eyes* series, it may be useful to review some recent Japanese theorisations of anime fandom that suggest a more self-conscious audience for these works. As mentioned above, one of the terms most often associated with the negative image of anime and manga fans is '*otaku*'. In Japan, the word denotes mostly male fans who have an obsessive interestin, and encyclopedic knowledge of, anime or other media- or hobby-oriented subcultures. Like 'geek', its more pejorative implications include not only an unhealthy interest in a unworthy subject, but also a lack of social skills, a sexual immaturity and a detachment from reality that prevents the *otaku* from participating in society and forming authentic relationships.

Originally *otaku* is a deferential version of the Japanese second-person pronoun 'you'. From its use among anime and manga fans, it was eventually applied to those fans as a blanket pejorative.[9] It took on its most negative associations after an infamous serial murder of four little girls in Tokyo in 1989. Seizing on the twenty-seven-year-old killer's interest in anime and manga devoted to horror and little-girl themes, the Japanese media linked this preoccupation to his social and physical isolation and to an amorality that seemed explicable only as a profound detachment from reality. In a twist on the *Dôjôji* legend, this murderer was cast as the demonic transformation of the maladjusted *otaku* male.

But more recently some fans have reclaimed the word *otaku* and spun it more positively; the vast number of female *otaku* has begun to be acknowledged, and critics studying anime's audiences have sought a more rigorous theorisation of the term. Okada Toshio, an anime producer turned pop theorist and self-anointed 'Ota-King', defines *otaku* by their sensitivity to visual media. He has his own version of 'the otaku's 3 eyes', which he labels 'an eye for style', 'an eye for technique' and 'the eye of a connoisseur'.[10] These correspond to an appreciation of film not only for its narrative, but also for its formal visual style and for the technical processes involved in producing those images.

Actually, Okada's examples rarely seem to rise above trivial behind-the-scenes details about the making of the films and texts he critiques. But this approach at least hints at a certain kind of sophistication, a meta-textual perspective on anime's construction and consumption that belies the criticism of *otaku* as thoughtless consumers whose desires are readily manipulated by the texts because they are unable to distinguish the real from the created.

Other theorists have developed this idea to suggest that *otaku* in fact have a better understanding than most readers of the blurry boundary between reality and representation in postmodern society. Saitô Tamaki's notable book, *Fighting Beauties: A Psychoanalysis,* argues that *otaku* confusion between the worlds inside and outside the text is the product not of myopia, but of an intuitive and ultimately savvy understanding of the ways that reality is always mediated, first by sensation and consciousness, and then by electronic media like television and video. It is this higher perspective which causes the *otaku* to 'regard reality itself as a species of fantasy'.[11]

> In that sense otaku are definitely not 'confusing fantasy and reality,' but neither do they place much importance on the opposition between the two . . . This does not mean that they are swallowed up in the world of a text they love, but that they take a posture of open-eyed enthusiasm toward it.[12]

Saitô suggests that what marks the *otaku*'s sophisticated combination of the real and fictional is none other than a sexual attraction to charmingly dangerous anime characters like Pai/Sanjiyan. These 'phallic girls', as Saitô terms them, are not Freud's phallic mothers (masculinely powerful women who regain the phallus); nor are they Creed's feminine castrators, who take over the paternal role of instituting the system of signification at the same time that they defy it or cut it off. Instead, the phallic girl represents a kind of essential fiction. Saitô says she 'becomes the phallus', which seems intended to identify her with the Lacanian phallus that marks the operation of significa-tion itself.[13] For Lacan, that phallus represents the desire for the other and for a whole present meaning; these are made possible and come into being at the same time they are endlessly deferred by the disjunction between signifier and signified.[14] In this way, Saitô seems to draw a parallel between the Lacanian phallus and the *otaku*'s coolly savvy, but still frustratingly unconsummated, desire for the animated body.

Saitô concludes that the *otaku*'s physical sexual attraction to this empty referent productively grounds his experience in a world of dangerously shifting signifiers. This conclusion feels forced, but what Saitô does capture along the way is the uncomfortable sense of disjunction we have watching these soft-core heroes and heroines, the uneasy feeling that while the char-acters definitely seem less real, our feelings of arousal (or the feelings that are aroused) are the same. And I would suggest that this experience is not restricted to a small group of enthusiasts, but that many of us experience the animated body as simultaneously more and less immediate than live action film.[15]

True to its origins as a pronoun of address, then, the *otaku* is 'you'. And '*otaku*' as I use it below indicates not a specific group or approach, but an element in the experience of anime that is present for many spectators. This is the experience of having that third eye open and becoming ambivalently aware of the artifice or artificiality, as we spy ourselves watching the text.

THE FORGETFUL PHALLUS

If we look again at *3x3 Eyes*, we can in fact discover something that encourages the spectator to look at him or herself. We see this awareness of shifting contexts in the second of the two series, *3x3 Eyes: Legend of the Divine Demon* (*Sazan aizu: seima densetsu*, 1995), made four years later by the same director. The story also picks up four years after the first series, which ends with a battle between Pai/Sanjiyan and her enemy Beneres. The outcome of that battle is uncertain, but Pai/Sanjiyan disappears, and as the second series opens, Yakumo, now twenty, has just located her again, after chancing on her picture in a soft-core porn magazine devoted to school-age girls. This kind of self-referentiality is ubiquitous in anime, and here it is a clue that the series will deal more explicitly with the issue of the audience's position and anime desire.

Pai/Sanjiyan's third eye has been sealed over by an evil charm that takes the form of a scale-like covering on her forehead, robbing her of her memory and her powers. She is now living as an ordinary schoolgirl and the adopted daughter of a kindly old couple named Ayanokôji, with no knowledge of her origins or her abilities. It is Yakumo, the *otaku* viewer's newly matured stand-in, who is charged with jogging her memory and sorting out reality from fantasy.

Saitô associates the fighting beauties' simulacrum-like quality with a lack of psychological depth. Unlike the phallic mother, who fights to avenge past wounds, his phallic girls lack history, memory and profound psychology. Their flexible identities may combine many different personalities, but each is no more than a thin set of 'specs' without depth. Weightier motivations are replaced by the 'pleasure of combat as she becomes the phallus', and a hysterical 'jouissance purified in the space of fantasy'.[16] The multiple personality of Pai/Sanjiyan/Ayanokôji Pai is similarly deprived of her past and her memory, and she literally becomes the phallus in the course of the story when we learn that there is actually a fourth character inside her, the consciousness of a giant snake named Howasho, the servant of her masculine nemesis Beneres.

In the climax, it is revealed that after her defeat in the battle that ends the first series, Beneres overlaid her personality with the snake's (hence the scaly shield that covers her third eye); the snake's identity was supposed to replace her own and take over her body, making her a puppet. But because of the complicated combination of identities already present inside her, this overlay instead produced the schoolgirl personality of Ayanokôji Pai, who can remember neither her past as Pai/Sanjiyan, nor his (?) past as Howasho. Pai/Sanjiyan/Ayanokôji Pai/Howasho's final dilemma is whether to remember his or her real pasts and surrender the fictional ones; if she does, she risks turning from a little girl back into a demon or an 'ugly monster snake'. Even after the denouement, some of these pasts, personalities and genders remain tangled together.

It is not happenstance that Pai/Sanjiyan/Ayanokôji Pai becomes the snake/phallus of Howasho, just as Saitô predicts. In the second *3x3 Eyes* series, this twist on the phallic imagery represents a multiplication of the heroine's personalities and their putatative genders in a way that serves to confuse the gender identities and anxieties that seemed much more transparent in the original series. This is wholly analogous to Saitô's effort to place these figures on the bar between deep meaning and empty signification (with regard to their language and their gender) by saying that they 'become the phallus'.

The Puppet's Last Dance

Before concluding, I would like to revisit the puppet image once more. Like Saitô's phallic girl, the puppet can be seen as a figure for the split bodies of anime, suspended between real and unreal. But to the extent that *otaku* are involuntarily aroused by these mediated subjects and manipulated as consumers, perhaps the puppet is a better figure for the spectator him or herself. In fact, *3x3 Eyes* and other anime titles use the puppet as an explicit figure for characters who find themselves in thrall to these transforming men and women. This, too, opens a third eye on the text, and it forces a recognition and response to the viewer's own manipulation by this media.

The theme of a fiction that manipulates its audience is never far from the surface in *Legend of the Divine Demon*, where Howasho's attempted manipulation of the heroine plunges both into amnesiac fantasy. But one of the pivotal scenes in the series is an episode where Yakumo literally battles this sense of manipulation and fictionality by engaging in combat with a series of demons shaped like giant dolls and puppets. Ayanokôji Pai's adoptive father, Mr Ayanokôji, is a doll-maker, but Yakumo discovers that the dolls in the house are actually demon puppets with the power to become puppeteers and to manipulate the humans around them. They are placed there to control the old couple and to keep the couple's adopted daughter in the world of fiction, ensuring that her memories do not awaken. By doing battle with these puppet- and doll-bodied monsters, Yakumo struggles to free Pai/Sanjiyan from the fiction that controls her, the false identity of Ayanokôji Pai.

These motifs of phallic and puppet transformation also occur in other horror anime, such as *Vampire Princess Miyu*, a four-part OAV series directed by Hirano Toshiki under the name Hirano Toshihiro. This series was also the model for a twenty-five-episode television show (not treated here) and a manga series by Kakinouchi Narumi.[17] The title character is a vampire in the body of a little girl. Part human and part monster, Miyu is charged with hunting down 'shinma', supernatural creatures that have strayed into the human sphere. She is thus cast in the role of humanity's protector, but she also hunts humans herself, and Napier sees in her anime's characteristic combination of danger and cuteness.[18]

Yet *Vampire Princess Miyu* is less about the battle between good and evil than about the contest between delusion and reality. Several of the *shinma* and Miyu herself act by wrapping their victims in some kind of fantasy. For example, a little girl in the first episode is revealed to be in the grip of the dream-eating demon Baku, whose true form is yet another variation on the giant demon worm. In return for the girl's soul, Baku keeps her in a dream in which her dead parents are still alive. Once again we have this motif of the girl cut off from a past and sunk in a fiction, combined with a literally phallic transformation *à la* Saitô, in which the worm-like or snake-like demon represents the world of forgetful fantasy.

The parallels between Baku's or Miyu's victims and *otaku* stereotypes are not accidental. In *otaku* fashion, the victims want to possess or regain a love object that is unreachable in real life. In return for their souls, they are reduced to a state of childlike catatonia, reminiscent of a media loop, in which they relive fond episodes over and over. At several points these dreams are associated explicitly with fiction, suggesting a direct engagement with the question of whether these texts themselves bewitch the reader or viewer and substitute empty sexual fantasies for real relationships. In one episode of the manga, for example, a *shinma* in the shape of a beautiful young boy imprisons his girlfriends on the pages of an illustrated storybook.[19]

But the most striking example is a *shinma* called Ranka, whose costume and theme music associate her with the traditional Japanese theatre, and who turns her lover-victims into puppets. In 'Banquet of the Marionettes [*Ayatsuri no utage*]', episode two of the OAV, she and Miyu compete for the soul and the affections of yet another weak but beautiful young boy who might constitute a stand-in for the *otaku* viewer. In the final showdown, Ranka transforms her body into a puppet's, and the boy chooses Ranka over Miyu, allowing himself to become a puppet too so he can join his wooden love. As the episode ends, Ranka and the boy perform a dance that consciously recalls Japanese theatre and a traditional stage curtain falls across the camera. This scene returns us to the motif with which this essay began, foregrounding the issue of representation at the same moment it asks whether we too will become lost in fiction.

Of course, the question this chapter cannot answer is whether a given viewer will take the cues present in scenes like these and consider his or her own position with respect to the text. Many anime texts offer an opportunity for that kind of examination, but they do not force it, and the *otaku*'s third eye that I have posited may in fact remain closed or sealed over. But it is important to acknowledge a potential in anime and in its audience for this broader perspective. Every once in a while that third eye may open unexpectedly and reveal a hidden insight, a hidden strength.

NOTES

1. Bolton, Christopher (2002) 'From Wooden Cyborgs to Celluloid Souls: Mechanical Bodies in Anime and Japanese Puppet Theater', *Positions: East Asia Cultures Critique*, 10:3, Winter, pp. 729–71.
2. Napier, Susan J. (2001b) *Anime from* Akira *to* Princess Mononoke, New York: Palgrave, p. 71.
3. Pointon, Susan (1997) 'Transcultural Orgasm as Apocalypse: *Urotsukidoji: The Legend of the Overfiend*', *Wide Angle*, 19:3, July, pp. 41–63; Newitz, Annalee (1995) 'Magical Girls and Atomic Bomb Sperm: Japanese Animation in America', *Film Quarterly*, 49:1, Fall, pp. 2–15. Napier herself takes issue with these critics (*Anime*, pp. 241–2).
4. Creed, Barbara (1993) *The Monstrous-Feminine: Film, Feminism, Psychoanalysis*, London and New York: Routledge; Napier, p. 72.
5. Willemen, Paul (1994) 'The Fourth Look', in *Looks and Frictions: Essays in Cultural Studies and Film Theory*, Bloomington and London: Indiana University Press and British Film Institute, pp. 99–110. Willemen's 'fourth look' is also cited by Creed (*Monstrous Feminine*, p. 29), as well as by Napier, whose more specific discussions of audience suggest that there is indeed a 'heightened self-consciousness to watching anime' (*Anime*, p. 242).
6. *Vampire Princess Miyu. Vanpaia Miyu.* Hirano Toshihiro, AIC/Sôeishinsha/Pony Canyon, 1988; OAV, available on two subtitled DVDs as *Vampire Princess Miyu*, vols. 1–2 (Animeigo, 1996); *3x3 Eyes*, Nishio Daisuke, Takenouchi Kazuhisa et. al., Kôdansha/Tavac/Tôei, 1991 and 1995; OAVs, available on two subtitled DVDs as *3x3 Eyes*, Collector's Edition (Pioneer, 2000).
7. Takada Yûzô (1988–9), *3x3 Eyes*, vols 1–3, Tokyo: Kôdansha, translated as *3x3 Eyes*, Milwaukie, OR: Dark Horse Comics, 2001–3.
8. Newitz, p. 5; Pointon, p. 55.
9. Okada Toshio (2000) *Otaku gaku nyûmon* [*Introduction to Otakuology*], Tokyo: Shinchôsha OH! bunko, pp. 10–13.
10. In Japanese *iki no me, takumi no me,* and *tsû no me.* Okada, pp. 116–32.
11. Saitô Tamaki (2000) *Sentô bishôjo no seishin bunseki* [*Fighting Beauties: A Psycho-analysis*], Tokyo: Ôta Shuppan, p. 44.
12. Ibid., p. 44.
13. Ibid., pp. 273–4. Unfortunately, on some of these points, Saitô's argument itself is not quite as fleshed out as the reader might desire.
14. We could compare this with the phallic serpent transformation in stage productions of *Dôjôji*, which combines frustrated desire and self-conscious theatricality.
15. As William Gardner notes in a review of the book, even Saitô finds himself sliding back and forth between the first and third person when indicating the *otaku*. See Gardner, William (2002) 'Attack of the Phallic Girls', *Science Fiction Studies*, 29:3, p. 488.
16. Saitô, pp. 237–40, 273–4.

17. Kakinouchi Narumi (1989–98) *Vanpaia Miyu*, vols 1–3, Tokyo: Akita Shoten, translated as *Vampire Princess Miyu* (2001–2), Fredericksburg: Studio Ironcat/I. C. Entertainment.
18. Napier, Susan J. (1998) 'Vampires, Psychic Girls, Flying Women and Sailor Scouts: Four Faces of the Young Female in Japanese Popular Culture', in D. P. Martinez (ed.), *The Worlds of Japanese Popular Culture: Gender, Shifting Boundaries and Global Cultures*, Cambridge: Cambridge University Press, pp. 94–8.
19. Kakinouchi, *Vanpaia Miyu*, vol. 1, pp. 35–62.

6. CASE STUDY: ISHII TAKASHI'S *FREEZE ME* AND THE RAPE-REVENGE FILM

Frank Lafond

A large number of Ishii Takashi's manga and films (for example, *Angel Guts: Red Vertigo*, 1988; *A Night In Nude*, 1993; *Alone in the Night*, 1994; *Freeze Me*, 2000) concentrate on a female character, most frequently called Nami, who is the unfortunate victim of male violence. However, it would be misleading to label Ishii a feminist film-maker without any further examination, as his first films depict nothing but sexual stereotypes;[1] he has even gone on record as stating that he does not understand women at all:

> I've always wondered what kind of species women are [. . .] I don't understand even one single woman, so I thought it was pointless to name and create different women every time. I decided to draw one special woman, over and over, all the time. I could never understand her though – all I could do was continue drawing her.[2]

However, in a 1998 interview, Ishii appears to contradict this statement, suggesting that he is quite aware of the meaning inherent in this recurring female character:

> Nami always conveys the views of the woman who is raped, attacked, who suffers from male violence. It's the leitmotiv of the protestation of the women in general, who suffer from the violence of their relations, not only in the yakuza circles, but also in their family, with their boyfriend, etc. It's a protestation against the submission imposed on women.[3]

Freeze Me, which is also known under the alternative English title *Freezer*, clearly belongs to the rape-revenge cycle, a horror subgenre which has been notably tackled at some length by Carol J. Clover[4] and one that perfectly suits the raising of feminist issues. Indeed, the name of this particular group of films speaks for itself; each one of them is made up of two parts: part one, where a woman is sexually assaulted, and part two, where she takes revenge on her rapists by killing them. Against Clover, Jacinda Read has argued that the rape-revenge films are 'historically rather than generically specific'.[5] Most of Read's arguments appear quite convincing, but it would be problematic to base an analysis of a Japanese film on western socio-cultural moments, such as the rise of second-wave feminism in the 1970s. I would rather suggest here that *Freeze Me*, which the majority of movie-goers will apprehend as a truly horrific text, can be analysed by a close study of the (sub)generic components it borrows from the cycle in question. It is in the similarities or in the gaps between Ishii Takashi's film and canonical examples of the rape-revenge subgenre that we might then be able to bring to the forefront the film's specific social concerns.

Before going any further, though, I would like to give a brief synopsis of this little-known film. *Freeze Me* focuses on young office clerk Yamazaki Chihiro (played by model Inoue Harumi), who lives in Tokyo and is just about to get married to one of her colleagues, Nogami. One day, she is visited by one of the three men who raped her five years earlier in her hometown. The rapist forces his way into her apartment and informs her that the other two aggressors are coming for a foursome. Confronted with his demands – he subjects her to all of his sexual whims and desires – she has no alternative but to kill the thug and keep him in her freezer. When the two others settle in turn in her apartment, Chihiro is compelled to dispatch them as well.

More than any previous film written and directed by Ishii, *Freeze Me* seems to have its roots in western cinema, and especially in American rape-revenge films such as Meir Zarchi's *I Spit on Your Grave* (1978) and Abel Ferrara's *Ms. 45* (1981) – to name only two of the most notorious examples of the cycle. Like *I Spit on Your Grave*, though in a less gruesome and explicit fashion, *Freeze Me* has a bathtub scene which looks like a gender reversal of *Psycho*'s (Alfred Hitchcock, 1960) famous shower scene. And, like *Ms. 45*, Ishii's film manifests visual echoes of Hitchcock's proto-slasher film: the famous shot of the hand tearing off the curtains being displaced from the first to the third murder, for instance.

HORRIBLE THINGS PAST

From a narrative standpoint, one can discern in *Freeze Me* a crucial difference from the canonical examples of the aforementioned rape-revenge cycle. The very term 'rape-revenge' suggests that the film's narrative structure possesses a binary logic, but Jacinda Read claims, to the contrary, that they are based on a ternary structure of the 'rape-transformation-revenge' type. However, the transformation of the woman herself – mostly understood by Read in terms of sexualisation – often appears too closely linked with her vengeance on the men who sexually assaulted her to be clearly isolated from the rape and the revenge aspects. Besides, her murderous activities are obviously an integral part of her evolution from victim to avenger. Thus, whereas the plot of the films appears to be traditionally divided in two halves – the rape part chronologically as well as narratively appearing before the revenge part – the male violence is actualised throughout Ishii's film by means of various flashbacks to the initial gang-rape and by the repetition (three times) of the abuse. From this perspective, *Freeze Me* must be compared with Clint Eastwood's *Sudden Impact* (1983), where the spectator learns about the motive for the murders committed by Sondra Locke throughout the course of the narrative.

Ishii's film opens with shots of a very young woman standing alone in the night; the snow is coming down, and she stares strangely at a street lamp. However, the quietness of this opening scene is disturbed by the masculine and feminine voices that we hear fighting on the soundtrack. Later on, we will understand that these off-screen sounds of struggle belong to Chihiro's rape scene, but for the time being they remain quite mysterious. Are they linked to a murder attempt or a sexual assault? Who is the victim of the attack? These non-diegetic sounds can only provoke the desire to see the images that accompany them.

Finally, Ishii allows us to see something of Chihiro's rape, but the images are always presented through the video made by the rapists; thus the images do not really have the status of an event recollected. The first such occurrence happens when Chihiro tries to sneak out of the apartment; in three shots, we quickly see the faces of the rapists while they are committing their crime, and each time the frame freezes. Then, when Chihiro recounts her story by leaving a message on Nogami's answering machine,[6] the main flashback occurs and we learn all the details of the sexual assault. Although the whole film appears quite realistic, it is easy to understand that by filming the rape in lesser quality video, complete with their faded and unstable colours, Ishii intended to increase the assault's realism, but this assessment alone is probably insufficient. We can suggest two possibilities here: either the flashbacks are only intended for the spectators, or they really allow us to penetrate inside Chihiro's mind. Two elements can help us to make a decision. In the film's second scene, a close-up of Chihiro's face is suddenly and briefly interrupted by the same shot as if it was seen on a television set. For the spectator, this shot appears to be totally meaningless and only deepens the mystery produced by the opening scene; however, from the character's standpoint, it links this instance with the rape. During the main flashback, we first see things from Chihiro's point of view until she enters the bedroom where the aggressors are waiting. From that moment on, we witness the events through the lens of the camera. Via this video device, Chihiro takes the place of her assailants (they hold the camera in turn), the hundred or so persons who bought the recording sold by the rapists and, on a meta-cinematic level, *Freeze Me*'s audience. Therefore, Chihiro willingly puts herself in a somewhat surprising voyeuristic position, which probably enables her to ease the pain she feels as a victim.

Before focusing our attention on the rapists, our examination of the rape scene must consider whether or not the female body is eroticised in the film. If at certain times Ishii Takashi does indeed make the most of model Inoue Harumi's advantageous physical appearance, he only briefly shows the actress's naked body *when* she is being raped or brutalised by her aggressors. For instance, the director resorts to an ellipsis instead of showing, to the spectator, Chihiro's rape by the first man: the slow pan on her naked body which follows, although slightly indulgent, is here to let us know that the assault actually took place, as does the revelation of the dribble of blood at the corner of her lips when she finally turns her head towards the camera. What is more, throughout much of the film, Chihiro has a short, severe, almost masculine hairstyle, and from the moment the rapists invade her apartment, she wears a roomy tee-shirt or an apron. These two details clearly work against Jacinda Read's assertions that the female avenger of the rape-revenge cycle differs from the final girl of the slasher film, as defined by Carol Clover, because her transformation is an eroticisation. Contrary to the final girl, *Freeze Me*'s female character undergoes a transformation that is not so much a masculinisation as a containment of several, but by no means all, features (wardrobe and haircut) usually associated, and even confused with, femininity under patriarchal ideology.

MASCULINE BEHAVIOURS

A pattern of repetition lies in the very heart of the rape-revenge cycle as well as in the slasher film, and sometimes the chain of events itself seems to be on the verge of absurdity when it does not purely and simply cross the line of verisimilitude. For instance, Thana in *Ms. 45* is raped twice in a row: she is first assaulted in an alley on her way home, and then she is raped by the burglar that she surprises in her apartment. In *Freeze Me*, Chihiro is not only attacked three times at her place but, by a strange coincidence, attacked by the second assailant on the very same day she returns home with a saw intended to cut into pieces the body of the first man who raped her.

Through the process of repetition, Ishii Takashi is able to display various psychological motivations for the rapists' behaviour, since they are never seen together – except of course during the initial rape – and, thus, they are not considered as a group, as is very often the case in the other films belonging to the cycle. The first rapist, Hirokawa, feels resentment concerning Chihiro's social superiority: although they were raised in the same town outside Tokyo, he now lives by his wits (borrowing money from friends, selling illegal videotapes, etc.), whereas she has a steady job in a bank. After a very short time, he manages to cause Chihiro's dismissal by making a scene in the office where she works, which brings about her social decline. Later on, she will have to move to a smaller apartment and accept to be employed – and underpaid – as a dishwasher. While Hirokawa looks and behaves like a hoodlum, Kojima, the second man who assaults Chihiro, is a salesman in a suit and tie who was fired when his company downsized. At first, he shows gentleness and even apologises for the rape, but as soon as he gets drunk, we understand that he has a strong feeling of sexual inferiority most probably linked to his social insecurity. For instance, he reproaches Chihiro for having supposedly laughed at the size of his penis, which she, of course, denies. *Freeze Me* then foregrounds one of the most widespread male justifications for sexual violence towards women, when Kojima blames Chihiro for the rape by saying: 'It's your fault, you're too sexy.' According to certain patriarchal ideologies, men can't control their sexual impulses, so it is up to the women to not arouse them. Lastly, Baba, the third rapist, is a one-dimensional character, a brute who becomes so fascinated by a videogame in which all he has to do is kill people (the kind of game appropriately called a 'shoot 'em all') that he gradually cuts all ties with the world surrounding him, immersing himself to such a point that Chihiro gives him headphones. The fact that, in the end, he prefers playing his game to taking advantage of Chihiro illustrates that raping her is just one outlet for his constitutive violence.

Despite all the obvious differences between them, the three men not only abuse Chihiro, but they also transform this independent young woman – who even financially supports her mother – into a submissive housewife. In so doing, they treat Chihiro like a kind of slave who cannot have a life of her own anymore; when she is not sexually assaulted, she spends a lot of time in the kitchen cooking meals for them and handing them alcoholic drinks, and she even sleeps on the kitchen floor. Her work itself becomes much less important than her so-called female duties – that is, sexually pleasing and taking care of the men. The film furthermore demonstrates the total alienation of women under patriarchal ideology, a condition best evidenced when Hirokawa asks Nogami for money to sleep with Chihiro, as if she were his property. It appears quite clearly in *Freeze Me* that masculine oppression must also be partially understood as a form of childish behaviour, since men only acknowledge their own unbound desire and need the woman to play a maternal role. It is not surprising, then, that Hirokawa plays with a toy when we see him taking a bath and that Baba spends all his time playing a video game in front of the television.

Lastly, it should be noted that when Chihiro tells how she was raped, she goes as far as talking about Hirokawa and his *yakuza* friends. In this way, she describes her rapists as 'abnormal'; they are outlaws, a categorisation that is, in fact, undermined elsewhere in the film. *Freeze Me* indeed reveals that male violence can be perpetuated by common people and not only by drop-outs (similar, in some ways, to the rednecks of *I Spit on Your Grave*). According to Peter Lehman, the characterisation of the rapists in the rape-revenge cycle usually displays stereotypes of class and ethnicity and, most of all, insists on their abnormality in order to distance the male spectators from their actions.[7] In Ishii's film, even the so-called normal man, the victim's love interest, is shown to possess the potential to assault women. At the very beginning of the film, before the spectator knows everything about the rape, Nogami pretends to attack Chihiro, who balks at leaving the office at the same time as her colleagues. He sneaks up behind her, grabs one of her breasts and puts his hand on her mouth. We can interpret this practical joke as an unconscious punishment for the overtime Chihiro is doing: Nogami probably thinks that a woman should not devote herself to a job outside the home. Moreover, unlike his fiancée, the young man has an interest in a violent video game, a detail that closely links him with Baba who will later become obsessed by the very same game. The discourse held by the film is that the rapist is not inherently different from the 'average' male, embodied by Chihiro's boyfriend.

CONTROLLING AND GIVING UP

It is in fact Nogami's reaction that marks the turning point of *Freeze Me*, the transformation of the female character from victim to avenging murderess. When he learns about Chihiro's rape, Nogami screws up his face in disgust and finally leaves her alone with Hirokawa: he disappears off screen without a word, and the apartment's door slowly shuts. Confronted with the egoism and lack of understanding of the man she was going to marry, Chihiro stands completely still, staring at the closed door for a rather long time, and in the end utters a single word: 'goodbye'. The camera shows us a medium close-up of the young woman from a very low-angle shot and then slowly tracks in to a close-up of her eyes, as we understand that she is suddenly deciding that she will have to fight for herself. What appears to be at stake in this scene is that *Freeze Me* does not rely on a radical version of feminism, in so far as man is not presented as the enemy in essence. On the contrary, Chihiro turns towards Nogami, who said he would protect her in any circumstances, before realising that she can only count on herself, since he holds her responsible for what happened to her like Kojima did before him.[8] Chihiro's isolation is confirmed in the next scene, which begins with an obvious image of castration: we see Chihiro once more preparing a meal in the kitchen, but this time she is slicing some kind of phallic cucumber. The close link between the two shots is further reinforced by the sound of the cutting knife, heard over Chihiro's close-up.

Having taken care of the three aggressors, Chihiro seems to arrive at a dead end, since she is at a loss as to how to get rid of the frozen bodies which clutter up her minuscule apartment and which, consuming most of the electric power allocated to her housing unit, eventually – and quite literally – transform her everyday life into an air-conditioned nightmare: she has to choose between supplying electricity to the three freezers or cooling her apartment. But why does Chihiro decide to keep her victims in her freezers? Does she act on purpose (in other words, for practical and objective reasons) or is she psychologically and irrationally compelled to do it? After all, in *Ms. 45*, Thana *temporarily* does the same thing with her second rapist-turned-victim, but she easily manages to rid herself of the body parts by spreading them all across Manhattan.

At one point, Chihiro looks at Hirokawa's body stuck into her freezer and observes with some surprise: 'They're so beautiful when you freeze them,' an assertion which is certainly quite intriguing. Later on, the cumbersome electric coffins become pieces of furniture and are used by Chihiro to store food and drinks as well as to provide ice. In a strange way, the three rapists henceforth perform the nourishing function previously carried out by their victim. What is more, because they are frozen, they are now totally under Chihiro's control. If we keep in mind the director's resort to video images during the flashbacks of the rape, it seems that the word 'freeze', as used by Chihiro in her comment, has to be understood in two ways.[9] Here the verb can not only signify 'to turn into ice', but also 'to stop a moving image at a particular frame'. Thus, by freezing her aggressors Chihiro is also metaphorically able to definitively stop them *in the past* and finally have a hold on the sexual assault to which she was submitted.

The end of the film seems to suddenly reposition the female victim as a 'good' girl in Nogami's eyes. Smitten with remorse, he reappears one day out of the blue, offers his apologies to Chihiro and they have make-up sex.[10] But the scene turns out to be much more ambiguous than it first appears, notably since a problematic reference to the beginning of the film is made. At one point, Nogami tells Chihiro that his rejecting her made him similar to the rapists, that he became a 'co-conspirator', but he sneaks up behind her like he previously did to frighten her. In fact, Nogami's acts are clearly at variance with his declaration of intent: he pretends to be concerned about Chihiro's problem, although he is clearly much more interested in her body as he keeps fondling her breasts during his whole monologue. Finally, Chihiro's calls for help never receive any appropriate answer: even when they are making love, she keeps repeating them. Bloody stains on the apartment's floor ultimately lead to the discovery of the dead bodies by Nogami, and the female avenger has to kill him in order to protect her secret and, more importantly, to get rid of this man who seemed to give her a new hope for a few moments but was in fact too selfish to really understand her.

Each time there are crimes committed in a film, one should look at its ending and examine the fate of the perpetrator, especially when a female protagonist has dispatched male victims and thus undermined masculine supremacy. Jacinda Read has stressed the fact that in rape-revenge films the 'vengeful rape victim' is 'rarely shown to be punished for her violent attacks on men',[11] and consequently the brutal death of Thana in *Ms. 45* has to be understood as one of the few exceptions which prove the rule. Whereas the last shot of *I Spit on Your Grave* shows the film's heroine making her way towards the camera in a resolute manner and in broad daylight, *Freeze Me* ends with Chihiro's mysterious disappearance in a flash of lightning as she is seen from behind, standing naked on a balcony overhanging a darkened Tokyo. Ishii chooses to show the aftermath of Chihiro's revenge and might even be seen as questioning the relevance of the murders committed by his heroine. Far from freeing her – from her painful past, from her present condition as woman – these murders seem, on the contrary, to lead to her withdrawal from the world and to her eventual self-destruction.

Freeze Me clearly articulates a condemnation of masculine violence towards women in contemporary Japanese society, unambiguously linking Chihiro's rape with men's behaviour in the domestic realm. Thus, the murderous activities of the young woman can be interpreted not only as a vengeance on specific individuals – that is, on her three rapists – but more generally as vengeance on the whole male sex. However, this violent attack on patriarchal oppression is but an act of despair, since there is no activism for women's rights in the film. Ishii's feminist point of view is not a pessimistic one, but a nihilistic one. Nobody really understood Chihiro's agony and, most likely, nobody ever will.

NOTES

1. Bowyer, Justin (2002) 'Film Notes', in *Freeze Me*, DVD, Tartan Video.
2. Stephens, Chuck (2003) 'What's in a Nami?: Takashi Ishii's Brief History of Women', *Pulp*, 4:09, http://www.pulp-mag.com/archives/4.09/reviews_film.shtml. Page accessed in October 2003.
3. Lachize, Sylvie (2001), 'Interview: Takashi Ishii', *Radio Canada*. http://radio-canada.ca/culture/evenements/fantasia/ishii.html. This page, accessed in September 2001, is unfortunately down at the present time.
4. Clover, Carol J. (1992) *Men, Women and Chainsaws: Gender in the Modern Horror Film*, London: BFI; Princeton, NJ: Princeton University Press.
5. Read, Jacinda (2000) *The New Avengers: Feminism, Femininity and the Rape-*

Revenge Cycle, Manchester and New York: Manchester University Press, p. 22. Read admits on p. 36, however, that 'the origins of the rape-revenge structure *do* lie in the horror genre'.

6. This scene exemplifies the lack of communication between the two characters: Chihiro is talking to a brick wall when she is confessing her agony to someone for the very first time, and we will never be able to see Nogami's reaction at this message, although at some point he says that he did listen to it.

7. Lehman, Peter (1993) ' "Don't Blame This on a Girl": Female Rape-revenge Films', in Steven Cohan and Ina Rae Hark (eds), *Screening the Male: Exploring Masculinities in Hollywood Cinema*, London and New York: Routledge, pp. 103–17.

8. At least, that's one possible interpretation of Nogami's silent reaction. Another possible explanation could be that he considers Chihiro to have been tarnished by the rape, which basically amounts to the same thing: the young woman is punished by Nogami while the rapists are not.

9. Since I haven't any notion of the Japanese language, I can't of course guarantee that the pun is conveyed by Chihiro's original line. In any case, the idea still remains valid in the film's context.

10. At this point, Chihiro takes off the tee-shirt and puts on a sexy dress.

11. Read, p. 48.

PART 3

NATIONAL ANXIETIES
AND CULTURAL FEARS
IN JAPANESE HORROR CINEMA

INTRODUCTION

In her essay, 'Horror and the Carnivalesque', Barbara Creed notes that '[t]he image of the transforming body is central to the horror genre' in that '[t]he possibility of bodily metamorphosis attacks the foundations of the symbolic order which signifies law, rationality, logic, truth'.[1] In other words, cinematic representations of radical biological malleability or violent corporeal disintegration disrupt notions of identity (national, cultural, gendered) as 'fixed' or 'natural', even as some artists and cultural critics with variably conservative, reactionary or intransigent subject positions mobilise such imagery to reify their political agendas. For instance, one can clearly discern a discourse of 'monstrosity' and dangerous transmutations underlying contesting interpretations of Japan's so-called 'modernisation' in the years following the Meiji restoration of 1868, a tumultuous period during which Japan emerged from a relatively isolationist paradigm as a response to not only the impact of western cultural and military imperialism, but also the rapid process of industrialisation it engendered.[2] As Ramie Tateishi notes, Inoue Tetsujiro, in his writings on 'monsterology' during the 1890s, merges metaphors of monstrosity with a pathologisation of pre-'modern' Japanese theological (or 'superstitious') precepts in an attempt to reify convictions that 'the conflict between the past and the modern' represented 'a battle against monstrous forces', and that the 'eradication of superstition . . . was instrumental to the constitution of a healthy, modern Japanese state'.[3] Marilyn Ivy advances a similar thesis in her description of the construction of an increasingly discrete Japanese social body during the mid- to late-nineteenth century. In particular, Ivy links

Japan's self-identification as a 'nation-state' with 'the threat of domination by European and American powers'.[4] In this sense, one can understand the very idea of a 'Japanese culture' as 'entirely *modern*'.[5] A response to colonialist overtures, the creation and maintenance of a definitive Japanese social body evolved within the cultural imaginary even as the trappings (both material and ideological) of western culture became progressively familiar.

In contrast to writers like Inoue, twentieth-century Japanese scholars and cultural theorists like Katsuichiro Kamei and Hayashi Fusao perceived the introduction/incursion of western (largely US) culture as contributing to a dissolution of a 'sense of "wholeness" in life among the Japanese'.[6] From this perspective, westernising forces are a deforming and disintegrating influence;[7] the impact of Western culture disrupts a spiritually and socially coded 'Japanese-ness' that, as Darrell William Davis asserts, had been shaped and reshaped 'for a very long time, even before Japan's mid-nineteenth-century encounter with American gunboats and the Meiji restoration of 1868'.[8] Even to this day, over a half-century after the Allied occupation further facilitated the proliferation of western cultural hegemony, this impulse to recover a perceived sense of social cohesion can still be observed:

> In contemporary Japan there has been a relentlessly obsessive 'return' to 'origins': an orchestrated attempt by the state to compensate for the dissolution of the social by resurrecting 'lost' traditions against modernism itself, and by imposing a master code declaring 'homogeneity' in a 'heterogenous' present.[9]

Like Inoue's 'monsterology', which depicts enduring religious models (or 'superstitions') as a 'monstrous' pre-'modern' past threatening the emergence of a newly modernist, industrial and internationally engaged Japan, discourses that call for a resistance to western cultural and military imperialism through the restoration of a conspicuously unified and 'Japanese' past promote a narrative in which a return of a 'repressed' and/or 'oppressed' identity figures prominently.[10] Both ideologies, informed by metaphors of imperilled social bodies, coexist in the larger cultural imaginary. Likewise, as Davis shows, both positions depend upon an understanding of nationalism as an invention made possible only through the acknowledgment of a 'relative' (as opposed to binary) difference that reaffirms the inescapable permanence of cross-cultural 'syncretism'/contamination.[11] Furthermore, the contesting ideologies discussed above can be understood as having achieved varying degrees of metaphorical translation through the iconography and dominant scenarios of Japanese horror cinema, particularly those texts created in the tumultuous decades following the Second World War. Metaphors of the body, like bodies themselves, are surprisingly flexible and porous; as Matsui

Midori notes, '[a]ccording to each historical application, the return of the repressed Japanese "body" can be made either regressive or liberating, reactionary or revolutionary'.[12]

Of course, to contextualise not only the recent 'explosion' of Japanese horror cinema but also the general popularity of horror films in Japan over the last fifty years, one cannot underestimate the impact of such crucial events as Japan's catastrophic defeat in the Second World War (and the subsequent years of foreign occupation), the decades of dramatic economic recovery and the similarly spectacular financial recession of the 1990s upon both the national psyche and, consequently, the artistic creations that inevitably emerged. In addition, it is equally essential to recognise how these larger social transformations inform the shape and significance of those institutions and behavioural codes central to the development and preservation of a sense of national and cultural identity. As Tim Craig notes, large-scale political and economic shifts invariably produce 'new social conditions', including 'urbanization, consumer cultures, changing family structures and gender roles, and lifestyles and values that are less purely traditional and more influenced by outside information and trends'.[13] Correspondingly, given the influence of such novel 'social conditions' and transformations upon the cultural imaginary, it seems only fitting that they would find reflection within the 'popular culture' as well.

The chapters and case study that comprise this section of *Japanese Horror Cinema* engage explicitly with notions of social, cultural and physiological transformation. For instance, both Ian Conrich's contribution, 'Metal-Morphosis: Post-Industrial Crisis and the Tormented Body in the *Tetsuo* Films', and Graham Lewis's essay, '*Pinnochio 964, Death Powder* and the Post-Human Condition', use the intimate, if uneasy, relationship between technology and the body in recent Japanese history as a point of departure for two compelling explorations of the cyborg body as a monstrous, cinematic representation that reflects a late capitalist culture in flux. While by no means a filmic tradition that produces and circulates exclusively negative representations of biomechanical amalgamations, as recent scholarship by Susan J. Napier and Sharalyn Orbaugh has illustrated,[14] Japanese horror films frequently address anxieties surrounding rapid technologisation and its impact upon the all-too-human flesh. When one considers technology's paradoxical status in the Japanese popular imagination – a role conditioned by the nation's legacy as the only country attacked by atomic weapons, as well as by industrialisation's substantial contribution to the 'miraculous' postwar economic recovery – it should come as little surprise that the complex impact of technology upon the social and corporeal body informs much of the genre's output, particularly in the latter decades of the twentieth century. Thus, in his reading of Tsukamoto Shinya's *Tetsuo* films (*Tetsuo: The Iron Man*, 1988, and *Tetsuo II: Body Hammer*, 1992), Ian Conrich locates Tsukamoto's 'nightmarish cyberpunk vision' as 'transformation and incorporation narratives' that locate images of radical biomechanical horror within a larger nexus of machine-age superhero mythologies, recent urban renewal practices, emerging notions regarding the mechanisation of the body in production processes, and the emergence of new economies of eroticism (including techno-eroticism/ fetishism) that confound conventional notions of gender and sexuality.

While Ian Conrich's reading of the *Tetsuo* films both emerges from, and intersects with, recent theories of post-industrial politics, Graham Lewis grounds his investigation of Fukui Shokin's *Pinnochio 964* (1992) and Izumiya Shigeru's *Death Powder* (1986) in conceptualisations of post-human identity. Drawing upon precepts articulated by visionaries like the inimitable science fiction author Philip K. Dick and the incisive cultural critic N. Katherine Hayles, Lewis illustrates how Fukui and Izumiya's texts reveal the artificiality of narratives, be they grounded in traditional notions of linear continuity ('cause and effect') or encased within the flesh that far too many of us still imagine as an inviolable boundary. In the course of his argument, Lewis traces the 'Industrial Age Monster' back to its earlier incarnation in Mary Shelley's *Frankenstein* and declares that '[t]he day of monsters' is not an age of horrors that is yet to come, but, whether we like it or not, a moment that has long since arrived.

A consideration of the aesthetics of postmodern body horror is likewise central to Jay McRoy's chapter, 'Cultural Transformation, Corporeal Prohibitions and Body Horror in Sato Hisayasu's *Naked Blood*'. Located between the examinations of technology and monstrosity offered by Ian Conrich and Graham Lewis, McRoy's chapter focuses on a notoriously gruesome film that negotiates the by no means mutually exclusive political and aesthetic terrains of cyberpunk, splatterpunk and soft-core pornographic cinema, likewise exposing the human body as 'an infinitely unstable nexus of often contradictory social codes informed by the cultural logics of contemporary Japan'. In the process, McRoy investigates Sato's film as a commentary on the eroto-politics of spectatorship, an ingenious critique of Japanese censorship policies that have come to 'signify a set of privileged discourses embodying questions of cultural authenticity and anxieties about Western contamination', and an insightful analysis of the anxieties accompanying changes and continuities in 'gender roles and expectations as they relate to Japan's transforming social and economic landscape'.

Lastly, Tony Williams's case study of Fukasaku Kinji's controversial international sensation, *Battle Royale* (2001), provides us with exactly what the title of his essay promises, an 'Apocalyptic Millennial Warning'. Condemned as irredeemably violent and denied an official US release, *Battle Royale* (as well as the recent sequel briefly discussed by Christopher Sharrett in the preface to this volume) has quickly risen to 'cult classic' status, regularly appearing on course syllabi and dorm-room television screens in universities worldwide. Appropriately, Williams's chapter considers the film's national and international appeal through an expansive, and long overdue, analysis of this groundbreaking work of Japanese cinema. For example, Williams posits, the apocalyptic 'dystopian universe' central to *Battle Royale*'s narrative speaks to contemporary dilemmas pertinent to 'both Western society as well as their post-capitalist Eastern counterparts'. Furthermore, despite its staggering body count and graphic violence, *Battle Royale* occupies an important space in world cinematic traditions in its decidedly oppositional political stance. In this sense, Williams argues, Fukasaku's film is not only remarkably anti-violent, but also sensitive to the pressures resulting from the Japanese education system's competitive, 'zero-sum' organisational logic, the impact of recent downward turns in the national economy upon traditional gender roles and family structures, the persistent adherence to binary modes of thinking that divides humans into categories such as 'winners' and 'losers', and the struggle of citizens against systems of disciplinary power where outcomes may very well have been decided in advance. Ultimately, for Williams, *Battle Royale*'s message is a deadly serious one that we ignore 'at our peril'.

NOTES

1. Creed, Barbara (1995) 'Horror and the Carnivalesque: The Body Monstrous', in Leslie Devereaux and Roger Hillman (eds), *Fields of Vision: Essays in Film Studies, Visual Anthropology, and Photography*, Berkeley, CA and London: University of California Press.
2. As Elizabeth Ann Hull and Mark Siegel note, '[t]he industrial revolution was not simply imported by the Orient; it was forced upon it, either through imperialistic exploitation or, in the case of Japan, as a defense against exploitation.' See Hull, Elizabeth Ann and Mark Siegel (1989) 'Science Fiction', in Richard Gid Powers and Hidetoshi Kato (eds), *Handbook of Japanese Popular Culture*, New York and London: Greenwood Press, p. 245.
3. Ramie Tateishi (2003) 'The Contemporary Japanese Horror Film Series: *Ring* and *Eko Eko Azarak*', in Steven Jay Schneider (eds), *Fear Without Frontiers: Horror Cinema Across the Globe*, Guildford: FAB Press, p. 296.
4. Ivy Marilyn (1995) *Discourses of the Vanishing: Modernity, Phantasm, Japan*, Chicago: University of Chicago Press, p. 4.
5. Ibid., p. 4.
6. Harootunian, H. D. (1989) 'Visible Discourses/Invisible Ideologies', in Masao Miyoshi and H. D. Harootunian (ed.), *Postmodernism and Japan*, Durham, NC and London: Duke University Press, p. 70.
7. One manifestation of this 'disintegrating' effect was the apparent rise in individualised, 'autonomous disciplines', a system of social compartmentalisation in which an emerging concentration on specialised fields of 'knowledge' led to the establishment of 'barriers between different areas of culture, causing mutual isolation and preventing genuine self-understanding'. See Harootunian, p. 74.
8. Davis, Darrell William (2001) 'Reigniting Japanese Tradition within *Hana-Bi*', *Cinema Journal*, 40:4, Summer, pp. 60–1.

9. Harootunian, p. 66.
10. D. P. Martinez recognises the logic behind this narrative as a rhetorical (and frequently aesthetic) construct that presents an almost panicked reification of an illusory 'wholeness' through a depiction of the Japanese national identity as discrete and homogenous: 'Japan is similar to many modern nation-states in that it has had to construct a model of a unitary identity shared by all citizens. Identity no longer depends on religious models or on loyalty to one particular ruler, leader, but on the wider construct of the imagined national community. This nationalism depends on the mass production of mass culture and, while the logic of capitalism (late or otherwise) demands diversification, the underlying logic of one identity (the Japanese) as different from that of their neighbors (let us say, Korea or China) remains crucial to the nation state.' See Martinez, D. P. (1998) 'Introduction: Gender, Shifting Boundaries, and Global Cultures', in D. P. Martinez (ed.), *The Worlds of Japanese Popular Culture: Gender, Shifting Boundaries and Global Cultures*, Cambridge: Cambridge University Press, p. 10.
11. Davis, p. 65.
12. Matsui Midori (2002) 'The Place of Marginal Positionality: Legacies of Japanese Anti-Modernity', in Fran Lloyd (ed.), *Consuming Bodies: Sex and Contemporary Japanese Art*, London: Reaktion Books, pp. 142–65.
13. Craig, Tim (2000) 'Introduction', in Timothy J. Craig (ed.), *Japan Pop!: Inside the World of Japanese Popular Culture*, New York and London: M. E. Sharpe, p. 16.
14. See Napier, Susan J. (2002) 'When the Machines Stop: Fantasy, Reality, and Terminal Identity in *Neon Genesis Evangelion* and *Serial Experiments Lain*', *Science Fiction Studies,* 88, Vol. 29, Part 3, November, pp. 418–35, and Orbaugh, Sharalyn (2002) 'Sex and the Single Cyborg: Japanese Popular Culture Experiments in Subjectivity', *Science Fiction Studies*, 88, Vol. 29, Part 3, November, pp. 436–52.

7. METAL-MORPHOSIS: POST-INDUSTRIAL CRISIS AND THE TORMENTED BODY IN THE *TETSUO* FILMS

Ian Conrich

Tsukamoto Shinya's films, *Tetsuo: The Iron Man* (1988) and *Tetsuo II: Body Hammer* (1992), mark the beginning of the new wave of Japanese horror cinema. The nightmarish cyberpunk vision of these experimental films can be traced back to the dystopianism, fear of annihilation and threats of invasion of both manga comics and anime; the excess, monstrosity and mutations of the colossal creature films produced by the Toho and Daiei studios; and the perversity, obsessions and sadistic torment of many of the *pinku eiga* produced by Nikkatsu Studios. Moreover, parallels can be drawn between Tsukamoto's films and David Lynch's industrial gothic *Eraserhead* (1976) and the postmodernity of David Cronenberg's *Videodrome* (1982), while *Tetsuo* and *Tetsuo II* display an aesthetic concern similar to the alchemical adventures of the surrealist artist and film-maker, Jan Svankmajer. In the violence and unfamiliarity of the transformations of *Tetsuo*'s salaryman into a man-machine, a flesh-metal hybrid, the stability of the domestic and work spaces is removed – an explicit challenge to the traditional images of social harmony and value established in the classical films of a director such as Ozu Yasujiro. In the post-*Tetsuo* Japanese films that appeared to reflect the cultural changes, there was a shared interest in social disorder, family dysfunction and economic and political instability.

Tsukamoto's cinema is distinctly located in the modern fantasies of brutality and destruction, which were regularly part of Japanese popular culture in his youth. Tony Rayns writes that Tsukamoto, who was born in 1960, 'clearly went through the standard Japanese infatuations with Godzilla movies, s-f *manga*, [and] video-game arcades'.[1] In interviews, Tsukamoto gives initial emphasis to the Godzilla movies – 'like other kids of my generation, I grew up with Toho monsters. They were a big part of my childhood reality'.[2] However, he is also keen to stress the diversity of cultural references that have affected the unique vision and design of his productions:

> Later my interests broadened to take in everything from Italian futurism to 'Metropolis', from Helmut Newton's photos to the cyberpunk sensibility, and all that fed into my Tetsuo movies. The destruction has something to do with the childish pleasure of building sand-castles and knocking them down, but I guess destruction has a special meaning for my generation.[3]

Any childish play within the *Tetsuo* films is absorbed into Tsukamoto's adult experiments in painful mutation and his ambitious explorations into scrapyard mayhem, where metal-man monstrosities are compelled into conflict. It is an impressive battle set against an overwhelming city, a bewildering Tokyo of rampant urban development that dominates its inhabitants. The urban jungle of this sprawling metropolis, like Tsukamoto's characters, is in a state of constant expansion and continuous transformation, with an ever-modified and ever-extended constructed form changing as each new element or dimension is composed. In a way, the *Tetsuo* films themselves are not unlike these creations, as each component or layer in Tsukamoto's imagination is connected for a startling filmic effect. To approach these films as the mythical constructs that they are perhaps necessitates that each key connection is detached and detailed. Addressing the individual components, this chapter locates the *Tetsuo* films in relation to Japanese cinema and contemporary productions. It also considers the *Tetsuo* films as part of an emerging post-industrial crisis in Japanese culture.

INCEPTION/RECEPTION

Tsukamoto studied painting in the Fine Arts Department of Nihon University, from where he graduated in 1982 and thereupon moved into the world of advertising. He founded the Tokyo-based Kaiju Theatre group in 1986, which soon after performed his play *Denchu-Kozo no Boken*, a live-action video-game fantasy in which a boy is transported via an electronic device into an alternative environment to do battle with a variety of foes. The play was made into a short film by Tsukamoto – *Denchu-Kozo no Boken* (*Adventures of Denchu-Kozo*, 1987) – the critical success of which inspired him to make *Tetsuo*. Tsukamoto had already made the short film *Futsu-size no Kaijin* (*The Phantom of Regular Size*, 1986), which exhibited in an early form the aggressive, experimental and hyper-charged nihilistic narratives that were to be a feature of his first full-length movies. Most noticeably, *Futsu-size no Kaijin* and *Denchu-Kozo no Boken* contain concepts that Tsukamoto was to return to in making the *Tetsuo* films. The titanic battles and degrees of combat which form a seemingly unending series of physical tests – *Tetsuo* ends with the message 'GAME OVER' – can be observed within the more recent work of Ishii Sogo, especially the film *Electric Dragon 80.000 V* (2001), and the movies of emerging director Kitamura Ryuhei, in particular his 2000 production *Versus*.

Cult director Ishii, however, was most likely an inspiration for Tsukamoto rather than the other way around. His film *Bakuretsu Toshi* (*Burst City*, 1982) depicts an urban centre in chaos and violent disorder, where rioting and gang warfare are as frequent as the acts of police brutality. An imploded city of alienation and destruction, Ishii's early example of a post-punk cinema is feverishly edited and supported by a loud soundtrack of Japanese punk rock. But then if this film inspired Tsukamoto, it would seem it was not the only one to do so. Noting the myriad cultural references, potential film influences and similarities to previous productions – such as *Akira* (1988 – Tetsuo is the name of the film's destructive and metamorphic main mutant), *The Terminator* (James Cameron, 1984) and *Robocop* (Paul Verhoeven, 1986), the work of film-makers David Cronenberg, Alejandro Jodorowsky, Jack Smith, Kenneth Anger, Norman McLaren and Sam Raimi, cartoonist Tex Avery and writer William S. Burroughs – was a prominent aspect of the reviews of the *Tetsuo* films on their release to western cinema audiences. The comparisons are very much part of the film's fan and Internet reaction too. Alison Jobling, on the *Heroic Cinema* website, attempted to define Tsukamoto as a director by suggesting 'you took David Cronenberg and force-fed him LSD from birth, then spliced his genes with those of David Lynch'. The experience of watching *Tetsuo* certainly affected Jobling: '[t]he film damn near sucked my brain out like a whelk'.[4]

The *Tetsuo* films had a limited initial release in British cinemas where, restricted to arthouse venues, they benefited from the support of London's ICA (Institute for Contemporary Arts), and, subsequently, received UK video distribution through ICA Projects. In the main, critics were unused to viewing such extreme examples of Japanese film-making and found the unconventional and low-budget narratives, demanding rapid editing and heightened soundtracks, to be both a curiosity and a challenge, as well as an uncomfortable sensory assault. Derek Malcolm, writing in the *Guardian*, described

Tetsuo II as having 'pounding music and frenetic, edgy camerawork';[5] Jonathan Romney of the *New Statesman* considered the same film as containing 'MTV-pace jumpcutting' and saw Tsukamoto 'in his delirious cutting . . . treat[ing] raw celluloid as infinitely maleable, scrappable stuff'. Romney adjudged the film as 'powerful', with the 'feeling that material – both metal and celluloid – is being allowed to run wild'.[6] Other critics found the film experience more an endurance test, though one that remained rewarding. Geoff Andrew, in his review of the first *Tetsuo* for *Time Out*, wrote that '[a] colleague has likened watching the relentless stream of startling images to being hammered on the head for an hour, and enjoying it'.[7] With such an intense experience, the imaginary clash of flesh and metal had apparently gone beyond the film itself.

Critics were unsettled not just by the kinetic force of the film and the bizarre series of monstrous creations; they also reacted against the levels of crude violence, the improvisational nature of the effects and the perceived weakened storyline. Sue Heal[8] mistakenly said *Tetsuo II* was 'for the ten pints of Special Brew and vindaloo crowd',[9] while Sheila Johnston unfairly described the first *Tetsuo* film as displaying 'worse production values and a feebler grasp of narrative than the most humble student movie'.[10] To the latter, Angus Wolfe Murray added that the '[c]ut-price special effects are neither special, nor effective',[11] and Christopher Tookey simply described it as 'tosh'.[12] If only these critics had not been so rash in their reviews, for as Hugo Davenport wrote in his response for *The Daily Telegraph*, 'it is possible to find a twisted allegory of modern Japan in all this'.[13]

TRANSFORMATION/INCORPORATION

Tetsuo II is not, as some have argued, a sequel to *Tetsuo*, nor is it a remake. Like the man-machine monstrosities at the centre of each production, *Tetsuo II* represents the continuous growth of an idea begun in the first film. The films, with minimal dialogue, are essentially quite simple stories with maximum consideration given to a free-flow of visual ideas. The first *Tetsuo* film presents the transformation of an ordinary Japanese salaryman (Tomoroh Taguchi) into an immense man-machine, after having knocked down an extreme metal fetishist (played by Tsukamoto) while driving his car. The fetishist undergoes metamorphosis too, bringing these metal mutants to clash in the film's finale. *Tetsuo II* multiplies the man-machines through the idea that Yatsu (played by Tsukamoto), a power-hungry leader of a small army of *übermensch* fanatics, desires to test out his new device for mutating men with metal (complete with explosive weaponry) on an innocent member of the public. The chosen individual, Taniguchi Tomoo (Tomoroh Taguchi), twice witnesses the kidnapping of his son Minori (Keinosuke Tomioka), an act designed to induce in him the necessary Hulk-like anger to trigger the flesh-to-metal reaction within his body. Later it is revealed that Yatsu and Taniguchi are in fact brothers who have already been mutated in their childhood through the experimentations of their father (Sujin Kim). There is, however, only room for one mutant, and the indomitable Taniguchi, having defeated his brother, mutates with the army of fanatics into a fearsome man-tank which rumbles onto the streets of Tokyo.

These films function as transformation and incorporation narratives. Tom Gill writes that while such narratives exist worldwide, they are repeatedly found at the heart of Japanese fiction and folklore, most noticeably in children's media. Gill considers the Japanese word for transformation – *henshin* or *henkei* – and for incorporation – *gatai* – and notes that the former translates as 'change body' or 'change form', while the latter means 'combine bodies'.[14] He also writes that incorporation 'looks like a much more modern, machine-age myth' and that transformation and incorporation 'come together in most modern tales of super-heroes'.[15]

The *Tetsuo* films in their machine-age myths depict the protagonists as transforming from the inside out, with wiring, metal pipes, tubing, bolts, drills, cannons and guns protruding, erupting and wrapping themselves around the body. The body size increases as the metal parts add a pulsating bulk to the torso, arms and legs. It is a spectacle of growth, enormity or excessiveness that is also a feature of the Ultraman stories in Japan, of the giant turtle Gamera series of films produced by Daiei, and Toho studio's creation, Godzilla.[16] There is incorporation too in the first *Tetsuo* as the salaryman, within his domestic space, attracts magnetically an array of kitchen and household objects – which, though mostly metal, includes a cat – and which add irregular shape and definition to the mutation. By combining with this hardware he gains a capacity to energise the body through electricity points by inserting his knives-for-fingers extensions into plug sockets. Later, as more metal is assimilated from the surrounding industrial wasteland, the salaryman almost becomes lost under a frenzied mass of metallic parts. Nevertheless, like Taniguchi in *Tetsuo II*, no matter how much metal is acquired, the man in the centre of the metallic form remains discernible.

Within the pile of metal is the supreme Superman, a mutated character who is the man of steel (and other metals), seemingly invincible and protected by a vast layer of exceptional plating, which will only keep increasing. More precisely, Tetsuo is the man of iron, 'tetsu' meaning 'iron' and 'o' meaning 'male'. He is also, perversely, a challenge to L. Frank Baum's gentle metallic-man, the Tin Man. In *The Wizard of Oz*, the Tin Man desires a heart so he can love; in the *Tetsuo* films, the clanging metallic-man has a heart but rages and destroys. Most explicitly, at the start of *Tetsuo II* we are introduced to Yatsu as a cold killer who literally has a pumping metal heart, which the film shows in close-up.

Yatsu kills with his extended finger, which has the capacity to shoot bullets. Yet while mutating towards weapons of emphatic destruction in *Tetsuo II*, with a bigger personal arsenal of guns and cannons, the horrific nature of the monstrous transformations remains largely the same. The metamorphical form with the capacity for infinite possibilities of mutation continues to be all-threatening in its unrelenting capacity to create the unexpected. Rage fuels its transformations and in this form is not dissimilar to Ang Lee's filmic representation of the Marvel comics creation, the Incredible Hulk.[17] The mutation here originates in childhood, from the experiments of a father intent on unconventional scientific research. A similar narrative is presented in *Tetsuo II*, where, like Ang Lee's Hulk, 'transformation is involuntary and convulsive'.[18] Gill argues that in American comic fiction, extreme body alteration is the result of bio-transformation, the mythology dependent on a serum for the power to change. In contrast, the Japanese tend to 'mecha-transform', employing a technological device to change size or appearance.[19] Gill's discussion addresses the superhero, which is clearly outside of the identity of the characters in *Tetsuo*. But as yet further additions to the Japanese cultural obsession with mythical monstrosities, the *Tetsuo* men are unusual as examples of bio-transformation, though the ability to incorporate and assimilate metal and industrial objects cannot exclude *Tetsuo* and *Tetsuo II* as examples also of mecha-transformation.

THE POST-INDUSTRIAL

In a culture in which the products of industry and technology are in abundance, it is not surprising that Japanese fantasies of growth and strength focus on mecha-transformation and incorporation. Reminders of a machine age occur throughout the *Tetsuo* films. Appearing near the start of the first film, the subway train and motorcar are markers of a modern culture. The passenger train supports the modern metropolis and transports the salaryman through the city; the motorcar similarly functions as a carrier, and like the train incorporates flesh within its metallic body when in service. A small group of model cars sit on top of the salaryman's television set in his home. They function as scaled mementos of the pleasing forms of designed car bodies; for the viewer they also serve as a reminder of the car accident with the body of the metal fetishist. This collision of man and steel, in which the fetishist is knocked down, leaves the salaryman 'infected' by the culture of metal. Soon after he finds a piercing shard of metal protruding through his cheek when shaving with his metal razor, and immediately hides it under a plaster. But the union of flesh and metal is too pervasive to be forgotten, and as the salaryman has sex with his girlfriend (Fujiwara Kei), taking her from behind, she likewise grabs a whirring metal fan. It gives her balance, but it also fastens the three into the physical act.

It is not the only example of what Claudia Springer considers as 'industrial-age techno-eroticism'.[20] As the salaryman feeds his girlfriend food he has just fried, including a cooked sausage, she bites down onto the fork with what appears to be unnecessary force. Her first mouthful is accompanied by a loud metallic pounding noise as her teeth chomp onto the utensil, while the second mouthful creates a sound of scraping metal as her teeth run along its surface. The unnatural and exaggerated sounds from using a fork may suggest the gradually transforming salaryman's newly heightened sensitivity to metallic noise, but it also draws attention to the penetration of the industrially manufactured into the fleshy orifice of the girlfriend. Moreover, the scene connects back with the earlier image of the fetishist, as he is introduced at the start of the film running some coiled piping through the clasp of his teeth before pushing it into the deep gash he has just cut into his thigh. Soon after, at the site of the crash, the desiring bodies of the salaryman and his girlfriend, seemingly charged by the impact, copulate close to the wreckage. The fetishist, who survives the accident, is then informed by a doctor (Naomasa Musaka) that a shard of metal from the car wreck penetrated his skull and is lodged in his brain. A piercing in the extreme, the fetishist perhaps achieves his desire to receive a rush of metal to the head.

In this post-industrial landscape, the human and the machine combine. In the mechanical age, machines were designed to serve and produce; in the post-industrial, advanced technology overtakes much of heavy industry and unites the operator and the product. With the change, though, comes loss and abandonment, and within the *Tetsuo* films there are many images of industrial decay and ruin. Various theoretical positions have been established in regard to post-industrialism, and these are discussed in Margaret A. Rose's work, where she locates the early uses of the idea in the writings of Arthur J. Penty (a key book being his 1922 text *Post-Industrialism*). Rose writes that 'Penty has been criticised in more recent years as offering a reactionary and unrealistic vision of the new post-industrial society as one in which the industrialism of the past will be "broken-up" '.[21] True, Penty may have created an 'unrealistic vision', but in Tsukamoto's imaginary Tokyo there are parallels between its neo-culture and Penty's defined 'state of society that will follow the break-up of Industrialism, and might therefore be used to cover the speculations of all who recognise Industrialism is doomed'.[22]

Japanese society is distinctly post-industrial with its excessive valuing of electronic and digital production and communication. Industrialism remains present in contemporary Japan, but in the *Tetsuo* films it is depicted, as Penty proposed, as doomed and broken up. The landscape of these films is one of metal and concrete. In the first *Tetsuo* film, Tokyo is a city of industrial abandonment, emptiness and collapse. The story takes place in derelict buildings, a forsaken railway station and disused warehouses or factories, where ruptured pipes and girders mark industrialism's doom. The streets of Tokyo, through which the protagonists move with great speed, appear maintained, but are largely devoid of life and activity. The protagonists rush (without any desire to pause) through streets of no traffic, under flyovers carrying no vehicles, alongside railway lines without trains, and past standing bicycles racked and unused. The scrapyards too are neglected, and the fragmented detritus of industry that are absorbed and attracted magnetically by the metal-men suggest dissolution. Moreover, the parts are reorganised, albeit in an unruly manner, into machines of destruction.

In *Tetsuo II*, the general emptiness of the metropolis remains, with a greater focus on the skyscrapers and office buildings, cavernous modern complexes and the vast, empty subways of central Tokyo. The coldness of this city void is emphasised through the icy blue filter that Tsukamoto employs for filming these images. As Donald Richie writes in his book-length reflection on Tokyo city, 'though now such permanent materials as stone, steel and marble [have been used] the city does not appear as though it has been built to last'.[23] The city sits on nineteen active fault-lines, each of which can trigger an earthquake, and Richie sees this 'apprehension of its own destruction' as part of the reason why Tokyo's buildings appear transient: '[n]ew buildings are constructed in fashions so flamboyantly modern that one cannot but expect them to be superseded'.[24] Such buildings lie in ruins in the apocalyptic coda to *Tetsuo II*, in which Taniguchi's wife Kana (Kanoka Nobu) declares 'It's so peaceful.' Tsukamoto repeatedly returns to images of the modern and heavily developed metropolis in *Tetsuo II*, and like the constant abstract inserted shots of machinery and metalwork in the first *Tetsuo* film, it is not always clear as to whether this director is fetishising or establishing a position of cool separation from industrial development. What is noticeable is the films' desire to probe and embrace the metallic form, functioning or fragmented, when linked with human flesh.

TECHNO-EROTICISM AND THE TORMENTED BODY

David Cronenberg's film *Videodrome* presents the idea of the 'New Flesh', the ability of the body to mutate and even to develop biological attachments that are not recognisably part of the human form. Cronenberg writes that '[t]he most accessible version of the "New Flesh" . . . would be that you can actually change what it means to be a human being in a physical way', and that '[s]heer force of will would allow you to change your physical self'.[25] The man-machine monstrosities of the *Tetsuo* films mutate through rage, which at a certain level of transformation would appear to be irrevocable. They are a version of Cronenberg's New Flesh and share a degree of *Videodrome*'s sexualisation of the effect of transmutation, and even its images of sadomasochism. Where the *Tetsuo* films differ most is perhaps in their continual emphasis on torment and their suggestions of homoeroticisation.

The sexualisation of the man as machine in the *Tetsuo* films connects with the techno-erotic values of the early twentieth-century Italian futurists, who Tsukamoto has acknowledged as an influence. As Springer writes, 'for example, [the futurists] fetishised the speed and powerful force of industrial machines from about 1909 until 1914, when World War I revealed the monstrously destructive aspect of technology and ended the lives of several futurist artists'.[26] Tsukamoto's machines are clearly monstrously destructive, but this appears to be an attraction for the director. As testosterone-fuelled killing machines, these creations recall the hyper-masculine forms of comic books and cult movies such as *The Terminator* and *Universal Soldier* (1992). Such fiction depicts the powerful male as a muscular and pumped-up body. In contrast, the *Tetsuo* films equate power with a hardened armoured body of metal that is an extensive series of odd attachments and that makes no attempt to appear biologically plausible. In *Tetsuo II*, a small army of well-built men exercises together; they relentlessly lift weights and pump iron to increase their body strength, but they remain inferior to the might of the iron man, who has no need for such discipline and dedicated training. The powerful bulk of the *Tetsuo* monstrosities lacks the toned physique of a bodybuilder, and they also lack the sleek and contoured shapes of the glorious machines so adored by futurists. Yet Tsukamoto still finds the metallic-man bodies in his films pleasing.

It is perhaps the power of going beyond the ordinary human, or of enhancing the normal body, that is a key to the *Tetsuo* films. However, the gain is not without immense pain, with the films depicting a tormented body located within the Japanese concept of *gaman* (or endurance), an important aspect of local cultural identity.[27] In particular, the *Tetsuo* films, with their sadistic and masochistic violence, can be traced back within Japanese cinema to when the tortured body regularly appeared in the *pinku eiga* (pink, or sex films) of the late 1960s and 1970s. They are also known as roman-porno (or romantic-pornographic). The main studio associated with these films, Nikkatsu, developed two subgenres in the mid-1970s – Best SM Pink and Violent Pink ('roughies' or rape films). Such productions predominantly showed male domination or violation of the female body.[28]

Nicholas Bornoff writes that '[t]he Japanese take sadistic fantasy – provided it remains only fantasy – in their stride'.[29] Bornoff also observes that in the Japanese sex clubs '[t]here is one thing . . . which one never, but absolutely never, sees in an SM show . . . and that is a man being pushed around by a woman'.[30] In the *Tetsuo* films, though, it is the male body that is mainly abused. The metal fetishist, in the first film, graphically splits open his thigh to allow him to thrust a sizeable pipe into his body (at the point of brutal success, of deep penetration, the 'enhanced' body of the fetishist is compared, perhaps ironically, with images of athletes). A nightmare experienced by the sleeping salaryman, post-collision with the fetishist, depicts further deep penetration of the male body. But the previous act of self-harm as an act of perceived self-enhancement is, in the nightmare, turned into a ferocious act of sodomy. The salaryman, unable to defend himself, is raped by a possessed woman who repeatedly thrusts into him an unfeasibly long strap-on extension that she wields. Upon awakening from this nightmare, and during a love-making session with his girlfriend, the salaryman discovers to his horror that a gigantic drill with a horrendously pointed burrowing head is protruding from his groin. Here, the protagonist may be struggling to control his rebellious body, but the role of the victim in this sadistic fantasy has now been reversed. Before the girlfriend is splattered apart by the drill, she is threatened by the salaryman: 'You want a taste of my sewage pipe?'

Rayns wrote that 'Tsukamoto is impressed that I had read "Tetsuo" as an expression of the space between phallic aggression and the fear of sodomy'.[31] In the original interview Rayns notes that '"Tetsuo" moves inexorably towards an all-male cataclysm (the antagonists finally merge in some bizarre metabolic copulation) and "Tetsuo II" is rife with Mapplethorpe like images of male torsos and muscles under duress'.[32] He asks Tsukamoto, '[w]here do the homoerotic elements come from?', to which Tsukamoto smiles and says:

> I wasn't aiming specifically for a homoerotic sensibility, more for a kind of polymorphous perversity with the sexual signals confused. But I like the way men's bodies have recently come to be objectified in art . . . In 'Tetsuo II', I wanted to go crazy with images of maleness. I guess the films could have ended with some kind of male-female fusion. But there's a feeling of purity when they're both men. I can't explain it.[33]

At the end of *Tetsuo*, where the two combatants have merged into one mighty man-machine, one turns to the other and declares 'we can mutate the whole world into metal.' This is followed by the statement 'our love can destroy the whole fucking world.' The dawn of Tsukamoto's New Flesh is a vision of global destruction, one where society has imploded and merged with industry, which is depicted within the *Tetsuo* films as inherently unstable.

Tetsuo II, with its trundling beast of a tank created from a fusion of bodybuilding men, suggests the New Flesh is unstoppable in its apocalyptic drive. Manoeuvring itself with ease through the emptied streets of Tokyo, community is notable by its absence. Such emptiness and depopulation has become an increasingly recurrent theme in recent Japanese films, with the director Kurosawa Kiyoshi, and his horror movie *Kaïro* (*Pulse*, 2001), receiving particular critical attention. Across many anime films, but also live-action features as diverse as *Yuriika* (*Eureka*, 2000), *Kakashi* (*Scarecrow*, 2001), *Honogurai Mizu no Soko Kara* (*Dark Water*, 2002) and *Border Line* (2002), the new Japan imagined, like the Neo Tokyo of *Akira*, is a tragic landscape, an overwhelming dystopia of alienation, loss, decay and dysfunction. The salaryman in *Tetsuo* brutally murders his girlfriend and invalidates his need for a domestic space. In *Tetsuo II*, Taniguchi is a loving father, but in his rage he accidentally obliterates his son, leaving only the hands as the surviving parts of the lost child. Taniguchi's own father had already destroyed him through unorthodox experimentation and the young Taniguchi's subsequent violent outburst leaves him orphaned and then adopted by foster parents. If there is a union it is around the man-tank: the army of bodybuilders permanently connected to each other and to a metal regime. Riding on the body of the tank is Taniguchi's wife Kana, who despite being a witness to all the destruction and the death of her son, remains attached to her husband. However, the union is forced, and if it is an allegory of modern Japan, then it depicts a future in crisis.

NOTES

I would like to thank Mette and Niels Weisberg for their helpful suggestions.

1. Rayns, Tony (1991a) 'Tetsuo', *Sight and Sound*, 1:5, September, p. 52.
2. Rayns, Tony (1992) 'Sodom and Tomorrow', *Time Out*, 8 November, p. 22.
3. Ibid, p. 22.
4. See http://www.heroic-cinema.com/review.php?ID=tetsuo.
5. Malcolm, Derek (1992) 'Tetsuo II: Body Hammer', *Guardian*, 19 November, p. 6.
6. Romney, Jonathan (1992) 'Tetsuo II: Body Hammer', *New Statesman*, 20 November, p. 33.
7. Andrew, Geoff (1991) *Time Out*, 4 September, p. 58.
8. See Heal, Sue (1992) 'Tetsuo II: Body Hammer', *Today*, 13 November, p. 38.
9. Special Brew is a very strong lager with a high alcoholic content. It is sold in Britain, where the myth is that it is consumed by people who wish to become drunk quickly. The vindaloo, or hot curry, is supposedly the traditional meal at the end of an evening of drinking and may be combined with the watching of late-night television programmes or a video of little value.
10. Johnston, Sheila (1991) 'Tetsuo II: Body Hammer', *The Independent*, 6 September, p. 16.
11. Wolfe Murray, Angus (1991) 'Tetsuo II: Body Hammer', *The Scotsman*, 21 September, p. 22.
12. Tookey, Christopher (1991) 'Tetsuo II: Body Hammer', *Sunday Telegraph*, 18 September, p. 44.
13. Davenport, Hugo (1991) 'Tetsuo II: Body Hammer', *The Daily Telegraph*, 5 September, p. 14.

14. Gill, Tom (1999) 'Transformational Magic: Some Japanese Super-heroes and Monsters', in D. P. Martinez (ed.), *The Worlds of Japanese Popular Culture: Gender, Shifting Boundaries and Global Cultures*, Cambridge: Cambridge University Press, p. 45.
15. Ibid., p. 46.
16. The *Tetsuo* films, *Tetsuo II* in particular, can be more closely compared with the Godzilla films, *Godzilla vs. The Cosmic Monster* (1974) and *Godzilla vs. Mecha-Godzilla* (1993). In these movies, a Godzilla imposter who combats the real Godzilla is revealed to be a bionic creation. In the first film, the cyborg is revealed only as the outer skin is cut. Inside is a formidable colossal creature with a body full of weapons; each finger is, for instance, a missile.
17. Anger similarly transforms the protagonist in Tsukamoto's film *Tokyo Fist* (1995) from a weak salaryman into a brutal boxer.
18. Gill, p. 46.
19. Ibid., pp. 46–7.
20. Springer, Claudia (1996) *Electronic Eros: Bodies and Desire in the Postindustrial Age*, London: Athlone Press, p. 4.
21. Rose, Margaret A. (1992) *The Post-Modern and the Post-Industrial*, Cambridge: Cambridge University Press, p. 24.
22. Ibid., p. 23.
23. Richie, Donald (1999) *Tokyo: A View of the City*, London: Reaktion Books, p. 44.
24. Ibid., p. 44.
25. Rodley, Chris (ed.) (1992) *Cronenberg on Cronenberg*, London and Boston: Faber and Faber, pp. 80, 82.
26. Springer, p. 3.
27. See Bornoff, Nicholas (1992) *Pink Samurai: The Pursuit and Politics of Sex in Japan*, London: Grafton, pp. 549–50.
28. See Hamamoto Maki (1998) 'Naomi Tani: An Interview with Nikkatsu Queen of SM', *Asian Cult Cinema*, 19 (April), pp. 39–48; Weisser, Thomas and Yuko Mihara Weisser (1998a) 'The Violent Pink Films of Yasuharu Hasebe', *Asian Cult Cinema*, 20 (June), pp. 32–36; and Rayns, Tony (1984), 'Nikkatsu's "Roman-Porno" Films' in Tony Rayns (ed.), *Eiga: 25 Years of Japanese Cinema*, Edinburgh: Edinburgh International Film Festival, p. 14.
29. Bornoff, p. 538.
30. Ibid., p. 547.
31. Rayns, Tony (1991b) 'Tokyo Stories', *Sight and Sound*, 1: 8 (December), p. 15.
32. Rayns (1992), p. 23.
33. Ibid., p. 23.

8. CULTURAL TRANSFORMATION, CORPOREAL PROHIBITIONS AND BODY HORROR IN SATO HISAYASU'S *NAKED BLOOD*

Jay McRoy

I want to make a film which has the influence to drive its audience mad, to make them commit murder. (Sato Hisayasu)

INTRODUCTION: SOCIAL (DIS)EASES AND THE BODY HORRIFIC

Sato Hisayasu's cinematic vision, particularly as visible in his 1995 film, *Naked Blood*, is often compared by western critics to that of Canadian-born director David Cronenberg. Though rarely explored beyond the basic acknowledgment that both filmmakers blend 'the visceral, the psychopathological and the metaphysical',[1] this association helps to point out that Sato, like Cronenberg, is a 'literalist of the body'.[2] Accordingly, Sato posits the body as an indiscrete, transformative and immanent space that reveals the potential for imagining new economies of identity. He is a film-maker who explores both the abject dread and infinite possibility of the human body in a state of dissolution, contributing an important and unique perspective to a familiar preoccupation within contemporary horror cinema. This chapter examines Sato Hisayasu's *Naked Blood* as a text that mobilises tropes frequently associated with the (by no means mutually exclusive) horror and science fiction genres in order to imagine the human body as an infinitely unstable nexus of often contradictory social codes informed by the cultural logics of contemporary Japan. Set within late-industrial landscapes where the flesh is at once agonisingly immediate and increasingly anachronistic, *Naked Blood* engages both the extreme dread and the 'extreme seductiveness' that, as Georges Bataille reminds us, may constitute 'the boundary of horror'.[3] Indeed, it is my ultimate contention that while Sato's film engages a multiplicity of territorialising cultural forces, his film revels in intensity until what emerges is a narrative of social and physical corporeality that allows viewers to conceive of an alternative existence that 'no longer resembles a neatly defined itinerary from one practical sign to another, but a sickly incandescence, a durable orgasm'.[4]

Locating the films of Sato Hisayasu within a particular cinematic genre is an especially frustrating endeavour. Indeed, even his most commercially accessible works, if in fact such texts can be said to exist, are largely exercises in generic and cultural cross-fertilisation. Though influenced by western literary and cinematic traditions, Sato's films reveal a myriad of social and political anxieties over the 'appearance' of the Japanese physical and social body. Emerging at the intersection of horror, science fiction, and Japanese softcore pornography, Sato's films are a veritable mélange of splatterpunk, cyberpunk and erotic cinema motifs that locate the body as a liminal construction. As a result, it is perhaps most accurate to examine Sato Hisayasu as one of cinema's most famous (infamous?) practitioners of 'body horror' – a hybrid, and thus somewhat more inclusive, category that, according to Kelly Hurley, 'recombines' multiple 'narrative and cinematic conventions of the science fiction, horror, and suspense film in order to stage a spectacle of the human body defamiliarized'.[5] A comprehensive term like 'body horror' is intensely appropriate in discussions of Sato's films, where the metaphoric implications of the splattered or transfigured body are central to his aesthetic and political agenda. Though frequently exploring the non-human topos of technology's complex role in the social imaginary of Japan's late capitalist political and ideological terrain, Sato's cinema simultaneously turns on foregrounded images of endangered physiognomies and corporeal disintegration. Even throughout the last ten years, as the circulation of capital, information and interpersonal communication has become increasingly *invisible* and *electronic*, Sato's films have continued to turn and return to the physical body, in all its visible, messy and all-too-vulnerable splendour, as a site of perpetual contestation. The body in his films provides a flexible and everencodable space that again recalls Cronenberg's cinema, where the body is 'at once a target for new biological and communicational technologies, a site of political conflict, and a limit point at which ideological oppositions collapse'.[6]

THE SEEN AND THE OBSCENE: SATO HISAYASU'S
NAKED BLOOD AND THE JAPANESE BODY

Naked Blood is perhaps one of Sato Hisayasu's most complex and visually arresting films. The plot revolves around a seventeen-year-old boy genius named Eiji. Inspired by his dead father's scientific and philosophic aspirations, which included a desire to better the world by helping humanity achieve a form of intensity akin to blinding light, Eiji creates the 'ultimate painkiller' to 'improve the happiness of mankind'. The fruit of his labour is a drug called Myson, a substance that causes the human brain to feel pain as pleasure. Seeking humans upon which to test his creation, Eiji sneaks his elixir into an intravenous contraceptive that his mother (an established scientist) administers to three young women. The test subjects include two unnamed women – a vain woman whose 'greatest pleasure[s]' are having an attractive body and wardrobe, and a food-obsessed woman whose 'greatest joy' is eating – and Mikami, a woman who hasn't slept since she was in the fifth grade, when the 'shock' of the onset of menses 'blocked' her 'sleep cycle'. Eiji chronicles Myson's impact by videotaping each woman from a distance, but his anonymity is compromised when Mikami catches him spying on her and confronts him. In part because Myson allows Mikami to experience her disdain for Eiji as attraction, they become romantically involved, and Mikami brings Eiji into her private world by showing him her 'sleeping installation', a virtual reality unit that allows her to experience a dreamlike state by showing her 'the scenery' of her heart.

Inevitably, Eiji's experiment goes horribly awry. The other two Myson test subjects become grotesquely self-destructive: the woman for whom beauty equals 'pleasure' slowly transforms herself into a bloody, albeit orgasmic, human pin-cushion, and the woman for whom eating is 'joy' literally consumes herself in what are undeniably some of the film's most unsettling moments. The narrative's climax occurs when Mikami, with whom Eiji has forged an uneasy yet intimate relationship, first kills her fellow test-subjects, then slices a gaping vaginal-shaped wound into Eiji's mother's stomach and, following a cyber-enhanced sexual encounter with Eiji, kills the young genius by first injecting him with Myson and then cutting his throat. In the film's final scene, set several years after Eiji's death, we learn that Mikami and her young, camcorder-wielding son – also named Eiji – are travelling about the land, spraying the air with a substance that might be herbicide or might be Myson. As Mikami drives off on a motorcycle equipped with a canister and spraying tube ('I think I'll go west today,' she tells her son, 'it hasn't spread there yet'), the child meets the viewers' gaze and says, 'The dream has not ended yet.'

Controversial both in Japan and in the few western markets and film festivals in which it was publicly screened, *Naked Blood* continues to provoke strong (if, at times, bewildered) reactions by film critics, movie reviewers and cinephiles, some of whom have left written reactions and thoughts about the film on the various on-line paracinema catalogues[7] and fan-based Internet websites dedicated to the celebration and circulation of 'shock' and 'gore' cinema. Thomas Weisser and Yuko Mihara Weisser, authors of *Japanese Cinema: The Essential Handbook* (1998), *Japanese Cinema Encyclopedia: Horror, Fantasy, Science Fiction* (1998) and *Japanese Cinema Encyclopedia: The Sex Films* (1998), label Sato's film-making as 'bitter' and composed in a 'sledgehammer style',[8] and describe *Naked Blood* as rating 'high on the gross-out level'.[9] Similarly, an online fan review called the film 'an incredibly transgressive horror film',[10] while a reviewer for the Sex Gore Mutants website, while lauding the film for being 'one of the most depressing movies ever', also characterises *Naked Blood*'s plot as 'raw, existing to frame a raw emotion, not to tell a story'.[11] This last observation is not surprising, especially given the film's surreal imagery and complicated storyline, as well as the movie's intentionally disorienting and ambiguous closing scenes that explore the tenuous distinction between what constitutes reality and what represents a part of virtual reality's 'consensual hallucination'.[12]

Manipulating audience understanding of what is real and what is imaginary is a popular narrative gesture in films that speculate upon the promises and pitfalls of an ever-emerging cyberculture.[13] What separates *Naked Blood* from many comparable western films, however, is that *Naked Blood*, as is the case with many of Sato's productions, was not backed by large budgets and extensive marketing strategies. Rather, *Naked Blood* emerges from Sato's work both within and against the Japanese *pinku eiga* cinema, a largely uniform and highly regulated tradition of 'soft core' films that, especially within the subgenres known as Best SM Pink or Violent Pink, have become increasingly notorious for emphasising partial male and female nudity coupled with narratives depicting 'the rape and brutalization of young girls'.[14]

In other words, unlike western films with comparable plots, Sato Hisaya-su's works arise from a largely low-budget cinematic tradition with a distinctly formulaic, yet surprisingly flexible, visual iconography. Yet, as I will demonstrate in the paragraphs to follow, *pinku eiga*'s frequently violent and misogynist tropes, coupled with prohibitions enforced by *Eirin* (Japan's censorship body which rules on 'decency' in film) against the depiction of pubic hair and genitalia, nevertheless allows for the possibility of a critique of dominant cultural power relations.[15] Sato Hisayasu, however, stands out among his fellow *pinku eiga* directors in both his detached, almost ambivalent cinematic vision of postmodern alienation (what Paula Felix-Didier calls the 'exposition of the existential emptiness of modern life'[16]) and the extent to which the splattered bodies in his texts function as subjects for political/cultural inquiry. In *Naked Blood*, Sato questions not only the politics of censorship in Japan and the cinematic tradition within, and against which, he toils, but also the impact of changing gender roles and the emergence of virtual technologies in late capitalist Japanese society.

DECONTEXTUALISED LIPS: CENSORSHIP AND THE NATIONAL BODY

To fully appreciate the ways in which Sato's *Naked Blood* functions as a critique of Japanese censorship policies, though, it is first necessary to explore how these regulations came to be established. In *Permitted and Prohibited Desires: Mothers, Comics, and Censorship in Japan*, Anne Allison locates the origin of contemporary standards regarding what can and cannot be shown on screens in Japan as originating from a nexus of concerns about national identity and the 'appearance' and 'purity' of the Japanese physical and social body. Much of this national focus on appropriate bodily representations, she argues, stems from a reaction to western orientalist imaginings of the Japanese biological and social body, particularly as they developed within the nineteenth century:

> It was as a corrective to this Western perception of Japanese 'primitiveness' that the modern laws against obscenity were first imposed: they were a means of covering the national body from charges that it was obscene . . . [I]n part, acquiring such an identity meant adopting Western standards of corporeal deportment. In part as well, it meant developing a notion of the public as a terrain that is monitored and administered by the state. Thus, the behavior of the Japanese, as state subjects, in this terrain is regulated and surveiled.[17]

Of course, policing (and prohibiting) certain modes of behaviour and visual representations of the human body and human sexuality, especially in reaction to a perceived 'dirtiness', also functions to 'protect what is "real"' – that is, 'unique to Japanese culture' – from 'outside contamination . . . from being infiltrated and deformed by Western influence'.[18] Some of the most heated debates about censorship in Japan have arisen in response to the controlled importation and, in several cases, subsequent visual alteration of western films and other media depicting genitalia and pubic hair.[19] In this complex history of negotiation over cultural value, pubic hair and genitalia have come to resonate beyond their prurient indexical value, signifying a set of privileged discourses embodying questions of cultural authenticity and anxieties about western contamination.

In *Naked Blood*, Sato operates within and, in some important ways, exceeds the conventions of *pinku eiga* cinema, including the foregrounding of nudity and graphic violence, to illustrate that censorship's function to territorialise 'national and public space according to body zones' is far more important than whether 'covered or uncovered sex organs are prohibited'[20] in Japan. By violently altering bodies in scenes that wed conventional signifiers of sexuality (such as moans of pleasure and ecstatic postures) with violent images of the human form turned horrifically against itself, Sato invests the body with the kind of 'radical otherness' that Jean Baudrillard locates at the 'epicenter' of 'terror';[21] the body is dis-/re-figured in a way that at once exposes (makes 'naked') and explodes (splatters) the social codes that inform its socially prescribed shape and meaning.

This oppositional politics behind *Naked Blood*'s scenes of body horror is perhaps best illustrated by a consideration of the scene in which one of the most memorable instances of self-cannibalisation in film history is performed by the Myson test-subject who equates joy with eating. Sitting naked upon her kitchen table, her body surrounded by plates and cutlery, she slowly moves a fork and knife into her genitalia, which is carefully concealed by the *mise-en-scène*. As she moans in ecstasy, her arms move in a manner that suggests that she is slicing something. It is at this precise point in the film that the Japanese censors' prohibition against the depiction of human pubic regions is radically and horrifyingly recontextualised and subverted: she slowly raises the fork and the camera focuses upon the bloody, quivering genital lips pierced on its tines. It is only at this point, when her lips meet lips, that the audience fully realises the extent of her orgasmically self-destructive action. Her self-consumption continues with a nipple and an eye, too, but it is the woman's consumption of her own vulval lips that most viewers will remember long after the film is over.

This scene offers what is perhaps Sato's most explicit example of how the violent dismantling of the human body provides a metaphor for the ways that disciplinary power in Japanese culture both grants and restricts personal expression, maintaining a notion of a cohesive national and cultural identity. By blatantly displaying that which cannot be shown (human genitalia) through a removal of the 'obscene' object from its traditional context, Sato simultaneously shocks his audience and reveals some of the logics at work in late capitalist Japanese culture. By revealing, through an ingenious process of decontextualisation, the very corporeal features rendered invisible by national censors, Sato forces his audience to confront the nationalist logics behind contemporary representations of the human body within Japanese visual culture, an image system designed to maintain a specifically 'Japanese' physical and social body free (at least theoretically) from western, orientalist notions of embodiment. The politics of censorship and (controlled) nudity in Japanese cinema is laid bare, exposed in a frenzy of the visible that ultimately discloses how the concerns over maintaining a consolidated social body are at once partially informed by, and yet ideally resistant to, western and other non-traditional concepts of social and cultural identity that inform how the human body is visually portrayed and ideologically invested. The quivering flesh at the end of the fork both *is* and *is not* genitalia; Sato is both revelling in the dangers of the body obscene and playing by the (or maybe creating new) rules. *Naked Blood*, then, pushes and deconstructs the boundaries of what can be seen – both making the logics of cultural negotiation visible as well as contesting them. *Naked Blood* skilfully directs the viewer's gaze, guiding his/her experience of this film about detached characters caught up in extreme events that, within the diegesis, unfold almost completely before the lenses of photograph and video equipment – including the meta-lens of Sato's own camera. As such, the film provides a commentary on bodily experiences, mediated visions and the eroto-politics of the gaze.

MOTHERS AND SONS: WOMEN AND WORK

Sato's depiction of the splattered body recognises social anxieties accompanying changes and continuities in gender roles and expectations as they relate to contemporary Japan's transforming social and economic landscape. Manipulated by the euphoric effects of Myson, the violence that the vain woman and the gluttonous woman perform against their own bodies can even be understood as a proto-feminist critique of the destructive impact of patriarchal authority and beauty ideals: the women literally self-destruct in a frenzy of body modification taken to near fatal extremes. In addition, *Naked Blood* addresses what Anne Allison describes as cultural apprehensions over the steadily emerging presence of women in the workplace and, by extension, the occasional reconfiguration of domestic space: 'In Japan in the 1990s . . . domestic labor is losing its moorings. Women are working in greater numbers, for more years, and with less inclination to quit at the point of marriage and motherhood.'[22] This gendered transformation of the social body finds cinematic articulation in the character of Eiji's mother. It is her position as a legitimately employed scientist, coupled with her son's familial, social and professional alienation (her son, after all, is still a teen and, thus, still under intense pressure to succeed in school), which results in the unauthorised delivery of Myson to the unwitting test subjects. This bodily chaos, engendered by the mother's Myson tests and mapped across explicitly feminine bodies, seems to suggest that women's participation in what was conventionally a masculine sphere can only result in catastrophe.

This social anxiety over women's transgressions of traditional feminine roles plays out in the Oedipal politics at work in Eiji's dysfunctional family. Eiji's desire to become a scientist and develop the aptly named Myson stems from his desire to follow in his deceased (and, thus, 'absent') father's footsteps. Like his father before him, Eiji longs to achieve a form of intensity; his desire to create a drug to 'improve the happiness of mankind' mirrors his father's quasi-scientific quest for a form of immortality through intensity – 'We'll break through time and space,' his father wrote prior to his disappearance, 'and head for the kingdom of light.' Consequently, it is his anger over what he perceives as his mother's failure to assume the traditional female role and support her husband's 'dream' that Eiji cites as a contributing factor to his emotional distance from his mother. The social implications of her refusal to blindly comply with gender expectations derived from a traditional patriarchal economy are intensified when one considers that Eiji's mother, as a scientist working towards the development of a more effective method of contraception, is in a position to further usurp conventionally masculine cultural roles by literally controlling biological, and by extension ideological, reproduction.

Additionally, throughout the majority of *Naked Blood*, Eiji, like his father before him (and like any member of a capitalist society), is denied the satisfaction he seeks: by consistently assuming the role of voyeur, his observations are perpetually mediated by technology, either in the form of cameras or virtual reality equipment. This, too, speaks to changing gender roles in Japanese society, given that, as formulated by Allison, 'situating the male subject as viewer and voyeur is not necessarily or unquestionably a practice of scopophilia that empowers him'.[23] Consistently removed from the objects of his desire by cameras and other technological devices, Eiji looks but does not actually reach out and touch. Even his act of sexual intercourse towards the film's conclusion is mediated by virtual reality goggles that project surreal images upon his retinas, resulting in a conflation of generic signifiers that provides the closest thing to a 'money shot' in Sato's film . . . the image of Eiji's arterial blood spraying Mikami's breasts and euphoric expression.

TECHNOLOGY, EAST/WEST BORDER CROSSING AND CYBERPUNK

Like many western works of speculative fiction, *Naked Blood* engages cultural trepidations surrounding rapid increases in technological development. In its extensive depictions of computers, video equipment, designer drugs and virtual reality, Sato's film has many similarities with the tropes that have come to constitute the genre of cyberpunk. As scholars like Joshua La Bare and Tatsumi Takayuki have illustrated, Japanese science fiction and its western counterpart have existed in a strange state of symbiosis in which each tradition borrows from the other, with various orientalist and occidentalist consequences. The scope of this ideological cross-fertilisation is quite extensive; however; even a perfunctory survey of western and Japanese cyberpunk texts reveals the degree to which these traditions inform one another. William

Gibson's novel *Neuromancer* (1984) and Ridley Scott's film *Blade Runner* (1982) are merely two examples of well-known western cyberpunk texts that are particularly rich with orientalist imaginings of Japanese culture as simultaneously mysterious, seductive, apocalyptic and technophilic. When these motifs find their way into contemporary Japanese science fiction, a recursive pattern of cultural inflection occurs, in which Japanese works of speculative fiction simultaneously perpetuate and condition operant tropologies. Certain familiar motifs emerge, but they are frequently invested with cultural codings that often confound western viewers. Thus, while many western cyberpunk narratives tend to adopt a largely cautionary, if not outright pessimistic view towards the conflation of the 'human' and the 'technological', the 'extrapolative tendency' in Japanese science fiction 'seems more oriented towards enthusiasm for the benefits or potential consequences [of technology] than for any social changes likely to be caused by that technology'.[24]

The cross-cultural transfusion of science fiction tropes extends back at least to post-Second World War Japanese importations of 'a huge variety of Anglo-American cultural products',[25] including numerous literary and cinematic works of speculative fiction. In turn, this new and, given Japan's steady re-emergence as a global economic power, increasingly expansive consumer base impacted how numerous western and Japanese authors and filmmakers imagined the shape and content of multiple genres, especially those dealing with the fantastic. Tatsumi Takayuki describes this symbiotic relationship in 'Generations and Controversies: An Overview of Japanese Science Fiction, 1957–1997':

> Given that science fiction is a literature reflecting the frontiers of techno-capitalism, it was inevitable that Japanese writers of the 1960s would follow the original literary examples produced by the Pax Americana in the West. In the 80s . . . a revolutionary paradigm shift took place: Anglo-American writers began appropriating Japanese images as often as the reverse, while Japanese writers came to understand that writing post-cyberpunk science fiction meant locating the radically science fictional within the semiosis of 'Japan'. Of course, Anglo-American representations of Japan appeal to readers largely by distorting Japanese culture, much as the Japanese people in the 50s and 60s . . . unwittingly misread their Occidentalism as genuine internationalism.[26]

To this day, science fiction and horror texts emerging on both sides of the Pacific frequently reflect complex economic, cultural and historical tensions. Analysing representations of human (and posthuman) embodiment within these texts provides a method for gaining insight into identity politics at the local, national and transnational levels.

Furthermore, in both Japanese and western science fiction, the dominant tropology of scientific extrapolation provides compelling insight into larger societal concerns related to technological advancement. If, as Elizabeth Anne Hull and Mark Seigel argue, modern Japanese industrialisation occurred 'as a defense' against western 'exploitation',[27] then the cyberpunk aspects of *Naked Blood* reveal not only cultural concerns over the extent to which technology has impacted and/or may impact how Japanese people view both their own bodies and their relationship to the larger social body, but also a compelling ambivalence, on the part of Sato as an artist, towards the infusion of technology in society. As Thomas Weisser and Yuko Mihara Weisser have noted, 'electronic tools and media gadgets' are crucial props in many of Sato's films. 'Besides being critical of . . . "dehumanizing pop culture"', they argue, '[Sato] is fascinated by it'.[28] The extent to which *Naked Blood* exemplifies this ambivalence is evidenced when one considers how technological advances constitute both a destructive force (Myson – the ultimately destructive pain killer 'tested' upon unsuspecting human guinea pigs) and a potential solace (the 'sleeping installation' – the only way that, given her insomnia, Mikami can attain the rest she needs). Technology, then, functions paradoxically in Sato's film. Despite its effects on the various characters, Myson was seemingly created with the best of intentions. In contrast, Mikami's virtual reality 'sleeping installation', like Eiji's ever-present video camera, provides yet another barrier to conventional interpersonal contact, thus heightening the film's theme of postmodern alienation.

Going Too Far: Intensity and the Body Horrific

Sato Hisayasu's *Naked Blood* weds horror with science fiction, or, more specifically, splatterpunk with cyberpunk. As such, it is a text that reduces the biological and the mechanical to an infinite set of surfaces upon which it is possible to recognise some of the effects of the circulation of late capitalist disciplinary power within Japanese culture and the oppressive exercise of those systems that endeavour to control how people think and act. While acknowledging the tyrannical and alienating potential of video, pharmacological and virtual technologies, *Naked Blood* does not completely disavow the possibility that these technologies may provide alternatives to traditional notions of identity. True, Myson's side effects have disastrous results, and often what characters see and remember is mediated by screens and lenses or experienced through filmed or recorded images. Nevertheless, it is also possible to understand the mixture of the physical and mechanical in *Naked Blood* as revealing a space where holistic, humanist notions of corporeal (and, by extension, social) embodiment collapse. As Michael Ryan and Douglas Kellner suggest, 'technology represents the possibility that nature might be reconstructable'.[29] In this sense, then, Sato's film explores what Scott Bukatman calls 'terminal identity', that 'unmistakable double articulation in which we find both the end of the subject and a new subjectivity constructed' through technology and media.[30] Thus, *Naked Blood*, like that hybrid cinematic genre known as body-horror, challenges the very notion of limits, exposing the borders mobilised to delineate genres, bodies and nations as not only constructed, but far more permeable than previously imagined.

Consequently, a discourse of intensity informs both the film's plot and presentation: from Eiji's father's quest to achieve immortality through becoming light to the narrative's collapsing of pain into pleasure and sexuality into violence; from Eiji's desire to attain 'eternal happiness' to Sato's aforementioned use of corporeal mutilation as a springboard for political inquiry. The multi-generational, (father–son–grandson[?]) pursuit of eternity through intensity (the name 'Eiji', we are told, means 'eternity's child') runs parallel to the violent, orgasmic destruction of the human body, that most basic locus of societal control; images of apparent limitlessness – oceans, static-filled screens, the blinding light of the sun or of bulbs burning through celluloid – correspond with gruesome instances of corporeal destruction that, in the quintessential splatterpunk tradition, evokes the notion of 'going too far',[31] of reimagining physiology as a 'field of immanence'[32] that rejects technocratic control over the subject. As Georges Bataille notes in his ruminations upon the power that rests within visual representations of the physical body (in this case the eye) punctured and slashed, horror 'alone is brutal enough to break everything that stifles'.[33]

In its exploration of intensity as a discontinuous and non-totalisable phenomenon, Sato's film advances an oppositional politics. It is in these moments that Sato reveals the potential of imagining an identity outside of culturally prescribed parameters, or, at the very least, gestures towards the potential for the conceptualisation of such a space. In their quests for eternal happiness, a philosophical (and biological) mission to literally discover 'the blinding flashes of lightning that transform the most withering storm into transports of joy',[34] Eiji and his father demonstrate and embody those 'impulses' that Georges Bataille describes in his essay, 'The Use Value of D. A. F. de Sade', as having 'social revolution as their end' in that they 'go against the interests of a society in a state of stagnation'.[35]

This is not to suggest that *Naked Blood* is by any means an exclusively progressive body horror film. Although *Naked Blood* advances an oppositional politics of identity, the film does not necessarily end on an optimistic note. In the film's final moments, when little Eiji tells us that 'the dream has not ended yet' and raises his camcorder to follow Mikami's progress as she rides her motorcycle westward, the audience feels a palpable sense of dis-ease well in keeping with the discomforting tone of the film's previous seventy-five minutes. Social theory has long contended that 'the growth of civilization requires simultaneously the restraint of the body and the cultivation of character in the interests of social stability';[36] texts that render human corporeal and social formations indiscrete – displaying, in the process, the various ideological veins and cultural sinews that keep the fragile, and yet alarmingly resilient, physiognomies intact – disturb, if only momentarily, this 'stability'. Confronting heterogeneity – that first step towards attaining Bataille's 'durable orgasm' – is a messy business. Sooner or later you're bound to get some on you.

NOTES

1. Hunter, Jack (1998) *Eros in Hell: Sex, Blood, and Madness in Japanese Cinema*, London and New York: Creation Books International, p. 139.
2. Shaviro, Steven (1993) *The Cinematic Body*, Minneapolis, MN and London: University of Minnesota Press, p. 128.
3. Bataille, Georges [1929–30] (1994) 'The Use Value of D. A .F. de Sade', in Allan Stoekl (ed.), *Visions of Excess: Selected Writings, 1927–1939*, Minneapolis, MN: University of Minnesota Press, p. 17.
4. Ibid., p. 82.
5. Hurley, Kelly (1995) 'Reading Like an Alien: PostHuman Identity in Ridley Scott's *Alien* and David Cronenberg's *Rabid*', in Judith Halberstam and Ira Livingston (eds), *PostHuman Bodies*, Bloomington and Indianapolis, IN: Indiana University Press, p. 203.
6. Shaviro, pp. 133–4.
7. 'Paracinema' is Jeffrey Sconce's term for a set of reading practices clustered around a variety of film texts that lend themselves to ironic and/or counter-hegemonic reading protocols in the hands of viewers who focus their sophisticated reading skills on texts usually ignored by 'legitimate' taste cultures. See Sconce, Jeffrey (1995) "Trashing" the Academy: Taste, Excess and an Emerging Politics of Cinematic Style', in *Screen*, 36:4, Winter, p. 372.
8. Weisser, Thomas and Yuko Mihara Weisser (1998c) *Japanese Cinema Encyclopedia: Horror, Fantasy, Science Fiction*, Miami, FL: Vital Books, p. 463.
9. Ibid., p. 417.
10. white pongo (2000) 'Essential Viewing', posted on the *Internet Movie Database* (User Comments), 3 October, http://us.imdb.com/Title?0217679#comment.
11. Gruenberger, Harald (2002) '*Naked Blood/Splatter*', 5 July, http://www.metamovie.de/.
12. Gibson, William (1984) *Neuromancer*, New York: Berkeley, p. 51.
13. See, among others, such high-profile films as Kathryn Bigelow's *Strange Days* (1995), Josef Rusnak's *The Thirteenth Floor* (1999), Alejandro Amenabar's *Abre Los Ojos* (1997) and its 2001 remake, Cameron Crowe's *Vanilla Sky*, the Wachowski Brothers' *The Matrix* (1999) and its two sequels, David Cronenberg's *eXistenZ* (1999) and Tarsem Singh's *The Cell* (2000). The theme of 'illusion'/ 'hallucination' versus 'reality'also appears in Sato's *Genuine Rape* (1987), the film from which many of the concepts behind *Naked Blood* eventually developed, and *The Bedroom*, a.k.a. *Promiscuous Wife: Disgraceful Torture* (1992).
14. Alexander, James R. (2001) 'Obscenity, Pornography, and Violence: Rethinking Oshima's *In the Realm of the Senses*', July, http://www.pitt.edu/~zander/Obscenity&Oshima.html.
15. Paula Felix-Didier argues that such erotic and pornographic cinema can frequently

function as a weapon for interrogating traditional cultural values. See Felix-Didier, Paula (2000) 'Cine y sexo en Japón', in Film: On Line, 15 April, http://www.filmonline.com.ar/40/dossier/40dossier3.htm.

16. Ibid. (my translation).
17. Allison, Anne (2000) Permitted and Prohibited Desires: Mothers, Comics, and Censorship in Japan, Berkeley and Los Angeles, CA: University of California Press, p. 163.
18. Ibid., p. 164. However, I must add that it would be a mistake to assume that this reactionary internal and external 'othering' is limited to visual culture. Identities are, after all, constructs with borders that are often reified/reinforced, sometimes violently so, when exposed as illusory. As such, when cultures come into contact, there are bound to be varying degrees of appropriation, reactionary attitudes and, as Tatsumi Takayuki posits, 'fabulous negotiations between Orientalism and Occidentalism'. See Tatsumi Takayuki (2000) 'Generations and Controversies: An Overview of Japanese Science Fiction', Science Fiction Studies, 80, 27:1 (March), p. 113. It is also important to note that certain behavioural prohibitions related to sexuality were long a part of Shinto mythology. See Allison, p. 163.
19. One Western film that sparked such a controversy was Pier Paolo Pasolini's Salo: 120 Days of Sodom (1975). Allowed into Japan by Japanese Customs and subsequently 'rubber stamp[ed]' (Weisser and Weisser (1998c), p. 24) by Eirin, the film's critique of the abuses of power, as well as its extreme impact upon the Japanese viewing public, had a profound influence upon Sato's development as a film-maker. His movie Muscle, a.k.a. Mad Ballroom Gala, a.k.a. Asti: Lunar Eclipse Theater (1988; 1994) is a 'loving salute' (p. 467) to Pasolini.
20. Allison, p. 161.
21. See Baudrillard, Jean (1990) The Transparency of Evil: Essays on Extreme Phenomena, London and New York: Verso.
22. Allison, p. 174.
23. Ibid., p. 49.
24. Hull, Elizabeth Anne and Mark Siegel (1989) 'Science Fiction', in Richard Gid Powers and Hidetoshi Kato (eds), Handbook of Japanese Popular Culture. New York and London: Greenwood Press, p. 262.
25. Tatsumi, p. 113.
26. Ibid., p. 113.
27. Hull and Seigel, p. 245.
28. Weisser and Weisser (1998c), p. 463.
29. Kellner, Douglas and Michael Ryan (1990) 'Technophobia', in Annette Kuhn (ed.), Alien Zone: Cultural Theory and Contemporary Science Fiction Cinema, London and New York: Verso, p. 58.
30. Bukatman, Scott (1990) Terminal Identity: The Virtual Subject in Post-Modern Science Fiction, Durham, NC and London: Duke University Press, p. 9.
31. Skipp, John and Craig Spector (1989) 'On Going Too Far, or Flesh-Eating Fiction: New Hope for the Future', in John Skipp and Craig Spector (eds), Book of the Dead, New York: Bantam Books, p. 10.
32. Deleuze, Gilles and Félix Guattari (1987) A Thousand Plateaus: Capitalism and Schizophrenia, Minneapolis, MN: University of Minnesota Press, p. 157.
33. Bataille, p. 19.
34. Ibid., p. 69.
35. Ibid., p. 100.
36. Turner, Bryan (1992) Regulating Bodies: Essays in Medical Sociology, London: Routledge, pp. 14–15.

9. *PINNOCHIO 964, DEATH POWDER* AND THE POST-HUMAN CONDITION

Graham Lewis

> Culture can be interpreted through its representations of monstrosity: the forbidden, the unruly, those among the secure genealogies who appear misbegotten, those who are composed of pieces that are unharmonious assemblages of incompatible categories. Yet it is precisely by embodying such paradoxes, of incorporating seemingly discordant fragments, that these beings call into question the categories according to which a culture defines the boundaries between normal and pathological. The monster's very existence subverts taxa of exclusion, enclosure and containment and challenges the givenness of the supposedly 'objective' orderings at the heart of science and culture. Monsters bear witness to the power of the marginal, the Other, to demarcate the known and the unknown, the acceptable and the deviant. Monsters are keepers of the boundaries between human and Other, yet by virtue of their inhabiting the 'borderlands' they promise liberation from the very strictures of binary definition. Their hybridity challenges our ontological hygiene.[1]

Humans have always been obsessed with ideas of our own transformation. Every culture had and still has its vampires, its werewolves, its zombies, its monsters. For the most part, these monsters were and are products of the human melded to the non-human or creations of science or the supernatural. While the human imagination also conceives readily enough of evil (or benign) space aliens, as well as entirely supernatural entities, nothing seems to terrify or beguile so much as the monsters we can make with our hands or become in our bodies, minds and souls.

The ancient world was rife with tales of the human melded to the animal. One need look only to cave paintings, the Sphinx and world mythologies in general (all ancient tales even by the time they were finally recorded) to realise how long humankind's collective imagination has been captivated by this subject matter. The western world has been particularly fertile ground for such tales. As Elaine Graham proposes in the rather lengthy epigraph that opens this chapter, the history of a culture can be understood through the study of its monsters. It is no surprise then that with the advent of the Industrial Age came the birth of the Industrial Age Monster: part human, part machine. And now that incredibly powerful computers have finally become commonplace household items, the once fantastic idea of artificial intelligence has become inevitable. Modern science fiction and horror cinema, often concerned with revealing the human fear of becoming anachronistic to our own technology, has, perhaps more than any other artistic medium, investigated the possibilities and horrors of the age we are now entering, the age of the Post-Human.

According to N. Katherine Hayles, there are four basic tenents that characterise the Post-Human Age:

> First, the posthuman view privileges informational pattern over material instantiation, so that embodiment in a biological substrate is seen as an accident of history rather than an inevitability of life. Second, the posthuman view considers consciousness, regarded as the seat of human identity in the western tradition long before Descartes thought he was a mind thinking, as an epiphenomenon, as an evolutionary upstart trying to claim that it is the whole show when in actuality it is only a minor sideshow. Third, the posthuman view thinks of the body as the original prosthesis we all learn to manipulate, so that extending or replacing the body with other prostheses becomes a continuation of a process that began before we were born. Fourth, and most important, by these and other means, the posthuman view configures human being so that it can be seamlessly articulated with intelligent machines. In the posthuman, there are no essential differences or absolute demarcations between bodily existence and computer simulation, cybernetic mechanism and biological organism, robot teleology and human goals.[2]

In the sphere of cinema, the physical representation of these ideas has its focal point in the characterisation of the cyborg (a being that is part human, part machine) and the android (a being that is wholly machine but is created in the image of man). Part psuedo-science and part real or soon-to-be-real technology, the cyborg is perhaps the most frightening of all movie monsters because of its verisimilitude:

> Cyborgs actually exist. About ten percent of the current U.S. population are estimated to be cyborgs in the technical sense, including people with electronic pacemakers, artificial joints, drug-implant systems, implanted corneal lenses, and artificial skin. A much higher percentage participates in occupations that make them into metaphoric cyborgs, including the computer keyboarder joined in a cybernetic circuit with the screen, the neurosurgeon guided by fiber-optic microscopy during an operation, and the adolescent game player in the local arcade.[3]

Projecting a future when a being like the *Star Trek: The Next Generation* character Data could actually exist is not difficult. But Data represents the optimists' side of such projections, as he is a creature created for good and, barring incidents of espionage beyond his control, all his works and deeds are depicted as aiding in the betterment of his human counterparts. In this respect, Data is a rare example of a positive characterisation of the android. Much more common in the realm of science fiction, to use another *Next Generation* example, is the Borg: part human(oid), part machine, but depicted as completely 'evil' and hell-bent on conquering and 'assimilating' any species it encounters. This is the typical science-fiction characterisation of the cyborg (even the name of their race is a shortened version of the term). In a world where technological wonders are announced almost daily, it follows that our anxiety concerning machines would grow alongside (and sometimes surpass) our delight.

This anxiety, however, is by no means limited to critics, philosophers, writers or film-makers in the west. Most technological wonders of our age are produced, or at least popularised, by Japanese companies and consumers who are far more savvy than westerners in their expectations and uses of new technologies. By the time a new device is introduced in the West, it has been in the hands of Japanese consumers for months if not years. This is due, in no small part, to the willingness, the hunger of the Japanese people to retain their standing in the world economy. A smaller country can compete with the industrial giants of the world only by remaining on the cutting edge of technological innovation. The Japanese are also the only people on earth to have first-hand experience on the receiving end of nuclear warfare: a tragic distinction, but one that has informed their science-fiction cinema since Honda Ishiro's *Gojira* debuted in 1954, a mere nine years after America's bombs changed Japanese life forever. *Gojira* may not have been the first '*kaiju eiga*' (giant monster) film in world cinema, but it was the first cautionary tale of the atomic age to come directly from the people who suffered devastation at the hands of atomic technology. Thus it only makes sense that Japanese artists would continue to produce particularly powerful visions when expressing anxieties and fears of technology run amok.

Since the 1980s and 1990s, Japan has produced numerous entries in what has come to be known as the 'cyberpunk' genre of literature and film. The most well-known (at least in the west) of the cyberpunk film directors is Tsukamoto Shinya, whose *Tetsuo: Iron Man* (1988) and *Tetsuo II: Body Hammer* (1992) enjoyed much well-deserved success in the West. But Tsukamoto isn't alone in his pursuit of these themes. Two other directors, Izumiya Shigeru and Fukui Shozin, have helmed important films that posit a grim future in which the idea of the Post-Human is anything but positive.

In its conception, the term 'cyberpunk' was coined by author William Gibson. With the first three (and most well known) books of his 'Sprawl Trilogy', *Neuromancer* (1984), *Count Zero* (1986), and *Mona Lisa Overdrive* (1988) Gibson became the first western writer of popular fiction to display keen insight into the Post-Human, post-apocalyptic near future our present pace of technological invention suggests. Though the term 'cyberpunk' has been overused to the point where any novel or film set in the future and featuring a computer is consigned to that genre, there are certain signposts in Gibson's work that can guide us to recognise more accurate representations of his ideas:

> The physical environment is either that of urban decay and social disintegration or computer-generated virtual worlds. Nature, unless heavily adulterated, does not feature in cyberpunk. In contrast to earlier science-fiction genres, Gibson's mood is dystopian and bleak. Transnational corporations, the media and religious cults have replaced any recognizable body politic. There is precious little altruism, charity or political will. Personal relationships are transitory, exploitative or dysfunctional and secretive, panoptic corporate power dominates the public domain. Gibson's chief protagonists are anti-hero(ine)s, fighting the anonymity of the system from the margins, living rootless, precarious lives on the verge of subsistence. Digital technologies, especially computers, artificial intelligence and cyberspace are ubiquitous; and the technologization of society extends to its human members, in the form of prosthetic limbs and implants, chemical enhancements, cloned or genetically engineered persons, organs and body parts.[4]

Gibson is our generation's H. G. Wells, in that many or most of his now imaginary cyber-nightmares will become realities by the end of this century (if not sooner). In the realm of hard science, one need look only to the successes of the Human Genome Project and the cloning of animals to see how close we really are to realising even the most speculative features in his fictions.

Director Izumiya Shigeru's 1986 film, *Death Powder*, displays all the above-mentioned traits and examines these horrors in a free-form series of scenes that explain little but reveal much about the whirlwind of Post-Human anxiety at the heart of this century's turning. Much like Buñuel and Dali's *Un Chien andalou* (1928) and David Lynch's *Eraserhead* (1976), *Death Powder* imagines an alternate reality more akin to a dream state: events play out in non-linear fashion, characters are ciphers, dialogue is absurd, and the symbolism obtuse and personal. In other words, it is a work of pure cinema. As with the directors named above, Izumiya's concerns lie in the abstract, the fragmented, the broken images that create both emotional and intellectual discord but cannot be explicated fully by either human faculty. Only in the subconscious interplay of visual images can a shred of 'truth' be understood, if not specifically known, by the conscious mind.

Izumiya's film contains a thread of a plot concerning the theft of a cyborg that is able to produce the drug that serves as the film's title, but Izumiya obviously couldn't care less about conventional narrative structure. What interests him is making a film that produces reactions in the viewer that mimic the effects of the drug. As one character advises, 'Just pretend like you understand what's going on. This, like life, makes no sense.' It would be easy to dismiss this approach as laziness or affectation, but, as with *Eraserhead*, the sheer beauty and care with which all the ugliness and chaos is presented support a more serious criticism.

In the character of Guernica the cyborg (obviously named after Picasso's famous cubist anti-war painting), we find the classic fear machine. It not only appears in the form of a beautiful woman, it also serves as a metaphor for the very drug it creates through a spore-like mist. Once 'infected', the user initially experiences godlike feelings but soon descends into a nightmarish hallucinatory hell, an alternate reality ruled by a nefarious gang called the Scar People. Their purpose, it seems, is to lead the 'infectees' through a painful and gory evolution process. Into what? Well, a large meaty amoeba. Is this what Guernica was created to do? Perhaps, or perhaps it is simply a defence mechanism. Either way, the Post-Human implications are clear: evolve or die. Science-fiction writer Philip K. Dick, no stranger to any of these ideas, once wrote, '[f]ake realities will create fake humans. Or, fake humans will generate fake realities and then sell them to other humans, turning them, eventually, into forgeries of themselves'.[5] Izumiya's film, then, may be considered as more of a 'documentary' of the new reality this evolution will generate than a 'dramatisation' of events explaining it. Considering the film's ultra-low budget, it is nothing short of miraculous that Izumiya was able to create such a vital, captivating and horrifying work of cinematic art.

*   *   *

Monsters are our children. They can be pushed to the farthest margins of geography and discourse, hidden away at the edges of the world and in the forbidden recesses of our minds, but they always return. And when they come back, they bring not just a fuller knowledge of our place in history and the history of knowing our place, but they bear self-knowledge, *human* knowledge – and a discourse all the more sacred as it arises from the outside. These monsters ask us how we perceive the world, and how we have misrepresented what we have attempted to place. They ask us to re-evaluate our cultural assumptions about race, gender, sexuality, our perceptions of difference, our tolerance towards its expression. They ask us why we have created them.[6]

Why have we created them? Indeed, this question is at the core of all horror and science-fiction literature and cinema related to the idea of the Post-Human. The west's most famous example of the Post-Human monster is, of course, Frankenstein's Monster. Certainly not the first 'man-made' monster of literature or film, it may be the first to pursue the question of why we fabricate such entities. And it is this creature's very ability to think of such a question that makes it so frightening:

As the story of a living being created not by conventional reproductive means but by scientific endeavor, *Frankenstein* stands as one of the quintessential representations of the fears and hopes engendered by new technologies. Insofar as the creature at the heart of the tale is both (and neither) alive nor dead, born nor made, natural nor artificial, he confuses many of the boundaries by which normative humanity has been delineated.[7]

Frankenstein's Monster is at once 'us' and the 'other', both and neither. Though it could not be called either a cyborg or an android, its creation through means of 'unholy science' has driven our fears of similar monsters since Shelley's novel first appeared in 1818. Why? Because inherent in these ideas is the concept of punishment. We create the monster, abhor it, teach it to hate us, and then are killed by it in an all too familiar realisation of 'divine justice'. When the laws of nature are transgressed, nature (or god) bites back.

The sex cyborg gone mad in Fukui Shozin's *Pinnochio 964* (1992) is a being cut from the same cloth as Frankenstein's Monster. Once a man, but then transformed into the first of a new line of pleasure devices for sexually frustrated women, it expects, if nothing else, to be accepted by its human masters on at least the level of a valued device: a car, a washing machine, a television. Unfortunately, like Frankenstein's Monster, Pinnochio finds nothing but human cruelty. His master is a spoiled, greedy, rich nymphomaniac whose bizarre tastes he simply can't satisfy. She sends him back to the company of his 'birth', where he is further lobotomised and thrown out onto the streets of Tokyo. The scientists, his 'parents', are embarrassed and appalled by his (and their) failure and, like Victor Frankenstein, have neither the guts nor compassion to simply put him out of his misery. They would rather just forget they created him.

Himiko, a street waif, spots Pinnochio wandering in a daze, pities him and gives him shelter in her makeshift sewer apartment. There she begins the labour of re-humanising Pinnochio, teaching him first to speak again, and then to remember who and what he is. Unlike the Murphy cyborg in Paul Verhoeven's *Robocop* (1987), Pinnochio does not come to terms with his recovered memories. When Pinnochio finally realises that his humanity has been forever altered, that he will never again know the simple joy of a human relationship, he is driven to complete despair and insanity.

When Himiko and Pinnochio attempt to make love, Fukui's fairly easy-to-follow plot suddenly veers into the realm of the surreal. It seems that Himiko's intimate contact with Pinnochio has a few unexpected side effects. For one, she begins behaving like Pinnochio. As his all-consuming hatred for his creators drives him further into madness, Himiko appears to be going insane as well. In an extended, very difficult-to-watch subway scene, Himiko purges herself by vomiting, literally, gallons of what may represent her humanity, the 'leakiness' of the human body. After this, Himiko becomes less and less human herself. Her compassion and love for Pinnochio disappear, and she begins to treat him as cruelly as his former master. This pushes Pinnochio over the edge. In one of the most interestingly filmed sequences, Pinnochio charges through the crowded streets of Tokyo (much to the obvious chagrin of real-life onlookers) while dragging a large concrete block like an old-fashioned ball and chain. Once he finds the company and scientists that transformed him, he, as expected, kills them. Then Fukui opts for what I'll call a classic Lynchian ending: Himiko plunges her hand into her midsection, pulls out an organ and tosses it to Pinnochio. Her head inflates to the size of a medicine ball, which Pinnochio promptly plucks from her body and places over his own head. Himiko's head grows back, and the scene switches to a shot of them both, restored to normal and saying in unison, 'Feels good. Everything is so clear. I love being with you.' The film's final image shows them slam dancing at a nightclub like a couple of normal punk-loving twentysomethings. True to his namesake, Pinnochio has become a real boy (again). I call this ending 'Lynchian' in that it reeks of false happiness and black humour, much like the endings of almost all David Lynch films. And from the bleak industrial atmosphere to the absurd behaviour of the characters, it is obvious that Fukui is no stranger to *Eraserhead*. Still, what does it all mean? Good question. I believe, though, we must examine Fukui's next film, 1997's *Rubber's Lover*, before attempting an answer.

If audiences were shocked by the 'wetness' of *Pinnochio 964*, the gore of *Rubber's Lover* must have sent them screaming from the theatres. Within ten minutes, the first subject of the film's central experiments literally explodes all over the 'mad scientists' presiding. The aforementioned experiments concern psychic powers and attempts at enhancing them. These scientists believe they can accelerate the evolution of psychic powers in certain people through such tortures as injecting them with ether, hooking them up to invasive mechanical devices, binding them into rubber sensory depravation suits, and blasting them with deafening white noise. So far, they haven't had much success (big surprise), and their corporate sponsor is about to scrap the project.

The sponsor sends his pretty secretary, Kiku, to relay that message to the scientists. But one of the more aggressive men of science, Motomiyo, has other plans. He beats and rapes Kiku and then turns his other colleagues against the former head scientist, Shimika. Motomiyo has the others place Shimika in the rubber suit and begins the experiments anew. When he decides to hook Kiku to Shimika, he actually succeeds in creating a powerful psychic bond between the two. Of course, his success proves to be his undoing. Kiku and Shimika join forces and kill the scientists in a psychic massacre much like those on display in David Cronenberg's *Scanners* (1981). Their victory, however, is bittersweet, as Shimika has been left an 'ether addict' and soon dies of an overdose. The final scene, a moment too similar to the scene introducing Himiko in *Pinnochio 964* to be mere coincidence, finds Kiku sitting on a crowded Tokyo sidewalk. *Rubber's Lover* seems to function as a prequel to *Pinnochio 964*, if not literally, then at least in spirit.

If this is so, it sheds much light on events surrounding Himiko's character in *Pinnochio 964*. Her psychic bond with Pinnochio now has a context, as does her seemingly fugitive lifestyle and initial attraction to Pinnochio. Fukui himself has not indicated such a connection in interviews concerning the two films, but like many directors he tends to be rather obtuse when asked about the 'meanings' of his films. Asked by interviewer Romain Slocombe to describe the 'theme' of *Pinnochio 964*, Fukui answered, 'Nothing. Attaining the state of nothing in Zen. I wanted crew, actors and audience all to feel that. To feel the tension building up to climax, to the point of ecstasy, where one feels transported.'[8] Here, too, is his answer to a similar question about *Rubber's Lover*: 'What I wanted to depict in that film is a new power human beings possess, in other words a hidden, unrealized potential power in ourselves. I wanted to show the impact such power has when it is finally released.'[9] Though the ideas of psychic and physical tension and release indicate a relationship between the two films on a metaphoric level, Fukui, like Izumiya, like Lynch, has little or no faith in such easy-to-decipher constructions as 'continuing narrative' and 'cause and effect'. Those ideas lie. They imply that there exist simple explanations for the human and inhuman within us. They speculate a traditional way to map non-traditional, unmappable territories at the joining of man and machine. And, perhaps most deceitfully of all, they provide intellectual comfort where no comfort is intended or should be found. Thus, though the ideas of prequel and sequel may find currency with viewers and critics (myself included), the director himself would probably find such a suggestion either humorous or annoying.

*   *   *

> The monster, that which refuses to abide by axiomatic orderings, carries a terrible threat to expose the fragility of its defining categories and thus the fiction of normality itself. Monstrosity is profoundly paradoxical, therefore, demonstrating both an illegitimate state of non-being and an indispensability to the very system that places the monstrous beyond the pale. Any creature that so capriciously defies the precision of nature's laws requires other schemes of placement and identification than those found on binary distinctions. New categories and ways of being have to be found.[10]

Here, I believe, is our answer to the question of meaning. What is it, exactly, that we truly fear about technology? Many of us would rejoice if we never had to leave our chairs again, so why fear that which brings us closer to the objective? Because works of art such as these constantly remind us that we, as sentient beings, are not simply our bodies. The true changes that present and future technologies threaten must take place in our souls. If we are to continue calling ourselves 'human', the old definitions, old modes of thought, old prejudices, old expectations, old gods must now be reconsidered and, ultimately, destroyed. The day of monsters among us is here. One must, then, view the films in the cyberpunk genre as contemporary cautionary tales, stories that reveal what will happen (or is happening now) if we insist upon remaining static in our beliefs of 'us' and 'them'. The human being as it now exists is doomed; we are dead men walking. Survival, as always, will depend upon our abilities to adapt and evolve. We must be prepared to accept the 'monster', the 'other'; indeed, we must be prepared to become it.

NOTES

1. Graham, Elaine L. (2002) *Representations of the Post/Human: Monsters, Aliens and Others in Popular Culture*, New Brunswick, NJ: Rutgers University Press, p. 60.
2. Hayles, N. Katherine (1999) *How We Became Post Human: Virtual Bodies in Cybernetics, Literature, and Informatics*, Chicago: University of Chicago Press, pp. 2–3.
3. Ibid., p. 115.

4. Graham, p. 194.
5. Dick, Philip K. (1995) 'How to Build a Universe That Doesn't Fall Apart Two Days Later', in Lawrence Sutin (ed.), *The Shifting Realities of Philip K. Dick: Selected Literary and Philosophical Writings*, New York: Pantheon Books, pp. 263–4.
6. Cohen, Jeffrey J. (1996) 'Monster Culture (Seven Theses)', in Jeffrey J. Cohen (ed.), *Monster Theory: Reading Culture*, Minneapolis, MN: University of Minnesota Press, p. 25.
7. Graham, p. 62.
8. See the Romain Slocombe interview with Tsukamoto in Hunter, Jack (1998) *Eros in Hell: Blood and Madness in Japanese Cinema*, London: Creation Books International, p. 202.
9. Ibid., p. 202.
10. Graham, p. 54.

10. CASE STUDY: *BATTLE ROYALE'S* APOCALYPTIC MILLENNIAL WARNING[1]

Tony Williams

The release of Fukasaku Kinji's *Battle Royale* (2000) on all-region DVD and VCD formats, coupled with the limited theatrical screenings it has received so far in North America, has evoked a storm of protest very similar to its opening reception in Japan. Conscious of the Columbine syndrome, which also influenced the reception of the markedly inferior *The Matrix* (1999), most western audiences and critics (who did not walk out of the film after the opening ten minutes) have condemned the film for its mindless and gratuitous violence in terms very reminiscent of the British attitude towards Sam Peckinpah's *Straw Dogs* (1971) on its initial release.[2] After a special screening in the Japanese Parliament, government officials labelled the film 'crude and tasteless' and regarded it as having 'no redeeming value' whatsoever.[3] With the exception of Andrew Britton and Robin Wood, similar assaults also affected the reception of *Mandingo* (1975), a film that deserved better analysis than it received either on its first release or now.[4]

Critical opinion is likely to become polarised between those condemning the film because of its gratuitous violence and South-East Asian critics such as Anthony Leong who look beneath the visceral features and see *Battle Royale* as a film holding 'a mirror up to the problems facing Japanese society, both in the present and the past'.[5] Despite being subjected to the usual charges of gratuitous violence and mindless entertainment, *Battle Royale* is actually a landmark film relevant to contemporary dilemmas in both western society and its post-capitalist eastern counterparts.

Over the past twenty years, western politicians have extolled the virtues of the South-East Asian 'tiger economy', despite the clear evidence of economic and psychological problems which have affected once-booming bastions of late capitalism such as Hong Kong and Taiwan. The reverence expressed by figures such as Bill Clinton, Al Gore, George Bush (Senior and Junior), Margaret Thatcher, John Major and Tony Blair for those orientalist capitalist utopias also extend to education. Both America and Britain now engage in attempts at controlling education through the adoption of quantitative and statistical standards of 'league tables' and associated utilitarian practices that would cause Mr Gradgrind of *Hard Times* to roll in envy within his grave. Despite the clear evidence of psychological stress involving mental strain, classroom violence and teacher/student suicide, especially in Japan, the new world order millennium sees more of an extension rather than the removal of such harmful practices.

Although *Battle Royale* may not initially seem to qualify as an artistically elevated 'pattern' or 'landmark' in world cinema, it is much more than just another example of a nasty and gratuitously violent Japanese film appearing to embody the worst elements of a cinematic culture eagerly embraced by audiences whose sensitivities have already become jaded in a post-Tarantino/ Guy Ritchie climate of screen violence. As Lisa Stokes and Michael Hoover cogently argue, South-East Asian economies are often cited as shining examples for western corporate-minded politicians engaged in destroying their national education systems, as well as dismantling welfare safety nets. Popular examples of South-East Asian cinemas often present the dark underside of what embracing post-capitalism really involves, in imagery strongly reminiscent of both classical Marxism and the nineteenth-century naturalist tradition represented by Emile Zola.[6] In this light, *Battle Royale* operates as a 'return of the repressed symptom' of a situation that can only lead to apocalyptic violence. Despite the *Survivor* aspects of this film, it is no '*Lord of the Flies* meets *Survivor* with guns',[7] but a dark end-of-the-millennium warning of what the twenty-first century might have in store for people of all nations.

Both educationally and economically, postwar Japanese society has always thrived on the competitive ethos. But, as historians such as Iris Chang have noted, the prewar culture contained several disturbing features, a certain number of which survived into the postwar era. After Japanese commercial and military expansionism in the late nineteenth century, the school system operated like miniature military units. Chang points out that the historical roots of militarism stretched back to the 1868 Meiji Restoration, when Japan embarked on a widespread process of modernisation both to avenge national humiliation by America and to extend Japanese hegemonic domination to other South-East Asian countries such as Korea and Taiwan. 'In the late nineteenth century the Japanese minister of education declared that schools were not run for the benefit of the students but for the good of the country.

Elementary school teachers were trained like military recruits, with student-teachers housed in barracks and subjected to harsh discipline and indoctrination'.[8] This feature explains why teacher Kitano's replacement, Hayashida, has been brutally murdered by the military before the 'Battle Royale' commences: he had vigorously opposed the inclusion of his new class in this exercise. Unlike Kitano, who is positioned as alienated from his students, Hayashida is shown in the bus during the school trip, conversing with his students as an equal and not isolated as an authoritarian figure. Significantly, this shot shows him playing with the six schoolgirls (including Utsumi) who are close friends, and whose later association suggests the faint possibility that their female bonding might lead to their eventual survival. But, as Kitano points out to his frightened students, Hayashida is a 'a no good adult', and he urges his prospective Battle Royale competitors 'to work hard not to become like [Hayashida]'. Quite obviously, Hayashida was not a 'team player' – to use a term so beloved of North American university administrators who expect their faculty to 'shut up and do as you're told'.

By 1930 the Japanese education system had become regimented and robotic. Chang sees these elements of cultural conditioning as responsible for the dehumanising holocaust that the Japanese military perpetuated on the inhabitants of Nanking in 1937.[9] The film's dystopian universe contains several of these militaristic elements. It is set in the near future, when Japan's economy is close to collapse with high unemployment; high-school students boycot classes and young people commit acts of violence against adults. As Sara Ellis points out, Battle Royale echoes a contemporary pessimistic mood in Japanese society involving economic decline, adolescent discontent within the pressure-cooker world of national education, and a growing level of violence among the school population who react in frustration to the fact that their social structure is rapidly breaking down. Ellis concludes her article by ironically noting the recent introduction of Japanese-influenced statistical modes of education by western leaders into their own national systems.[10]

Apart from Anthony Leong and Gary C. W. Chun, very few have seen the contemporary relevance of Battle Royale. The entire social structure in the film is a system in chaos. Instead of dealing with the roots of the dilemma, the system chooses to engage in an arbitrary and ruthless policy of 'zero tolerance' by enacting gratuitous revenge on students who do not conform to traditional Japanese precepts of obedience and reverence towards adults. As with the Nanking situation, a link clearly exists between the cultural system and the violence exploding on the screen. Leong notes that a 'zero sum' mindset, in which one country could only achieve its objectives at the expense and annihilation of another, dominated Japanese political expansionism prior to both World Wars.[11] This ideology affected Japanese foreign policy towards its own Asian neighbours. It also led to Pearl Harbor.

'Likewise, the players in *Battle Royale* are faced with a "zero sum" situation, where there can be only one winner, and the use of force becomes the currency for all transactions.'[12] Leong also notes that it is not coincidental that the students selected to play 'Battle Royale' are from the ninth grade. The Japanese education system does not stratify students into achievement levels for the first publicly-funded nine grades. As long as students turn up for classes, moving into a higher grade is automatic. However, by the ninth grade, students have to compete ferociously in nationwide examinations for placement into the more prestigious secondary schools that guarantee eventual entry into quality higher education. During this time, high-school students face great emotional pressures that often result in suicides. Significantly, Shuya's voiceover commentary during the bus trip mentions, '[A]nd so our compulsory education was coming to an end.' When Kitano meets his former students again he reintroduces himself as their 'seventh grade teacher'. When the anxiety-ridden Motobuchi confronts Shuya and Noriko later in the film, he insanely repeats an algebra formation in a parody of rote learning and announces his intention of surviving the Battle Royale; in order to 'go to a good school', he will kill as many of his former classmates as possible.

Although familiar to western audiences primarily as the co-director of the Japanese sequences in *Tora! Tora! Tora!* (1970), *Battle Royale*'s director Fukasaku Kinji is well known in Japan not only for a series of graphically violent films exploring the dark underside of his national culture during the 1960s and 1970s, but also for his role as a mentor for a future generation of Japanese directors such as Kitano Takeshi (who appears in *Battle Royale*) and Ishii Takashi.[13] Described by Tom and Yuko Mihara Weisser as 'often cited as the most consistently successful filmmaker in Japan',[14] Fukasaku is a veteran of the Japanese film industry, having worked in a number of diverse genres for over forty years, including co-productions featuring American actors. Throughout his career he has also worked with veterans of Japanese cinema such as Wakayama Tomisaburo and Tetsura Tanba (as well as Mishima Yukio in the 1968 classic *Black Lizard*) in genre films often implicitly critiquing the dark underside of the Japanese economic miracle. During several interviews, Fukasaku has mentioned that *Battle Royale* also echoes his own experience as a fifteen-year-old working in a munitions factory in the closing months of the Second World War, when he often saw his own friends literally blown up before his eyes during Allied bombing raids.[15] He has also stated that, as a third-year high school student, he was given the task of collecting dismembered body parts following Allied bombing raids, many of which belonged to his friends.[16]

It is also likely that *Battle Royale* is Fukasaku's violent reworking of the film version of Horace McCoy's 1935 novel *They Shoot Horses, Don't They?*, directed by Sydney Pollack in 1969. Set in the American Depression, both novel and film documented the brutal exploitation of the unemployed in a dance marathon presided over by a jaded entrepreneur played by Gig Young, whose callous exterior often masked his own contradictory feelings. Young's role may influence the portrayal of the corrupt and disillusioned teacher Kitano played by 'Beat' Kitano Takeshi. But whereas Pollack's film ended on a note of defeat and disillusion, *Battle Royale* concludes with some qualified hope for the future.

Despite the natural tendency of most viewers to feel outraged by the graphic displays of spectacular violence, Fukasaku's film mostly concentrates on the personal dilemmas of its young victims. A close analysis of the opening scenes is necessary here to elaborate on what most viewers miss. The film begins with the strains of Verdi's *Requiem* as waves crash against the seashore. The opening captions reveal a world in turmoil and a nation planning a special type of '*Dies Irae*' for its rebellious younger population: 'At the dawn of the millennium the nation collapsed. 15% unemployment, 10 million out of work. 800,000 students boycotted school. The adults lost confidence and, fearing the youth, passed the Millennium Educational Reform Act, aka The BR Act.'

An abrupt transition to the next sequence reveals a low-angle shot of a military helicopter dominating the screen, putting the audience into a submissive position as a television journalist gleefully announces to her viewers the appearance of the sole survivor (Iwamura Ai) of the last annual competition. The military display a traumatised young girl, bloodied from an unspeakable combat situation and clutching a doll. As the reporter ignorantly tells her audience, '[T]he girl definitely just smiled,' Fukasaku edits three jump cuts, bringing the audience closer to the girl's insane expression, each cut accompanied by the flash of a newsreel camera implicating the media in this appalling public exhibition. Since further media satire occurs later in the film, this editing sequence is not at all accidental.

After the insertion of a class photograph showing teacher Kitano ('Beat' Kitano Takeshi) and his students, the film uses the voiceover narrative by its leading character, Nanahara Shuya (Fujiwara Tatsuya), who informs the audience about the abandonment by his mother when he was in the fourth grade and the suicide of his father 'on my first day in the seventh grade'. It is not accidental that each tragic incident in Shuya's personal life relates to his school career, since the director clearly equates outside institutional pressures with the realm of personal chaos seen in *Battle Royale*. After attempting in vain to find employment, Shuya's distressed father commits suicide. Although this act leaves a traumatic mark on the son ('I didn't have a clue what to do and no one to show me the way'), the father attempts to encourage his son to avoid this fate in whatever way he can by leaving a farewell message: 'Go, Shuya. You can make it, Shuya.' The adult world can provide no answers and it is up to the younger generation (who may or may not succeed) to provide their own solution. But *Battle Royale* suggests that such a task is not going to be easy due to the violent nature of the system they face. Any optimism expressed in the film often faces contradiction and qualification by a system that controls the rules of the game.

The next scene shows another impotent father figure, teacher Kitano, who sits on his desk in an empty classroom before a blackboard with the chalked student message: 'Taking the day off 'cause we want to. Class B.' Noriko (Maeda Ai) arrives late. An exchange of looks occurs between the burned-out adult and the young girl (the significance of which the director leaves for the climax) before Kitano leaves the classroom. Outside, delinquent student Kuninobu (Kotani Yukihiro) rushes at Kitano and stabs him in the rear before running away. Noriko picks up Nobu's knife and conceals it behind her back. Another exchange of looks occurs between them as Kitano limps to a nearby sink to clean his wound. The sequence then changes to a shot of the school bus trip with Shuya's voiceover ominously commenting on the 'end of our compulsory education'.

This sequence may appear as just another repetition from an average juvenile delinquency movie were it not for several factors. Although Kitano gets his revenge on Nobu by first stabbing him in the same place Nobu had wounded him and then later setting off the explosive device in Nobu's necklace, this important scenario is complicated by various points. As played by Kotani Yukihiro, Nobu looks the least violent member of the entire group and obviously represents the director's comment that any child in this dystopian universe could become corrupted. As the *Battle Royale* website's 'Character Study' notes, when we see Nobu on the bus, he appears as a harmless juvenile trickster who has been encouraged by Noriko to return to school.[17] He clowns around and is associated visually with both Shuya and Noriko. However, while Noriko appeals to Nobu's good side, Kitano plays on his worst feelings by provoking him so that he will be the second victim in the *Battle Royale* contest, thus avenging his humiliation in the earlier attack. Furthermore, during a subsequent flashback, Shuya tells Noriko that Nobu taught him to play the guitar when he 'was busted after I quit baseball' – a telling reference to the fact that Shuya has chosen not to follow the 'jock' option in his high-school years. During the flashback, when the two boys share a room in a state foster home, Nobu appears as a sensitive young adolescent. Like Shuya, he is an orphan, but he expresses feelings of friendship and love for both his friends who significantly mourn his demise. It is clear that the system has alienated Nobu, who is really a sensitive individual with alternative potentials his society refuses to nurture.

During the bus trip, Noriko offers candy to Shuya and Nobu. However, the candy is later prominently shown to be in Kitano's possession during three scenes in the Battle Royale classroom headquarters. Unlike Shuya, who has had no opportunity to enjoy Noriko's gift, Kitano munches it constantly in a manner suggesting some form of perverse identification with his victims, as well as an unconscious recognition that he, also, has an inner child within his own repressed psyche. The Battle Royale headquarters is a schoolroom on a deserted island that the military has taken over. This location makes it evident that this 'most dangerous game' belongs to the everyday competitive system of Japanese education in which war and education belong together. When Kitano introduces the rules of the game to his victims, who include two older, less neatly attired 'transfer' students, Kawada (Yamamoto Taro) and Kiriyama (Ando Masanobu), he comments that the class's 'participation' results from their 'own damn fault. You guys mock grown ups. Go ahead and mock us. But don't you forget, Life is a game. So fight for survival and find out if you're worth it.' Each student is fitted with a necklace containing an explosive device to ensure that only one survivor remains. The device will explode if any decide to engage in a collective opposition to the rules of the game by working towards group rather than individual survival. Prior to the issuing of survival equipment and weapons to the students, Kitano plays an educational video articulating the rules of this game, featuring a chipper adolescent hostess (Miyamura Yuko). Her trivial comments parallel those of the television reporter in the film's opening scene. The game can have only one survivor, and the students are encouraged to take the logical implications of their role in a competitive system to the ultimate conclusion and kill each other. As Kitano tells his victims, who depart one by one as the military throw random weapon bags at them: 'Each weapon is different. You may be lucky or not.' As we later learn, these weapons range from the most deadly, such as machine guns, to the most useless, such as pot lids and binoculars. Ironically, Shuya and Noriko, who decide to 'trust' each other early in the contest, find they have these latter 'weapons'. The more streetwise Kawada makes Kiriyama take his pack containing a less deadly weapon. But one female student, Ogawa (Shimaki Tomomi), contemptuously throws her weapon pack back at Kitano and emphasises her refusal to play by these manipulative deadly rules. She later decides to commit suicide with her boyfriend Yamamoto. Before they jump from a cliff she throws his weapon pack into the raging sea below.

Not all the students decide to follow the rules of the game and engage in bloodlust. Although the deadly psychotic Kiriyama has volunteered for the contest, some (like Ogawa and Yamamoto) commit suicide, while others attempt in different ways to seek alternative solutions, not all of which are viable in a contest which has been fixed by the adult world. When Inada (Kinoshita Tsuyako) receives her summons, her best friend tells her, 'You're still my friend,' to which she poignantly replies, 'Yes, I know.' When four boys and one girl surround Kiriyama on the beach, they tell him, 'None of us is killing anybody.' However, Kiriyama's seizure of a machine gun (to replace the useless Harisen weapon given to him) curtails this possibility as he massacres all five. He later does the same to the two girls, Yukiko and Kusaka, who vainly appeal, over a bullhorn, for everyone to 'stop fighting'. Mimura and his group appear to offer the most viable alternative against Battle Royale. As the nephew of a 1960s activist who has written a book with the significant title *Turning the Clock Back*, he uses technological skills to hack into the military computers and cause confusion. Mimura (Tsukamoto Takaashi) operates according to a collective philosophy, encouraging his companions, '[w]hen we escape, it will be together.' He hopes that the fifteen-minute hacking interference will allow him to begin his own version of 1960s revolution by blowing up the school headquarters to end the game. 'It's time we started our own struggle. But there's not much time.' His attitude contrasts with the equally accomplished class nerd Motobuchi (Nitta Ryou), who fawns before Kitano in the opening classroom scene and only thinks about his individual survival. However, Mimura's own attempt at following his uncle's philosophy of 'turning the clock back' is brief. Kiriyama suddenly appears on the scene to cut off this alternative avenue by shooting Mimura and his companions. Motobuchi is later killed by Kawada, who saves Shuya and Noriko. Both transfer students have been placed there to fix the game by preventing the possibility of collective action. While Kawada acts as a mentor to both Shuya and Noriko by helping them survive, the authorities use Kiriyama's psychotically aberrant loner character to demolish the possibilities of the participants moving towards any form of group solidarity.

The system represented by Kitano and the state plays upon the vulnerable qualities of adolescents whose personalities have already been affected by negative features of family and state, as well as the school's competitive ethos. The students react to their dilemmas according to programmed modes of behaviour, which are not often of their choosing. The most dangerous female in *Battle Royale* is Mitsuko (Shibaski Kou), who achieves the second most kills in the film, the highest tally naturally belonging to Kiriyama. When she introduces herself to her first victim Megumi (Ikeda Sayaka) at night, she flashes a torch under her face so that she resembles the demonic being from Japanese films such as *Onibaba*; indeed, she is one of the most dangerous and treacherous students. At first her motivations seem confusing, but her line to Anna Nagata's Hirono, 'Why is everybody picking on me?' and her dying words 'I just didn't want to be a loser anymore' imply that she is a victim of certain classroom peer groups and, consequently, wishes to take revenge on her persecutors. However, the expanded director's cut of the film explains her deadly actions as resulting from her social status. Mitsuko belongs to a dysfunctional family and was subject to sexual abuse from an early age. We also learn from the film that she has pimped girls in her class. As the outsider in her group, she thus sees Battle Royale as offering the possibilities of revenge upon a peer group that has tormented her for so long. Although this does not excuse her actions, it does allow further insight into her motivations. Like everyone, she is a victim of the system. But, unlike Shuya, Nobu and Kawada, who also come from dysfunctional families, her emotional scars are too deeply embedded within her psyche for her to consider any alternatives. Ironically, in an act of poetic justice, she is dispatched by Kiriyama, who will himself perish at the hands of his fellow transfer student Kawada.

Sometimes victims express regret at the wrong choices they have made. For example, fat schoolboy Akamatsu (Kusaka Shin) achieves the first score by killing vulnerable schoolgirl Tendou (Noriyama Haruka). However, before suffering the same fate with the same implement (an arrow) he used against Tendou, Akamatsu cries out, 'Shit. What am I doing?' When Oki (Nishimujra Gouki) attempts to attack Shuya with an axe, he accidentally kills himself during a fall and utters the apologetic lines, 'I'm sorry. I'm fine. I'm fine,' before he dies. The most poignant example of lost potential appears in the lighthouse sequence. When Utsumi (Ishikawa Eri) tends to Shuya's wounds, she informs him that the other female members of her group wish to isolate themselves from male influence. 'Some of them don't trust guys.' Like Mimura, she is clearly one of the leading figures in this group. However, like the society to which they belong, their group is already fraught with mutually aggressive tensions that reach their logical culmination in self-destructive violence. Two of her friends, Satomi (Kamiysa Sayaka) and Chisato (Kanai Asami), criticise her leadership. Having earlier witnessed Oki's accidental death, Yuko (Hyaga Hitomi) inserts poison in the meal intended for Shuya, but she only succeeds in poisoning Yuka (Hanamura Satomi) before the rest of her companions. This leads to a bloodbath when the group turns on each other. Utsumi's dying words poignantly express the waste of lost potentials: 'What idiots! We might have survived here. Stupid! Stupid!' Following this statement, Fukusaku inserts a caption twice in a manner akin to the dialectical concepts of silent Soviet Cinema – 'You know what that means?' – as if challenging his audience to consider the real implications behind this display of screen violence. Likewise, before she commits suicide, Yuko regrets the trajectory to which her actions have led her: 'I even forgot that they're all my friends.'

Battle Royale eventually moves towards the final encounter. Although resembling Gig Young's Rocky from *They Shoot Horses, Don't They?*, Kitano Takeshi's performance is not exclusively a one-dimensional exercise in patriarchal sadism. While he clearly relishes taking revenge upon his unruly class and avenging his humiliation by Nobu, he is a complex character in many ways. Like his students, he has been psychologically scarred by his national culture. But rather than retiring from the profession, he has decided to return and act as a more deadly mentor than ever before. He tells his class, 'I missed you guys,' a remark which is not entirely one-sided. Although relishing announcing the daily tally of casualties on the public address system, his attitude is ambivalent. During scenes featuring him relaxing on the sofa, Kitano consumes the candy Noriko offered Shuya and Nobu earlier in the film. Significantly, Kitano does not share this candy with any of the military. He has an ambiguous relationship with Noriko, who sees him in a dream as a 'lonely figure' on a riverbank. Importantly, her dream follows a sequence revealing Kitano as a failed parental figure. When his daughter, Shiori, phones to inform him that 'Mother's feeling bad again,' she concludes her call by insulting him when she learns that he cannot return until Battle Royale is over. Later in the film, Kitano protects Noriko from Mitsuko (who runs away when he appears) and gives her an umbrella with the tender fatherly words, 'Don't catch cold.' Significantly, the sequence ends with Kawada standing in the same area Kitano had left, the director clearly comparing the film's two mentor figures.

As the film moves to its conclusion, the audience eventually understands that Kitano's offering of an umbrella, as well as the exchange of looks with Noriko, presents the teacher as faintly conscious of contradictions within his own persona. He sees Noriko as an ideal daughter, but he also realises that his state-appointed role places him within the realm of the Death Instinct in terms familiar from the work of Norman O. Brown.[18] Like his students, Kitano's personality has suffered from the system. He not only looks on Noriko with love in a perverse embodiment of Freud's Eros principle, but, dominated by the Death Instinct, he hopes that she will finally put him out of his misery by killing him in a manner of a dutiful daughter. Kitano's personality has masochistic, as well as sadistic, overtones, resulting from a situation that is as much social as individual. Kitano is both a sadistically punitive father as well as a socially compliant victim harbouring masochistic desires engendered by his allegiance to a corrupt and violent system. He is a walking embodiment of the close relationship between those sadistic and masochistic features Freud describes in his 1915 essay 'Instincts and their Vicissitudes', which may equally oscillate between each other given the appropriate circumstances.[19] These elements are part of social conditioning as well as individual psycho-pathology. They are particularly prominent within *Battle Royale*'s society, which represents an apocalyptic version of the situation described by Freud in his essay 'Civilization and Its Discontents'.[20] Furthermore, Kitano moves from being the sadistic father in Freud's 1919 essay 'A Child is Being Beaten' towards becoming a masochistic parental figure desiring that the child 'beat *him*', no matter how much the psychological costs of this act will affect his chosen executioner.[21] Kitano sees Noriko as both his saviour and '*Dies Irae*' figure. She is his chosen judicial executioner who performs an act he feels himself incapable of doing. He is too contaminated by a system whose corruption he intuitively recognises but against which he finds himself too passive to fight.

Desiring oblivion at the hands of a daughter substitute in a perverse act of masochistic desire, Kitano attempts to provoke Noriko with the words, 'I've had it. The kids make fun of me and my own kid hates me. I might as well take you with me.' Kitano also astonishes the trio by showing them a childlike painting of the Battle Royale devastation. It depicts Noriko in the angelic posture of a pubescent saint whom Kitano obviously hopes will put him out of his misery. However, realising the psychological damage this will cause Noriko (who has not killed anyone in the film up to this point), Shuya performs the act for her. He hesitates until the last flashback of his dead father appears in the film, providing him with the answer to his dilemma. Up to this point, Shuya has only accidentally killed one person. His father's message, 'Go, Shuya. You can make it, Shuya,' motivates him into action. It is the last testament from a parent who, like Kitano, has also been psychologically destroyed by the system. But when Shuya fires his gun, he finds that Kitano's gun is a water pistol. Several traits in Kitano's personality represent a yearning for a type of childhood innocence which both his personality and an oppressive social structure makes absolutely impossible. Kitano finally expires after consuming the last of Noriko's candy and, following a final contemptuous message from his rebellious daughter, shooting his mobile phone.

The film concludes with the two survivors, Shuya and Noriko, fleeing like the 'last romantic couple' familiar to us from the films of Nicholas Ray and Jean-Luc Godard. But in this case, both partners survive and run towards an uncertain future as fugitives from a system blaming them as murderers. Kawada has died on the boat from wounds caused by Kiriyama, and his last words, 'I'm glad I found true friends,' express the need for trust that many of the deceased Battle Royale protagonists fail to enact. These words have a particularly powerful resonance, since during a flashback we learn that Kawada was a previous winner of the Battle Royale, having killed not only a friend, but his girlfriend, Keiko, in a situation in which only one person could survive. Although the system forced Keiko to shoot Kawada, her dying words to the lover who also shot her, '[t]hank you,' are ambiguous. As Kawada comments, '[r]eally trusting someone is a hard thing to do.' Keiko may see her death as a final release from the competitive nature of the game. Since it has finally turned her against Kawada, she may thank him for putting her out of the future misery of facing feelings of guilt over a situation she was not responsible for in the first place.

Kidnapped and thrown again within the deadly Battle Royale contest by authorities who have no intention of playing by the rules they have instituted (by putting both Kawada and Kiriyama there to 'fix' the whole system),

Kawada decides to act as a mentor to Shuya and Noriko, who represent the lost relationship he once had with Keiko. As a result, he uses his survival skills (including succeeding in Mimura's goal of hacking into the system) to both achieve his revenge on Kitano and help two survivors realise the goal of 'trust' he has articulated throughout the film. When Kawada saves Shuya and Noriko from Motobuchi, he points out to them the two choices awaiting those who do not decide to participate in the deadly game. These involve either suicide (which several students have already chosen) or a rational recognition of the odds facing them. 'If you can't trust anyone, just run.' During the beach scene towards the end of the film, Kawada tells Shuya and Moriko: 'I've never really trusted adults. My Mom and my Dad ran off or died because they couldn't take it. But I'll keep fighting even though I don't know how until I become a real adult.' Significantly, most of Kawada's speech occurs as a voiceover during a scene showing Kitano, as if the director expresses certain reservations over a younger generation growing up to become other versions of Kitano. Kawada's speech expresses an uncertainty over formulating definite strategies for survival, since *Battle Royale* has depicted most of them as futile. This speech influences the film's concluding scene, which shows Shuya and Noriko as fugitives from civilisation. When Noriko returns to Shuya after saying farewell to her sleeping parents, she shows him Nobu's knife, which she has kept since her deceased friend's attack on Kitano. The knife opens, but Shuya closes the blade and returns it to her. His voiceover comments, 'Each of us has a weapon now. Even if the time comes to use them again, *it'll never be an easy choice.* But we've no choice now but to keep moving forward. No matter how far, run for all you're worth.'[22] *Battle Royale* then abruptly concludes with the caption 'RUN!' appearing before the end credits.

Despite its graphic violence, *Battle Royale* is a more serious film than its detractors realise. However, by employing spectacular violence, it falls into the same dilemma Stephen Prince and Claudia Springer note as affecting works that are often anti-violence and oppositional in nature. By distracting the spectator from considering important issues in the text, spectacular devices may dilute a director's socially oppositional intention. However, as Charles Barr notes in his analysis of the contemporary British critical response to *Straw Dogs*, the usual comments involving 'gratuitous violence' and abhorrence at certain types of over-the-top cinematic representations can also hinder the appreciation of the total message of any particular film.[23] But *Battle Royale* is too important to be neglected at the mere level of viewer sensitivity. It fictionally presents a particular warning which has relevance to the western world as well as Japan. The film's message is clear for those choosing to explore beneath the graphically violent spectacular surface. If capitalism kills, so does its associated philosophy of individual competition, which sets one person against another. *Battle Royale* is not a film in which viewers may choose to exercise the privileged option of moral disgust and walk out of the theatre after ten minutes. Although its fictional practices are absent from the real world – at the moment – its premises are already operant. Competitive quiz shows involving the humiliation of masochistically compliant participants encouraged to engage in backstabbing practices are now common on most television screens. Soap operas set in a corporate world bear the logo: 'Being Good Doesn't Pay'. Talk-shows involving the denigration of people (or actors) displaying their personal problems for audience gratification litter the globe. Finally, a British newspaper recently announced that a television company would be adapting a programme that its American counterpart turned down – a *Survivor*-type game show involving individuals placed in a prison situation and subjected to frequent humiliations and strip searches. Although situations depicted in films such as *The Most Dangerous Game* (Irving Pichel and Ernest B. Schoedsack, 1932), *The Running Man* (Paul Michael Glaser, 1987) and *Hard Target* (John Woo, 1993) once seemed far removed from reality, grim developments in the twenty-first century are quickly removing those boundaries between fact and fiction. It is not surprising that the recent cover of *Psychotronic* contains a 'Wanted' poster featuring *Flash Gordon*'s villain Ming the Merciless with the caption 'Bring Back the 20th Century'. We ignore the warning signs contained in *Battle Royale* at our peril.

NOTES

1. I wish to express my debts to Anthony Leong, Tom Weisser and the *Battle Royale* web page.
2. See Barr, Charles (1972) '*Straw Dogs, A Clockwork Orange*, and the Critics', *Screen*, 13:2, pp. 17–32.
3. Leong, Anthony (2001) 'Those Who Are About to Die: *Battle Royale*', *Asian Cult Cinema*, 33, p. 38.
4. Wood, Robin (1998) *Sexual Politics and Narrative Film: Hollywood and Beyond*, New York: Columbia University Press, pp. 265–82.
5. Leong, p. 39.
6. See Stokes, Lisa Odham and Michael Hoover (1999) *City on Fire: Hong Kong Cinema*, London: Verso.
7. Leong, p. 35.
8. Chang, Iris (1997) *The Rape of Nanking*, New York, Basic Books, p. 31.
9. Ibid., p. 31.
10. Ellis, Sara (2001) 'Teenage Wasteland: Battling the Royale Mess of Japanese Education', 31 December, http://www.authorsden.com/visit/viewaricle.asp?AuthorID=6139.
11. Leong, p. 38.
12. Ibid., p. 40.
13. Leong, p. 38.
14. Weisser, Thomas and Yuko Mihara Weisser (1998b) *Japanese Cinema: The Essential Handbook*, Miami, FL: Vital Books, p. 99.

15. Mesure, Tom (2000) '*Battle Royale*', in *Midnight Eye: The Latest and Best in Japanese Cinema*, www.midnighteye.com.
16. See Ellis.
17. See *Battle Royale*'s official website at www.battleroyale.com.
18. See Brown, Norman O. (1959) *Life Against Death*, Middletown, CT: Wesleyan University Press.
19. See Freud, Sigmund [1915] (1984) 'Instincts and Their Vicissitudes. On Metapsychology', *The Penguin Freud Library, Volume 11*, London: Penguin, pp. 105–38.
20. See Freud, Sigmund [1930] (1985) 'Civilization and Its Discontents', *Civilization, Society and Religion. The Penguin Freud Library, Volume 12*, London: Penguin, pp. 235–340.
21. See Freud, Sigmund [1919] (1990) 'A Child is Being Beaten', *A Contribution to the Study of the Origin of Sexual Perversion. The Penguin Freud Library, Volume 10*, London: Penguin, pp. 159–93.
22. Italics mine.
23. Barr, pp. 17–32.

PART 4

JAPANESE HORROR CINEMA AND THE PRODUCTION AND CONSUMPTION OF FEAR

INTRODUCTION

Discussions of film production and reception are invariably restricted by a plethora of technological and temporal factors. This is due, in large part, to the seemingly inexhaustible aesthetic approaches available to film-makers, as well as the plurality of potential, often contradictory reactions members of a single audience can have to a cinematic text. Further complicating such readings are the myriad ways an individual spectator's experience of a film may alter over time. Nevertheless, such investigations are crucial to the study not only of individual films, but also of specific cinematic genres, since these critical inquiries provide invaluable insight into how different directors construct their works to elicit particular emotional responses from their audiences. In the chapters that comprise this last section of *Japanese Horror Cinema*, Philip Brophy, Matt Hills and Jay McRoy engage with issues surrounding the production and consumption of key Japanese horror films, exploring how technological innovations and manipulations have contributed to the rise of Japanese horror as a major tradition in world cinema.

For example, in his chapter, '*Arashi ga oka (Onimaru)*: The Sound of the World Turned Inside Out', Philip Brophy reads Yoshida Kiju's 1988 film as a specifically 'Japanese Gothic' text inspired by an assortment of European Gothic tropes, including tropological and structural elements arising from Emily Brontë's celebrated contribution to British Romanticism, *Wuthering Heights*. What makes Yoshida's film exceptionally compelling, Brophy argues, is how the director 'orchestrates and arranges the thematic levels of Brontë's tale via Takemitsu Toru's musical score'. A carefully composed sonic miasma that may initially confound audiences more accustomed to arrangements designed within a primarily western musical paradigm, Takemitsu's work successfully complements *Arashi ga oka*'s Gothic narrative and characterisations, as well as Yoshida Kiju's striking visuals. Consequently, Brophy suggests, *Arashi ga oka* is a cinematic offering created not so much in response to western film and musical motifs, but rather as a result of a direct infection by the European 'Gothic germ'. Complementing the film's action in vital yet complicated ways, Takemitsu's score resonates in its positioning of ' "music as *mise-en-scène*": a staging of sound that becomes a plane upon which theatrics are played out'. In this sense, the music accompanying the images in Yoshida's film does not arise in a conventionally non-diegetic fashion. Rather, Brophy contends, it 'turns the cinematic world inside-out'. Thus Takemitsu's score operates as a vital part of the world of the film, emerging 'from the abject materiality of the components existing within the diegesis of the depicted world on screen'.

Technology in the form of Internet message boards provides the foundation of Matt Hills' contribution, 'Ringing the Changes: Cult Distinctions and Cultural Differences in US Fans' Readings of Japanese Horror Cinema'. In this enlightening piece, Hills states that 'the US cult status of Japanese horror cinema needs to be related not simply to the "virtual unobtainability" and "marginality" of its texts, but also to discussions of Japanese–US cultural differences and homologies, as well as to time-sensitive re-constructions of Japanese horror cinema's status as beyond-the-mainstream.' Through a careful analysis of the complex dynamics of fan discourse, with an extensive focus on the assorted debates surrounding discussions over the merits of Nakata Hideo's 'original' *Ringu* and Gore Verbinski's recent US 'remake', Hills relates these on-line discussions to Internet fandom's tendency towards initiating dialogues on cultural differences. Interestingly, such conversations become problematic when one dissects the stereotypes and totalising assumptions behind such perceived disparities. Furthermore, Hills provides valuable insight into the hierarchies of knowledge and authority that arise based on *when* a fan saw the 'original' film, as well as the fine points of 'bias theory', which contends that preferences for Nakata's 'original' *Ringu* versus the Verbinski 'remake' are often determined by which version an individual viewed first. Perhaps one of Hills' most intriguing observations, however, is his recognition of the establishment and policing of 'boundary-marking practices' enacted by fans in a gesture that at once privileges their identities as expert cinephiles in possession of specialised knowledge, and as consumers defined by the avid consumption of 'different', 'difficult' and 'foreign' cultural products.

Finally, in the case study that concludes this section, Jay McRoy analyses Shimizu Takashi's *Ju-on: The Grudge* (2002) as a work of cinematic hybridity in its fusion of the *mise-en-scène* of US slasher films, like the *Friday the 13th* and *A Nightmare on Elm Street* series, with the visual logics informing works of Japanese horror cinema constructed around the *onryou*, or avenging ghost, motif. Such an approach, McRoy argues, is important to consider for several reasons. First, this visual style seems particularly appropriate given the hybridity embodied by the supernatural mother and son whose unquenchable rage give the film its title; not merely spectral beings, but 'not fully monsters in the term's most conventional sense', their restless spirits haunt the house in which they suffered at the hands of the family's murderous patriarch. In some of the most unsettling moments in Japanese horror cinema, the mother and son bring paralysing fear and death to those who enter their abode and, consequently, perpetuate further curses in an almost viral fashion. Additionally, McRoy claims, *Ju-on: The Grudge*'s theme of hybridity allows for a simultaneously conservative and progressive exploration of 'a radically transforming Japanese culture in which tensions between an undead past and an unborn future find articulation in the transforming family of a haunted, interstitial present'. In the process, the film provides valuable insights into shifting social and gender roles in the years following the bursting of the Japanese 'bubble economy'. Lastly, the film's visual mélange marks Shimizu Takashi's unique cinematic vision, an arresting style that will be put to an interesting and potentially groundbreaking test with his forthcoming Hollywood remake of *Ju-on: The Grudge*, starring *Buffy the Vampire Slayer*'s Sarah Michelle Gellar.

11. *ARASHI GA OKA (ONIMARU)*: THE SOUND OF THE WORLD TURNED INSIDE OUT[1]

Philip Brophy

SPEAKING JAPANESE AND SOUNDING GOTHIC

The Gothic is attracted to decay like maggots to a corpse. And like flies carrying airborne disease, the Gothic vaporises. It floats along the global trade winds that breathe death through the fetid national identities which distinguish each country's cinema. The Gothic may be Germanic in its morphological origination; it might be English in its formulation of a literary obesity; it might be American in its slippage toward social decline. Its constancy is its suffixing to any cultural identity as a means of decaying that which it touches.

'Japanese Gothic' is a symptom of this affectation. The mutative outgrowth of European tropes, figures and icons from noticeably Japanese environs, architecture and landscape is a clear demonstration of how the Gothic performs more as wormwood and less as a rhizome. It atrophies from within to create new chimeraesque shapes rather than sprouting forth additional structures. While European and Occidental Gothic expressions are the result of importation, the Gothic in Japanese guise is the result of direct injection and a consequent inability to digest. The spectre of Japan's unnerving isolationism governs Japanese aesthetics to such an extent that transcultural occurrences like the Gothic are never subsumed, fused or blended: they curdle, pock and mar their reflecting surfaces into microterrains of cultural mutation.[2]

Yoshida Kiju's *Arashi ga oka* (1988, also known as *Onimaru*) announces itself as a contorted duality of Gothic imposition, with opening credits declaring its basis as Emily Brontë's *Wuthering Heights*, and then cutting to an *obayashi* – the traditional narrational figure in Japanese ghost stories from the medieval period. As she tells the tale of Onimaru to a blind monk, her archetypically rasping voice sucks in the Gothic and expels it through a uniquely Japanese dialect. The Occidental vanishes; the Oriental materialises. The Japanese voice that speaks this versioning of Brontë's novel serves as a sign of its generative Gothic apparition to such an extent that 'voice' becomes both metaphor and metonym in the play between sound and image that characterises *Arashi ga oka* as a complex audiovisual text. No mere transposition, interpretation or translation of Brontë's tale of displaced souls, windstrewn romance and diminishing vitality, *Arashi ga oka* eschews all recourse to 'staging' its para-Gothic literary origins. In place of nominal literary and theatrical strategies employed in cinematic novelisations, *Arashi ga oka* orchestrates and arranges the thematic levels of Brontë's tale via Takemitsu Toru's musical score.

COLLAPSING THE ORCHESTRA INTO SOUND

The first point to make about the score to *Arashi ga oka* is an obvious one: it is performed by an orchestra. This central detail might fall on deaf western ears who are happy with 'film music' as unending echoic strains of Wagnerian clichés and gross operatic gestures. But the point is arch: to employ a European orchestra for a Japanese film is a high-relief effect comparable to scoring *Schindler's List* with *koto* (a traditional Japanese instrument). Takemitsu amplifies the musicological schisms that arise from his adoption of the orchestra by employing Japanese technique in the performance and 'sounding' of the orchestral elements. Largely bypassing the linguistic strictures of western harmony, which tend to apply a default setting to the harmonic building blocks in orchestral writing and performance, instrumental identity in *Arashi ga oka* is always blurred, diffused, aerated. Flutes behave like whistling kettles; timpani like rolling boulders; horns like tuned wood resonance. No instrument in *Arashi ga oka*'s score presents itself as recognisable. True to the film's ingestion of the Gothic, Takemitsu's orchestration is the result of the orchestra being transformed from within, at the level of tactile performance. No mere vaudevillian mimicry and spookery blasted from the pit below the screen, the score conjures a spectral being living and breathing upon the stage, spot-lit with make-up melting in the lights.

The tactile timbres and seeping sensory nature of the score is always at the fore, accenting the physicality of the orchestral apparatus. In the conjoined history of western musical progression, the shift from the musical to the sonic is perceived as either an unwanted aberration, a sign of ineptness or an act of wilful destruction. The evacuation of controlled musical expression and its collapse into tonal impurity, sonic irritation and harmonic degeneration have long formed critical paradigms that qualify 'music' as a grand and noble pursuit. But to a western ear not exposed to Japanese music, the highly skilled performance of a lute (*biwa*), flute (*shakauhachi*) or guitar (*shimasen*) might sound identical to a three-year old western child tearing apart a violin. *Arashi ga oka* features superb solo performances of all these instruments atop the aforementioned orchestral arrangements. Boldly laid across the splayed fields of European instrumentation that squirm like carpets of maggots on moist earth, these uniquely Japanese signifiers of musicianship and performance are emblematic of the 'voice' which 'sounds' the score, and serve to continually remind the ear that they mix with a lush European string section like oil with water.[3]

But *Arashi ga oka* is a film, not a concert. The score then is affected by, and in turn modulates, the dramaturgy of the film. And it is precisely here that the power of *Arashi ga oka* as a Japanese Gothic scenario is discerned. A reading of how the music relates to (a) the interior spatial design and depiction of exterior locations; (b) the psychological development (or deterioration) of the enmeshed characters; and (c) the shimmering and wavering dissolution between sonic atmospheres and temperate musicality, uncovers the musicological map upon which *Arashi ga oka* is audiovisually staged. Despite the bloody *chambara* explosiveness and the bodily corruption which posit *Arashi ga oka* as a dimensional shift beyond the original film version of *Wuthering Heights* (directed by William Wyler in 1939), the dissolution of the score – its creeping, weeping palpability – is the prime signifier of the Gothic germ that has overtaken this highly mannered Japanese film.

MAPPING THE TERRAIN OF *ARASHI GA OKA*

Brontë's *Wuthering Heights* is as much neglected as it is referenced by *Arashi ga oka*. This sixteenth-century feudal story details the slow descent into madness of the brutish Onimaru (Matsuda Yusaku) – an unwanted heir to the Yamabe family fortune after the death of Lord Takamaru Yamabe (Mikuni Rentaro) to whom Onimaru has been utterly loyal. The central cause of Onimaru's madness is his frayed bonding to Kinu Yamabe (Tanaka Yuko) after she gives herself over to him following her father Takamaru's death at the hands of passing soldiers. She does so prior to leaving to marry her cousin, Lord Mitsuhiko. Both families belong to the Serpent Clan who live on the Sacred Mountain, each owning a huge mansion on opposite sides, and each wholly opposed to the other due to generations of feuding. Forced to become a Shinto priestess at the capital once she reaches womanhood, Kinu marries Mitsuhiko only so that she is allowed to stay on the mountain and, hence, near Onimaru, even though her marriage to Mitsuhiko prevents her from seeing Onimaru again. Onimaru is angered by her marriage and leaves, only to return some years later from the capital as a Lord to whom dominion of the whole mountain – including the household of Kinu and Mitsuhiko – is bequeathed. During his absence, Kinu has had a daughter, Shino – likely from her past sole union with Onimaru.

Kinu dies; Mitsuhiko is slain by robbers who in turn are butchered by Onimaru. Deeply disturbed by the death of Kinu, Onimaru disinters her body from the mountain's Valley of the Dead, risking supreme damnation. A now-adult Shino (Ito Keiko) travels to Onimaru's mansion full of hatred toward Onimaru, as she believes he killed her father. Shino is intent on retrieving her mother's coffin and remains, and planning to drive Onimaru mad by reminding him of her mother. After first finding and then hiding her mother's remains from Onimaru, Shino's attempt to seduce Onimaru backfires when he reveals his past affair with her mother. Onimaru reclaims Kinu's coffin and withdraws into deepening neuroses and visions. Aged and lost in his insane bond to Kinu's skeletal remains, he has his right arm severed in a conflict with Shino's young cousin, Yoshimaru (Furuoya Masato). Presumed dead, the one-armed Onimaru miraculously reappears as Shino and Yoshimaru are returning Kinu's coffin to the Valley of the Dead. Onimaru regains Kinu's coffin and drags it into the rising mist covering the upper reaches of the Sacred Mountain.[4]

The settings for *Arashi ga oka* are essentially polarised between the chiaroscuro interiors of the east/west mansions, and the unforgiving volcanic landscape of the Sacred Mountain (also referred to as a 'fire mountain'). The figures of Onimaru, Kinu and so on are positioned within these settings as delicate gestural shapes, mostly layered in relief against massive and expansive backdrops of colour and texture. They are materialisations of the solo traditional instruments (including *biwa*, *shimasen*, *shakauhachi*, *koto* and *taiko*), dancing atop the seething density of the orchestral murmuring which represents the haunting terrain of the Scared Mountain and the penumbral gloom of the east/west mansions. While visual grandeur and 'opulent minimalism' is readily apparent, *Arashi ga oka*'s overall brooding tone arises from the way the sound design and film score interpolate these settings. Predominantly, when we are outside on the dark ashen mountain, the orchestra sounds like howling wind; when we are inside the cavernous mansions' rooms, we hear actual moaning wind. This is a major reversal of the dominant logic of western mimetic cinema (labelled, among other terms, 'realism' or 'naturalism') in that music is often deemed the voice of humanist enterprise and dramatic conflict, while landscapes are 'non-human' and thus often felt to require non-musical (that is, sonic) representation. *Arashi ga oka* consistently places sound as the backdrop to the chamber dramas in the mansions, while music is employed to speak the voice of the landscape. This conceptual technique is typical of much Japanese cinema, wherein land is inextricably linked to the psyche and spiritual tenets place the human and the non-human on a coexistent plane of energy.

Yet *Arashi ga oka* invigorates this Japanese cinematic template of audio-visual construction. Through Takemitsu's quasi-spectral compositional approach, the volcanic carpet of the Sacred Mountain becomes a mindscape for the characters as they are emptied of all social mores in their decline to madness; the composed silence of the mansions' rooms is amplified to form hollowed resonators for the characters' emptiness. Contrary to western notions of house design, the traditional Japanese domus welcomes sound rather than blocks it: paper walls allow sound to filter through; wooden floorboards create reverberant points of contact for sliding doors and walking feet; the sounds of nature outside flow throughout the house as a soundtrack to framed openings onto manicured gardens. The Japanese experience of what constitutes the relationship between the inside and outside of both the home and, more broadly, the environment, is substantially different from the experience of people raised within bricked and plastered walls and closed glass windows. Consequently, the symbolic role of interior and exterior sounds performs differently – especially in the film's imposition of the Gothic, whose symbolic codes accent the repression of the inside and sensationalise its unleashed rupture of the outside.

Arousing the Interior and Planing the Exterior

Arashi ga oka sounds this difference of the interior/exterior bind at two levels. First, the score charts the shift between the objective capture of scenes and the subjective impressions of being in those scenes. Soft timpani rolls fused with richly bowed double-bass against a panorama of the Sacred Mountain will simulate wind but also invoke the power its mass has on the minds of those who traverse its barren terrain. At other times, bass-heavy droning wind against the same panorama will simulate a *portamento* pitch drop of a bowed double-bass, but evoke the acoustic characteristics of wind travelling low to the ground to create an ominous hum typically felt on such terrain. The 'difference' between these two aural states concurs at the symbolic level, but their actualisation – their choice of aural rendering – reflects the angle at which the drama is positioned as it moves forward. In effect, this is 'music as *mis-en-scène*': a staging of sound that becomes a plane upon which theatrics are played out.

The second way in which the interior/exterior bind is articulated as different from conventional western modes of audiovisuality lies in the narrational aspects of the music. The score employs its solo instrumentation of traditional Japanese instruments to embody the psychological stature of its characters. For example, Onimaru is 'sonically signed' by growling low frequencies (drums, cellos, oboes) and a low *shakauhachi*; Kinu by a blend of *koto* and harp and a high *shakauhachi*. Now while this might seem standard practice in western cinema (thematic representation of characters through instrumentation), *Arashi ga oka* displaces these themes into a complex biorhythm that at times synchronises with the on-screen depiction of a character and at other times completely dislocates any continuity or simultaneity. Over a static shot of Onimaru might be the *shakauhachi* line of Kinu, which is then allowed to carry over into a landscape shot of the mountain. Contained within this complex interweaving of themes and their roving, shifting apparition is the way in which sound effects, atmospheres and foley will appear and disappear according to intensity or prominence of the psychological fissure being presented at any one moment. The mix of the film is thus a psychologically monitored one and accords little to the linguistic/ structural guidelines of realist/naturalist cinema. This is 'music as dramaturgy': an arousal of the characters' interiority expressed beyond and despite the plastics of the filmic construction (costume, sets, lights, camera, etc.).

Some detailed charting of the ways in which *Arashi ga oka*'s score articulates its weave of sonarised *mise-en-scène* and dramaturgy can now be undertaken. The terrain of *Arashi ga oka* is the breadth and depth of the Sacred Mountain. A volatile geography, its volcanic aspects figure it as unsettled earth whose ground is unfixed and whose fluctuating temperature suggest its living quality. Following folkloric tradition, the Lord of the Yamabe family must annually perform the Rite of the Serpent, designed to keep the serpent deep within the earth. Its symbolic rupture of the earth is deemed responsible for crop failure by the villagers, hence the need to repress its arousal. Yet the sexual symbolism of the rising serpent is the sediment to *Arashi ga oka*'s unending sexual tension. Read this way, the low rumbles which flow throughout the film like a sonar network of invisible ducting symbolise the earth as a living corpus which affects and controls those who touch its surface. From the occasional subsonic vibrations that shudder the mountain's slopes of dark gravel to the low-toned wind drafts surging throughout the mansion's wooden corridors, the earth is a responsive being triggering states of arousal in its denizens.

While such a view of the earth aligns with mystical and fantastical tropes in western storytelling, Japanese culture supports the animist notion of spiritual energy contained within the apparently 'inanimate'. The earth and all its discontents are as alive as any human. When Kinu and Mitsuhiko discuss the bond each of their clan shares with the mountain and its serpent essence, low-pitched oboes and clarinets swirl around each other in snaking lines to musically represent and symbolically evidence their awareness of the mysterious power embodied by the mountain. Notably, the volume level of this theme almost overcomes the dialogue track, indicating how elemental energies can overpower the human.

BECOMING THE OTHER AND VISCERAL RENDERING

The core of *Arashi ga oka*'s drama is the 'love action' between Onimaru and Kinu. This actioning of desire, consummation and obsession is concentrated in their lovemaking scenes. Prior to their first physical encounter, each bathes in seclusion. A naked Onimaru roughly pours buckets of water over himself, the bursts of white noise gashing the silence of the mansion. Earlier, clothed in white muslin, Kinu has had cupfuls of water carefully poured down her lithe form by her attendant. The water barely makes a trickling noise; in place is a series of delicately plucked *koto* notes and tinkling chimes. This musical tinkling represents the upper filature that breaks free from the corporeality of the earth: Kinu is hovering on the transcendental cusp of becoming 'other' than the identity that the Shinto priestess custom dictates.

These tinkles also represent an inner nucleus to the swirling sexual energy that both attracts Onimaru and Kinu to each other and polarises them. After they have made love, Kinu is attended to by her maid while holding a mirror. She is transfixed by her own image (like she was as a child when first given the mirror by her father), yet narcissism and vanity have no play here. As her oval face hovers like a beautiful orb within the circular frame, Kinu chants softly to her reflection, 'He is here . . . I am Onimaru . . . Onimaru is me.' Not only has his seed taken hold in her body (symbolised by the mirror as womb), but she has given herself over to him as an act of self-erasure. When she departs to start a new life with Mitsuhiko, she is, as she says, Onimaru. The tinkling thus implies the presence of Onimaru in shots or sequences from which he is physically absent.

Kinu and Onimaru's lovemaking takes place in a glowing room tainted with smears that suggest dried blood. This rosewood-toned colourisation of the room's screens is never outrightly explained (Onimaru enters and declares, 'It's the smell of blood, not damp mould'), though when Kinu first encounters the space she clearly finds its aura unsettling. This humoral room is actually referred to as the Seclusion Room where household members are interred as acts of punishment. Kinu acknowledges her iniquity in seducing Onimaru by performing their sexual union in this Seclusion Room. When they have sex, a seductive 'dance' is first deployed, as each hovers around the contours of the other's body, suggestively following its lines with finger, hand, tongue, hair. They contort and entwine like two snakes, engorged by the energy of the serpent spirit of the mountain. Tuned wind drafts rise and fall in response to the intensity of their movements. Swirling around them like sonic smoke curls are two *shakauhachi* solos, a low flute and a high flute engaged in a sensual dialogue. Having conjured forth the serpent energy into the realm of the corporeal, the music represents this transformation of their selves by functioning as a form of oxidised sexuality: airborne, it molecularly transforms their space. These floating flutes are thus not symbolic of Onimaru and Kinu per se, but more so their transformation. As they move into tactile embrace, all foley sound effects disappear: they have absented themselves from the plane of physical existence to become the Other.

Apart from accompanying the rolling end credits, the only time the dual *shakauhachi* theme appears in full-bodied form is during the above love-making scene. Elsewhere, the flute solos are sounded alone. When Kinu dies, she is seen through a muslin gauze similar to the fabric she wore during her ritual bath prior to joining with Onimaru. Fevered and dying slowly from within ever since she left Onimaru, she now claims to hear the sound of Onimaru's horse's hooves. The deep timpani rolls we have heard many times now come to the fore; this is the spirit of the mountain sounded through the spectre of Onimaru, who has been possessed by the spirit of Kinu who seduced him as she, in turn, was controlled by the mountain's sexual energy. The looping here is important, recalling not only how Kinu perceives herself as one with Onimaru, but also how the low rumbles symbolise the way the mountain affects those who walk upon it. Crying that she'll drag Onimaru down to hell, her last words are spoken calmly: 'Onimaru, you are dead.' Throughout this scene, Onimaru's low *shakauhachi* plays the exact solo dance it performed during their lovemaking. Read through visuals alone, the scene would be one of desperate revenge. Acknowledging the transferrals that have occurred between Onimaru and Kinu, plus the presence of his sexual 'becoming' flute theme, the scene is actually a morbid sex scene – one that forecasts his descent into necrophilia.

Possessed by the spirit of Kinu – and equally dispossessed by not possessing her body following their sole night of love – Onimaru is driven to extend his consummation of her being after death. When he first opens her coffin, Kinu's decaying corpse is illuminated by lightning and revealed as an undulating spread of maggots. Mixed atop the sheets of lightning noise and deep thunder claps (prime sonic signifiers of rupture and transgression in global Gothic cinema) Kinu's high *shakauhachi* theme plays as Kinu drags Onimaru down to hell by sexually luring him to take her despite her state of decrepitude. Onimaru passes over to the other side in his expression of love here as he embraces both what he has become and what the mountain has made of the bond between him and Kinu. The breathiness of their shared *shakauhachi* sighs are so hot and moist that viewers can practically feel the exhalations against their necks, imbuing Onimaru and Kinu's musicality with a viscerality that allows the film to waver between erotic denouement and pornographic stimulation.

From this point on, Onimaru lives in his own 'Valley of the Dead'. Two notable scenes extol this in unsettling ways. The first is when Onimaru throws Mitsuhiko's sister, Tae (Ishida Eri), into the Seclusion Room after she travels to the east mansion in order to become Onimaru's bride. Sensing the spite that impels her desperation, he rejects the sexual advances she uses as a means to overcome and control him. A terse gender confrontation occurs, as she flaunts herself as a reappearance of the dead Kinu, not realising that he could *only* relate to her as the dead Kinu. Psychologically sparring with Tae, Onimaru is overwhelmed and rapes her as a vessel of 'not-being' Kinu, dry-humping the absence of Kinu embodied by Tae's physiognomy. Tae's face expresses not simply outrage at being raped, but revulsion at 'becoming symbolically dead' in the grasp of Onimaru. The depths of his madness shocks her so much she hangs herself at the gate of the east mansion the next morning. Throughout the rape scene, the *shakauhachi* lines affirm the presence and absence of Kinu as a dark shadow cast upon everyone. Thus the seemingly blood-stained walls of the Seclusion Room are less material residue and more a sexual ectoplasm that defines an epidermis to this erotic realm.

The second scene that depicts the morbid domus of Onimaru's mind occurs when Shino cloisters herself in the room – first lying in Kinu's coffin, and then later appearing naked and ready for sex. She taunts Onimaru by flaunting her physique; wind drafts sonically surge around the room and cause a candle Onimaru holds to lap and dance around her body like he once did with Kinu. As he eyes the genetic imprint of Kinu upon her daughter's form, Shino dares him, 'Come – hate me if you can.' This time Shino is a corporeal manifestation of Kinu's *shakauhachi* solo: Shino's erotic performance, reminiscent of Kinu's, is an act of becoming that haunts and lures the crazed Onimaru.

'TURNED INSIDE OUT' AND SONO-MUSICAL CONFLATION

The graveyard of the Yamabe clan on the Sacred Mountain – poetically named the Valley of the Dead – is often accompanied by swirling and slow-throbbing oboes and clarinets. This is possibly a straightforward choice of instrumentation, but the accent of woodwinds relates closely to the terrain as degraded wooden coffins. It is almost as if the wooden coffins have been remodelled into woodwinds in order to sound human breath through their morbid materiality. This is no overreactive reading of the use of woodwinds, as elsewhere in the film wind is the breath of the mountain, rumbling across the mountain's dales and troughs and tunnelling down the mansions' corridors. Takemitsu's approach to scoring is often based on an animist awareness of the materiality of chosen instruments, and clearly in *Arashi ga oka*, wood, wind and death are thematically and aurally fused.

Essentially, Takemitsu is less engaged in 'film scoring' as we know it and more absorbed in 'decomposing' music for the film's Gothic-infected scenario. Rather than presume the cinematographic scenario is somehow a 'photo-realist' dramatic document requiring the non-diegetic mode of musical discourse to articulate a human perceptiveness (the lofty yet limited quest of most classical western film scoring), Takemitsu's approach is to 'make sound' from the abject materiality of the components existing within the diegesis of the depicted world on screen. In doing so, he effectively turns the cinematic world inside out, hiding the thematic striations that obviously suggest dramaturgy to the film composer and revealing the sonic elemental nature of a film's fabric. This perception of the world is a key philosophical determinant in the sono-musical conflation strongly associated with Takemitsu.

Yet Takemitsu is not imposing on *Arashi ga oka*'s dramatic logic or fictional realm. His method of 'decomposition' is perfectly suited to the film's Gothic impulse, as well as its visceral rendering of suppressed thematics. Recalling the aforementioned 'aeration of musical themes', one must acknowledge how this 'decomposition' resonates with the central notion of decay that drives the Gothic in general and *Arashi ga oka* in particular. When the inside of the body is exposed through incision or rot, airborne germs gain access to that which hair and skin block and cover, causing decay of the most mortal kind. Onimaru experiences this potently when he disinters Kinu's body but, as also noted, he is affected by the psychic stench unleashed by Kinu's bodily decomposition. Inner and outer realms – their trembling disclosure, their acidic meld – are also at the base of the story's social construction. Takamaru holds an awesome power over the villagers by enacting the Serpent Rite to keep the mountain's serpent energy at bay and assuring their livelihood. However, he is acutely cogniscent of the theatrical charade he enacts, declaring, 'Now is an age of wars . . . Only fools worry about curses or divine punishment.' Yet true to the Gothic drive to prove that which one most denies or refuses to believe, he neglects to consider how the mountain's ominous form affects the sexual and psychological composure of the family he has built on its bed of volcanic rock. Desire, love and familial growth are thus affected at the micro-level, allowing for a fulsome decay and deterioration to take hold of everyone.

The Gothic – encompassing its criss-crossing folds of 'Neo-Gothicisation' that historically skirt both the sub-history of serialised romances and the validated examples of great nineteenth-century novels – returns uncontrollably to the sensational intersection of the morbid with the romantic. Never tragic but always titillating, the Gothic loves death and loves to count the ways a person can die. Its thrill within western modes is one of knowing the silent, hearing the mute and acknowledging the unspoken. Gothic literature's excessive descriptiveness (a precursor to a cinematic tradition that 'dwells on the unsavoury') is an erotic striptease of signification, through which the unutterable is framed and spotlit but never named or spoken. A complex of Judeo-Christian mores and Eurocentric morals might block the western Gothic from rendering the totality of its unspeakable action, but Japanese Gothic has neither qualms nor concerns about adhering to the caveats placed on the Gothic's propensity towards the lurid. Hence, the wuthering musical depths and psycho-sexual heights of *Arashi ga oka* truly constitutes a world turned inside out.

NOTES

1. Thanks to Chiaki Ajioka and Rosemary Dean.
2. Not a particularly official genre of horror, 'Japanese Gothic' would be ably demonstrated by notable films like Nakagawa Nobuo's *Kyuketsuki ga* (1956), *Kaidan kasanegafuchi* (1957), *Borei kaibyo yashiki* (1958) and *Takaido yatsuya Kaidan* (1959); Shindo Kaneto's *Onibaba* and Kobayashi Masaki's *Kaidan* (both 1964); Kobayashi Tsuneo's *Kaidan katame no otoko* and Sato Hajime's *Kaidan semushi otoko* (both 1965); Shindo Kaneto's *Kuroneko*, Yasuda Kimiyoshi's *Yokai hyaku monogatari*, Kuroda Yoshiyuki's *Yokai daisenso*, Yamamoto Satsuo's *Kaidan botandoro*, Tanaka Tokuzo's *Kaidan yukigoro* and Hase Kazuo's *Kaidan zankoku monogatari* (all 1968).
3. For more on Takemitsu Toru's approach to film-scoring, especially in relation to horror, see Brophy, Philip (2000) 'How Sound Floats On Land: The Suppression and Release of Indigenous Musics on the Cinematic Terrain', in Philip Brophy (ed.), *Cinesonic: Cinema and the Sound of Music*, Sydney: Australian Film TV & Radio School, pp. 191–215.
4. For an analysis of the depiction of Woman in *Arashi ga oka*, see Iwamura, Dean R. (1994) 'Letter from Japan: From Girls Who Dress Up Like Boys to Trussed-Up Porn Stars – Some Contemporary Heroines on the Japanese Screen', *Continuum: The Australian Journal of Media and Culture*, 7: 2, pp. 109–30.

12. RINGING THE CHANGES: CULT DISTINCTIONS AND CULTURAL DIFFERENCES IN US FANS' READINGS OF JAPANESE HORROR CINEMA

Matt Hills

As has been recently observed, 'in cult movie fandom, information and inaccessibility need to be carefully regulated . . . inaccessibility is maintained . . . not only through the selection of materials – they are not for everyone – but also through their virtual unobtainability'.[1] This argument undoubtedly rings true for a range of transnational cult movies – the Italian *giallo* in the US or UK,[2] and Hong Kong genre movies such as *The Killer* in the United States.[3] The distinctiveness required for cult status is, here, partly based on such films' cultural-textual differences from the 'mainstream' of Hollywood productions, given that 'a sense of what is marginal often has a national-contextual specificity, with the "foreignness" of some . . . film genres rendering them marginal [and cultish] in markets outside of their country of production.'[4]

An established body of academic work has explored the fact that 'cult' status often hinges, for fans, on an imagined or constructed distance from the status quo of 'mainstream' film culture.[5] If Japanese horror cinema has indeed been somewhat 'marginal' in the US, and has thus been cultishly appreciated by an interpretive community of like-minded fans, then what happens to this nationally contextualised cult distinctiveness when Japanese films become a source for commercially successful Hollywood remakes? This essay will consider the way in which recent Japanese horror has become more readily accessible and obtainable in the US, and the way in which this conditions its 'cult' status. Having been 'adapted' into major Hollywood releases (for example, *The Ring*, directed by Gore Verbinski, 2002), original Japanese texts such as *Ringu* (Nakata Hideo, 1998) are no longer securely or obviously outside the 'mainstream'. I will therefore argue that the US cult status of Japanese horror cinema needs to be related not simply to the 'virtual unobtainability' and 'marginality' of its texts, but also to discussions of Japanese–US cultural differences and homologies, as well as to time-sensitive reconstructions of Japanese horror cinema's status as beyond-the-mainstream.

In order to provide a focal point for discussion, I will take one online message board as a case study, the *Ringworld's Ring Forum* (accessible via http://ringworld. somrux.com). This board was established 21 May 2002 and had received 108,958 posts as of 12 January 2004. The majority of my analysis will focus on one thread, 'Remake vs. Original debate', which carried 315 replies (again as of 12 January 2004). I will discuss posters' comparisons of *The Ring* and *Ringu* as well as their wider reflections on live-action Japanese horror cinema in the US.[6]

My selection of *Ringu* as a case study is premised on the fact that it has been credited 'with sparking a Japanese trend for so-called "Psycho-Horror" films . . . [While i]n the West, . . . [it] . . . has provoked interest in Japanese genre films – the biggest beneficiaries . . . [being] . . . Miike Takashi's *Audition* [2000], and Kinji Fukasaku's *Battle Royale* (2000)'.[7] Or, as another film critic has put it: 'live-action thrillers from the genre called "psycho-horror" have found an eager audience in America . . . The spearhead of this invasion was the movie *Ring*, adapted by director Hideo Nakata from the bestselling novels by Suzuki Koji'.[8] Indeed, the success of Verbinski's *The Ring* was such that an American translation of Suzuki's original novel became available in 2003, proving to be far more uncomfortable in its representations of gender and sexuality than both Japanese and American film adaptations, with its male protagonist, Ryuji, being a self-professed rapist, and its monster, Sadako, a hermaphrodite.[9]

Several writers have previously analysed film-related online message boards[10] or horror-genre-related fan websites,[11] and this chapter adds to a burgeoning academic interest in fan audiences and their online self-representations and interpretive activities.[12] However, my intention here is not to explore notions of fan community per se. I am interested, instead, in how posters to the *Ringworld's Ring Forum*, and specifically its 'Theories and Debates' section dealing with the 'Remake vs. Original debate', construct subcultural fan distinctions while simultaneously positioning themselves in relation to Japanese–US cultural differences. The cult distinctions of horror fandom are, in this instance, mapped onto negotiations and discussions of cultural difference. Genre fandom is defended and valued by this fan group through its possibilities for provoking cross-cultural understanding.

In the first section of this chapter, I will address American fan audiences' cult distinctions – how these fans of Japanese horror cinema work to separate themselves out from 'the masses' or 'the mainstream' – before moving on to consider how these distinctions are also related to issues of cultural difference.

Cult Distinctions: First Viewers Versus 'Bias Theory'

Scholarly accounts of cult film fans as anti-mainstream or as 'resistive', subversive and transgressive audiences tend to implicitly construct this argument in spatial terms. 'Underground' cult films are said to circulate materially in distinctive cultural spaces (arthouse or indie/specialist cinemas rather than the nearest multiplex; specialist stores rather than high-street shops or the local Blockbuster). In such arguments, the distinctions of cult status are related to the texts' distance – in terms of their distribution and circulation – from mainstream cinemas and video/DVD outlets. Joanne Hollows has noted that cinemas specialising in screening cult movies have often been located

> in parts of the city's 'underbelly' or 'twilight zones'. This works to confirm the figure of the cult fan as a . . . 'manly adventurer' who sets out into the urban wilderness . . . [of] disreputable city spaces . . . [S]ome specialist cult outlets also take care to define themselves against more 'mainstream' shopping spaces; the interiors of cult shops are frequently painted in dark colours, dimly lit, with products . . . in . . . dusty plastic bags . . . these consumption spaces are based on a refusal of 'mainstream consumer culture'.[13]

However, this emphasis on cult 'anti-mainstream' distinctions as spatial distinctions is brought into question by Hollywood remakes of cult Japanese horror films (the 'Asian Horror Remake Watch' thread on the *Ring Forum* lists at least nine Hollywood remakes of Japanese or Korean films as actively in development, including Nakata's post-*Ringu* films, *Chaos* (1999) and *Dark Water* (2002)). Any Hollywood remake brings in its wake the possibility of wider distribution and accessibility – and thus a type of consumer-cultural 'mainstreaming' – for the original Japanese text. Indeed, this greater accessibility of the 'cult' object is welcomed by a number of posters to the Ring Forum who explicitly identify themselves as US-based fans of Japanese horror cinema:

the success of the remake does a couple things for those of us who live in the US . . . For one thing, it gets the original distributed more widely.[14]

I was extremely pleased when I overheard some clueless teens at my local blockbuster talking about how they've never heard of 'Ringu' but are now dying to see it. If a remake is what it takes to get people interested in the original, then I sincerely hope that . . . studios learn a lesson or two from Dreamworks.[15]

until there is a visible upswing in Asian horror [distribution in the US], we will probably have remakes first, then once the remake becomes popular or infamous then someone eventually creeps a distro out.[16]

For these fans of Japanese horror cinema in America, the mainstreaming of a 'marginal' Japanese text following on from its US remake is not seen as an inherent threat to cult status.[17] Rather, the remake's success is viewed positively, as providing a platform for the cult text's wider availability (both for these fans, and for the 'clueless teens at . . . Blockbuster' who still continue to be positioned as an imagined consumer-Other to the fans' expertise). Hollywood remakes are thus positioned as relatively inauthentic/inferior texts that nevertheless allow the 'cult' original to move beyond its initial underground status, a shift that is embraced, as if culturally validating the fans' love of *Ringu* et al.

However, if cult status cannot be securely anchored to spatial differences, given that *Ringu* becomes readily available within 'mainstream consumer culture' and no longer remains 'underground' after its Hollywood remake, then how can the 'niche market' of Asian horror fans in the US maintain its subcultural distinction from 'the masses'? In the absence of the spatial markers testified to by Hollows, this becomes a matter of temporal, or time-sensitive, cultural distinctions. Posters to the *Ring Forum* are often careful to differentiate themselves from audiences who saw the original only after initially viewing the remake:

Hollywood . . . has a tough time gauging [the] success of foreign films like *Ringu* and other Asian Horror because the niche market is very small in the US. Its cool that we, on this board and maybe thousands of others will hunt down original Asian works and *appreciate them for what they are before a remake is made, however we are not status quo*. Unlike Anime . . . [Asian] Horror is still very 'new' to the masses.[18]

The thing that occurred to me after the whole US Ring thing died down was that, *for people like us who usually find the originals first*, the remakes don't matter all that much.[19]

mostly the only people who had seen 'Ringu' over here in the states were underground/international film fanatics, japanese film fanatics, otakus . . . etc the average American Joe had, and probably never would see Ringu.[20]

While welcoming the later 'mainstreaming' of *Ringu* and its US DVD release, these fans continue to recuperate the cult distinctions of the film by referring to their own earlier or 'first' viewing. In this instance, subcultural distinctions are recontextualised as *pre-mainstream* instead of being monolithically and spatially anti-mainstream. These fans 'got there first', if you like, representing themselves as early adopters of a text that would only later go on to achieve widespread film-cultural notoriety. Such fans are hence able to display their status as having been 'in the know'[21] ahead of 'mainstream consumer culture' which is discursively figured via 'the average American Joe' as well as through 'clueless teens'.[22] Fannish early adoption is also represented, by one of the moderators on the *Ring Forum*, as nominally and knowingly 'subversive' due to its underground, tape-swapping activities:

> part of the mystique, for those of us who saw the original first (and before the remake came out) was getting our hands on this movie people were talking about but that no-one we knew IRL had seen, and the quality of the video added to the 'subversive' experience of watching the film.[23]

It is particularly striking here that viewing 'the original first' is an insufficient bid for subcultural distinction; mikejonas also adds the bracketed comment 'before the remake came out' to clinch a sense of pre-mainstream, temporal and subcultural authenticity. However, it could also be suggested that the additional, qualifying remark is necessary on this message board because of a further way in which the notion of 'first viewing' is commonly and communally used. Humorously referred to as the 'M J Axiom', and named after its originator mikejonas by a fellow moderator, Interferon,[24] this theory suggests that whichever version of a film (e.g. *Ringu/The Ring*) people personally see first will be the one they prefer. This is also referred to as 'bias theory': 'yes, I believe most peoples preference does depend most of the time on the "First Viewing" bias'.[25] Despite the fact that many posters disagree with this 'axiom', it continues to be debated on the message board and it frames many postings.

This use of the term 'first viewing' implies something very different from the statements of fans displaying their status as cult viewers who saw the original ahead of 'mainstream' or 'mass' audiences. By contrast, the 'bias theory' type of 'first viewing' is not inherently linked to any bid for cult or subcultural distinction; it works, instead, to psychologise and individualise debate. The original/remake discussion carried out on this board hence incorporates a discursive strategy for defusing one interpretive community's systematic bid for symbolic power, seeking to contextualise this within a broader framework of meaning which reduces differences in taste culture to the matter of whichever film is first seen in biographical/individual terms. While cult fans continue to champion the superiority of *Ringu* over the Hollywood version, other posters' views in favour of the remake can be contained and tolerated by referring to 'bias theory'. This demonstrates a deep-rooted tension within the *Ring Forum* between the need to maintain subcultural boundaries – such that posters refer to 'people like us who usually find the originals first' or 'we, on this board' while othering 'clueless teens' and 'the average American Joe' – and the apparently simultaneous need to maintain cultural notions of liberal individualism in which everyone is freely entitled to their opinion. This clash between subcultural distinctions and an ideology of liberal individualism is played out through discourses of 'first viewers' (that is, cultists) versus 'first viewings' (or, individual preference). Cult fans can partly defuse their bid for distinction and subcultural authenticity by relating it to individualised and psychologised notions that they happened to see the original film first, while also explaining away the views of other horror fans posting to the message board via the same discursive manoeuvre. This appears to provide a levelled playing field for the free expression of opinion. Yet such an appearance is deceptive, since the cult fans' bid for distinction systematically hinges not only on seeing the original first but, as mikejonas is seemingly compelled to add, on seeing it 'before the remake came out'. Psychologistic and individualising discourses therefore do not entirely win out over those of the Japanese horror cinema fans' interpretive community.

I have argued that, in this case, subcultural distinction seems to become primarily temporal rather than spatial, with fans of cult Japanese horror representing their tastes as pre-mainstream rather than wholly anti-main-stream, and celebrating the eventual wider dissemination and distribution of their favoured texts. However, there is another dimension to these cult fans' appreciation of Japanese horror. As well as bidding for subcultural distinction via their status as 'first viewers', these fans also discuss cultural differences between American and Japanese horror. It is to this aspect of fan debate – potentially operating to reinstate the 'spatial' differences of 'anti-mainstream' readings – that I will turn in the next section.

EXPLORING JAPANESE HORROR:
CULTURAL SIMILARITIES VERSUS DIFFERENCES

It is striking that the film *Ringu* deals not merely with supernatural themes, but is more precisely concerned with the mediation and technologisation of ghostly forces:

Sadako's manifestations in the present . . . are significant because of the ways in which they depict the past emerging into the present via technological means . . . it is the VCR in particular that is exemplary of Japan's presence in the technological 'modern', with nearly 70% of the videocassette recorders produced worldwide coming from Japan.[26]

It could therefore be suggested that one of the underlying factors in the transnational appeal of *Ringu* lies in its twin equation of Japanese identity with superstition and technology. Potentially, the film plays into what David Morley and Kevin Robins have identified as a western ideology of 'techno-orientalism' where, within 'the political and cultural unconscious of the west, Japan has come to exist as the figure of empty and dehumanised technological power'.[27] However, depicting this ideology as a negative western view of Japan misses the point that *Ringu* is a Japanese film critiquing views of technologised modernity. Furthermore, *Ringu* is not alone in this; other key entries in Japan's post-*Ringu* 'psycho-horror' cycle, such as Sono Shion's *Suicide Circle* (2002) and Kurosawa Kiyoshi's *Kaïro* (2001), have been described as surveying 'the potentially cataclysmic effect that technology and the desensitisation of modern life can have on the populace of Japan'.[28] Rather than arguing that these films therefore resonate with negative western stereotypes of Japaneseness, it could be countered that there is a cultural homology operating here between Japanese and western fears of technologised society, such that cultural differences may become less significant than shared, transnational anxieties over media distortions and corruptions of 'the real'.[29]

The issue of pervasive mediation and its 'dangerous' effects is far from being a nationally specific concern: 'The international appeal of horror is perhaps linked to its tendency to favor symbolic situations over particular ones.'[30] The specific 'symbolic situation' here focuses on the powers of symbol-carrying media to virally 'infect' their audiences. As a type of what might be dubbed 'media horror', *Ringu* shares thematic affinities with American indie-horror films such as *The Last Broadcast* (Stefan Avalos and Lance Weiler, 1998), *The Blair Witch Project* (Daniel Myrick and Eduardo Sánchez, 1999) and Hollywood fare such as *Feardotcom* (William Malone, 2002). Some posters to the *Ring Forum* do indeed stress that *Ringu*'s themes are not dissimilar to those in US horror, for example: 'really, how unfamiliar or alien was the backstory? Izu was just another name for "Shelter Mountain" and the psychic phenomenon is not at all lost to Americans . . .'[31] Or posters occasionally follow the 'symbolic situations' style of argument:

I am North American, yet I was able to relate easily to the Japanese characters in Ringu. I feel that the story of Ring (generally speaking all versions of the Ring story) is very primal and most people react . . . similarly in situations that are life-threatening.[32]

Interestingly, it is nevertheless cultural difference rather than media- or technology-based cultural similarities on which Japanese horror fans posting to the *Ring Forum* predominantly focus. Evocations of shared generic structures and common 'primal' situations are dominated on the message board by discussions of Japanese–US differences. *Ringu* and *The Ring* are nominated as

> two very different movies made for two different cultures, if you like. The original plays with Japanese supernatural folklore . . . The remake is more 'westernised' and to make money it has to be more mainstream, and as such has to give more answers.[33]

> the original plot: i understand that nensha and other paranormal things are taken differently in Japan . . . it's like, everyone believes in them to some extent, but not openly . . . but it's not something to be doubted or dismissed either. So drawing conclusions quickly from ESP, rather than deeply investigating facts, makes sense. The remake plot: we needed rational facts along with paranormal explanations. The characters needed to maintain a sense of disbelief even to the very end, rather than pure acceptance of their fate. This introduced the nensha more subtly, which actually makes it more creepy, for a Westerner.[34]

These cult fans' readings of *Ringu* versus *The Ring* tend to stress reading-for-cultural-difference, certainly to the extent that posters repeatedly discuss the films' representations of '*nensha*' (literally, the 'thought-writing' displayed by Sadako), and focus on differences between western 'rationalism' and what is construed as a broader acceptance of the supernatural in Japanese culture. Posters also frequently raise general issue of cultural difference between American and Japanese cinema.[35]

Why, then, might these fans typically read for cultural difference, noting that they could, as suggested above, read instead for similarity? I want to suggest that by emphasising an awareness of Japanese cultural differences, US fans of Japanese horror cinema are able to align their cult distinctions, as an interpretive community, with this second axis of difference. Reading-for-cultural-difference works, therefore, as a homologous part of this audience's bid for a subcultural identity opposed to mainstream 'American' culture. By discussing topics such as *nensha*, these fans construct a reading of *Ringu* and *The Ring* that seeks to recuperate and bolster their anti-mainstream status.

This opposition to mainstream consumer culture, figured specifically as 'American teen' culture, is captured in postings that contrast Japanese horror to 'MTV' remakes:

> The Ring is a film that is aimed towards the MTV generation, its aim was to keep the attention of teens and twenty something year olds in a theatrical setting. The long pauses of silence, etc, of the original were disregarded.[36]

Although such a contrast does not go uncontested on the board – one reply to this point argues that *The Ring* 'is in no way an "mtv" film. That's an EASY term that asian film enthusiasts like to slap on certain american films'[37] – this opposition between 'valued' Japanese horror films and devalued 'MTV' movies nevertheless appears to sustain cult distinctions for many posters. Whereas US horror, and especially the remaking of Japanese originals, is represented as juvenile, excessively fast-paced and self-consciously 'stylish', Japanese horror is instead constructed as serious, reflective and less accessible to (or not meant for) the American teen market. Posters therefore discursively construct 'serious', 'adult' identities for their genre fandom, as opposed to Othered, teen and mainstream audience identities. This sentiment also emerges via the Japanese film aesthetics defended by fans:

> About the cultural issue. Japanese film-making usually relies on implied meaning, in opposition to American/Western filmmaking, where everything has to be stated . . . The story is literally told by the silence, the noises, the colors, the picture framing and camera movement.[38]

Again, US films are positioned as 'obvious', and thus as requiring less thought. Everything is allegedly clearly signposted for the mainstream/teen viewer, whereas one of the key 'differences' stressed by posters is that, by contrast, Japanese film retains an enigmatic quality. Although this reading-for-difference may, at times, appear itself to draw implicitly on stereotypes of Japanese 'inscrutability', its subcultural effectiveness arises from the fact that it grounds the fan audience's bid for anti-mainstream distinction. Cult Japanese horror is defined here – seemingly as an 'objective' matter of cultural difference – as 'difficult' rather than as 'obvious', as requiring close attention rather than signalling diegetic events and motivations directly for its readers. It is thus demarcated as culturally and aesthetically valuable (requiring audience labour, knowledge and reflection) rather than as disposable or low-cultural (where these qualities are read into 'mainstream' consumer culture and into so-called 'MTV' film).

That many of the fans posting to the Ring Forum defend the distinctiveness of their 'cult' readings by invoking 'difficult' transcultural interpretation is, I would argue, not at all unique to this message board. For example, similar sentiments are iterated in John Paul Catton's column on Japanese cinema for fantasy/horror cult prozine *The Third Alternative*:

> what makes modern Japanese horror so different . . . In a Japanese film we see the characters, we read the subtitles, we follow what happens to them; but there are depths which are hidden from us. There are dramatic and cultural cues which are behind the main action . . . which are just as important to the drama as the foreground action.[39]

The implication here is that these 'cues' may be hidden from 'mainstream' audiences, but they are likely to be apprehended by Japanese film enthusiasts. The articulation of reading-for-cult-status and reading-for-cultural-difference leaves some fans, including the founder of *Ringworld*, open to accusations of elitism from their fellow posters:

> It wasn't meant to sound as if I was speaking from a position of elitism, or to imply that your opinion somehow means less because you can't speak the language – I was just trying to illustrate that fluency in language and culture gives one a far more intimate look at the goings-on of a situation (story, acting/reactions) than if one were to rely exclusively on some outside source (subtitles . . .) to understand what one were viewing . . . Nor do I subscribe to the ideas of cinema snobbery, or that American cinema = dumb.[40]

The explicit need to deflect allegations of 'cinema snobbery' arises due to the fact that reading-for-cultural-difference is privileged by this fan interpretive community as a strategy for securing the distinctiveness of cult fan identities and interpretations (cf. An's (2001) argument that cult readings of Hong Kong films such as *The Killer* are actually (mis)readings that fail to appreciate cultural difference). But if such a strategy is used to devalue fans of *The Ring* and *Ringu* who are imagined as being closer to 'mainstream' consumer culture, then it surely has to be perceived as a form of cultural elitism. This is a reading based on denigrating the projected tastes and cultural identities of 'the average American Joe', 'clueless teens' and 'MTV' film consumers, all construed as enjoying shallow and immediate pop culture. The ultimate logic of this interpretive position is that it also necessarily pits cult fans who can speak the Japanese language against those who remain reliant on subtitles. Greater subcultural authenticity accrues to those, such as 'ring rasen loop' (this name referring to Suzuki's three original novels) who can demonstrate textual understanding ever more distanced from 'mainstream' consumers depicted as mindlessly and unintelligently 'American' in their cultural outlook and consumption patterns.

Although it may be tempting to celebrate US fan audiences' active readings of *Ringu* precisely because they are sensitive to cultural differences, such a univocally positive conclusion would fail to address the articulation of cult distinctions and reading-for-cultural-difference that occupies a dominant position on the *Ring Forum*'s 'Remake vs. Original' thread. In this case, other possible readings of *Ringu* (for example, as sharing certain codes and conventions with US horror, or as sharing connotations of 'media horror') appear to be relatively marginalised in favour of stressing cultists' knowledge of Japanese cinema and culture. 'Pre-mainstream' re-cuperations of cult status are thus bolstered by a return to national/cultural/spatial models of cultural distinction. These fans' reading positions outside 'the mainstream' are based on their identification with, and of, Japanese cultural identities and aesthetics.

Although US 'mainstream' audiences may gain access to the texts of Japanese horror cinema in the wake of popularising remakes (and this newfound popularity may indeed be partly embraced by cult fans), such a situation renders it subculturally important for cult fans to demarcate the boundaries around their readings, tastes and interpretive community. The *Ring Forum*, I have argued here, operates as part of those boundary-marking practices. Its postings work to exclude and devalue the interpretations of Othered US-mainstream audiences in a reversal of the logic of Morley and Robins's 'techno-orientalism'[41] that could, perhaps somewhat provocatively, be termed 'consumer-occidentalism'.

NOTES

1. Jankovich, Mark (2002) 'Cult Fictions: Cult Movies, Subcultural Capital and the Production of Cultural Distinction', *Cultural Studies*, 16:2, pp. 318–19.
2. For example, consider films by Dario Argento and Mario Bava; see Hutchings, Peter (2003) 'The Argento Effect', in Mark Jancovich, Antonio Lázaro Reboll, Julian Stringer and Andy Willis (eds), *Defining Cult Movies: The Cultural Politics of Oppositional Taste*, Manchester: Manchester University Press, pp. 127–41, and Karola (2003) 'Italian Cinema Goes to the Drive-In: The Intercultural Horrors of Mario Bava', in Gary D. Rhodes (ed.), *Horror at the Drive-In: Essays in Popular Americana*, Jefferson, NC and London: McFarland, pp. 211–37.
3. See An Jinsoo (2001) '*The Killer*: Cult Film and Transcultural (Mis)Reading', in Esther C. M. Yau (ed.), *At Full Speed: Hong Kong Cinema in a Borderless World*, Minneapolis, MN: University of Minnesota Press, pp. 95–113.
4. Hutchings, p. 138.
5. See Hills, Matt (2002) *Fan Cultures*, London and New York: Routledge; Hills, Matt (2003) '*Star Wars* in Fandom, Film Theory, and the Museum: The Cultural

Status of the Cult Blockbuster', in Julian Stringer (ed.), *Movie Blockbusters*, New York and London: Routledge, pp. 178–89; Hollows, Joanne (2003) 'The Masculinity of Cult', in Mark Jancovich, Antonio Lázaro Reboll, Julian Stringer and Andy Willis (eds), *Defining Cult Movies: The Cultural Politics of Oppositional Taste*, Manchester: Manchester University Press, pp. 35–53; Jancovich, Mark (2000) ' "A Real Shocker": Authenticity, Genre and the Struggle for Distinction', *Continuum*, 14:1, pp. 23–35; Jancovich (2002); and Sconce, Jeffrey (1995) ' "Trashing the Academy": Taste, Excess, and an Emerging Politics of Cinematic Style', in *Screen*, 36:4, Winter, pp. 371–93.

6. As opposed to anime. For a study of anime and its reception by US fans, see Napier, Susan J. (2001b) *Anime from* Akira *to* Princess Mononoke: *Experiencing Contemporary Japanese Animation*, New York: Palgrave.

7. See Osmond, Andrew (2003) 'Ringing the Changes', in *Shivers*, 102, p. 20; and Daniel, Rob and Dave Wood (2003) 'Pain Threshold: The Cinema of Takashi Miike', in Steven Jay Schneider (ed.), *Fear Without Frontiers: Horror Cinema Across the Globe*, Guildford: FAB Press, pp. 285–91.

8. Catton, John Paul (2002) 'Japan's Dark Lanterns', *The Third Alternative*, 31, p. 31.

9. In fact, the Japanese-South Korean film version, *The Ring Virus* (dir: Kim Dong-bin, 1999) is actually more faithful to Suzuki's novel than Nakata's better-known Japanese version, both in its emphasis on connotations of the viral and in its representation of Sadako.

10. See Brooker, Will (2003) 'Rescuing *Strange Days*: Fan Reaction to a Critical and Commercial Failure', in Deborah Jermyn and Sean Redmond (eds), *The Cinema of Kathryn Bigelow: Hollywood Transgressor*, London and New York: Wallflower Press, pp. 198–219; and Gauntlett, David (2000) 'The Web Goes to the Pictures', in David Gauntlett (ed.) *web.studies*, London: Arnold, pp. 82–7.

11. See Hoxter, Julian (2000) 'Taking Possession: Cult Learning in *The Exorcist*', in Graeme Harper and Xavier Mendik (eds), *Unruly Pleasures: The Cult Film and Its Critics*, Guildford: FAB Press, pp. 173–85; Hutchings (2003); and Jancovich (2000).

12. See Baym, Nancy K. (2000) *Tune In, Log On: Soaps, Fandom and Online Community*, London: Sage; Bird, S. Elizabeth (2003) *The Audience in Everyday Life: Living in a Media World*, New York and London: Routledge; Hodkinson, Paul (2003) ' "Net.Goth": Internet Communication and (Sub)Cultural Boundaries', in David Muggleton and Rupert Weinzierl (eds), *The Post-Subcultures Reader*, Oxford and New York: Berg, pp. 285–98; Jenkins, Henry (2002), 'Interactive Audiences?', in Dan Harries (ed.), *The New Media Book*, London: BFI Publishing, pp. 157–70; Ross, Karen and Virginia Nightingale (2003) *Media and Audiences: New Perspectives*, Maidenhead: Open University Press; and Zweerink, Amanda and Sarah N. Gatson (2002) 'www.buffy.com: Cliques, Boundaries and Hierarchies in an Internet Community', in Rhonda V. Wilcox and David Lavery (eds.), *Fighting the Forces: What's at Stake in Buffy the Vampire Slayer*, New York and Oxford: Rowman and Littlefield, pp. 239–49.

13. Hollows, pp. 41 and 48.

14. Doria4 (2002) 'Remake versus Original debate', *Ringworld's Ring Forum*, http://ringworld.somrux.com. Posted 14 November.

15. NeighborTotoro (2003) 'Remake versus Original debate', *Ringworld's Ring Forum*, http://ringworld.somrux.com. Posted 10 March.

16. Isoline (2002) 'Asian Horror Remake Watch Thread', *Ringworld's Ring Forum*, http://ringworld.somrux.com. Posted 14 November.

17. See Hills (2003); Hunt, Nathan (2003) 'The Importance of Trivia: Ownership,

Exclusion and Authority in Science Fiction Fandom', in Mark Jancovich, Antonio Lázaro Reboll, Julian Stringer and Andy Willis (eds.), *Defining Cult Movies: The Cultural Politics of Oppositional Taste*, Manchester: Manchester University Press, pp. 185–201; and Wu, Harmony (2003) 'Trading in Horror, Cult and Matricide: Peter Jackson's Phenomenal Bad Taste and New Zealand Fantasies of Inter/National Cinematic Success', in Mark Jancovich, Antonio Lázaro Reboll, Julian Stringer and Andy Willis (eds), *Defining Cult Movies: The Cultural Politics of Oppositional Taste*, Manchester: Manchester University Press, pp. 84–108.

18. Isoline (2002) 'Asian Horror Remake Watch Thread', *Ringworld's Ring Forum*, http://ringworld.somrux.com. Posted 14 November. My italics.

19. Dogg Thang (2003) 'Remake versus Original debate', *Ringworld's Ring Forum*, http://ringworld.somrux.com. Posted 1 October. My italics.

20. Nox Noctus (2003) 'Remake versus Original debate', *Ringworld's Ring Forum*, http://ringworld.somrux.com. Posted 8 February.

21. See Thornton, Sarah (1995) *Club Cultures*, Cambridge: Polity Press.

22. Jancovich (2000) pp. 28–9.

23. mikejonas (2002) 'Remake versus Original debate', *Ringworld's Ring Forum*, http://ringworld.somrux.com. Posted 2 December.

24. Interferon (2003) 'Remake versus Original debate', *Ringworld's Ring Forum*, http://ringworld.somrux.com. Posted 3 July.

25. Tourneur Jr (2003) 'Remake versus Original debate', *Ringworld's Ring Forum*, http://ringworld.somrux.com. Posted 17 January.

26. Tateishi Ramie (2003) 'The Contemporary Japanese Horror Film Series: *Ring* and *Eko Eko Azarak*', in Steven Jay Schneider (ed.), *Fear Without Frontiers: Horror Cinema Across the Globe*, Guildford: FAB Press, p. 298.

27. Morley, David and Kevin Robins (1995) *Spaces of Identity: Global Media, Electronic Landscapes and Cultural Boundaries*, London and New York: Routledge, pp. 169–70.

28. Crawford, Travis (2003) 'The Urban Techno-Alienation of Sion Sono's *Suicide Club*', in Steven Jay Schneider (ed.), *Fear Without Frontiers: Horror Cinema Across the Globe*, Guildford: FAB Press, p. 305; see also Catton, p. 31.

29. Napier, Susan J. (1996) *The Fantastic in Modern Japanese Literature: The Subversion of Modernity*, London and New York: Routledge, p. 223.

30. Karola, p. 214.

31. mikejonas (2002) 'Remake versus Original debate', *Ringworld's Ring Forum*, http://ringworld.somrux.com. Posted 2 December.

32. Wizard2 (2002) 'Remake versus Original debate', *Ringworld's Ring Forum*, http://ringworld.somrux.com. Posted 2 December.

33. Gazmoviegeek (2002) 'Remake versus Original debate', *Ringworld's Ring Forum*, http://ringworld. somrux.com. Posted 27 February.

34. mellybeanTC (2003) 'Remake versus Original debate', *Ringworld's Ring Forum*, http://ringworld.somrux.com. Posted 2 June.

35. See, for instance, Interferon (2003) 'Remake versus Original debate', *Ringworld's Ring Forum*, http://ringworld. somrux.com. Posted 21 June.

36. Wizard2 (2003) 'Remake versus Original debate', *Ringworld's Ring Forum*, http://ringworld.somrux.com. Posted 2 December.

37. Nox Noctis (2002) 'Remake versus Original debate', *Ringworld's Ring Forum*, http://ringworld.somrux.com. Posted 9 December.

38. Kitano (2003) 'Remake versus Original debate', *Ringworld's Ring Forum*, http://ringworld.somrux.com. Posted 3 July.

39. Catton, p. 31.

40. ring rasen loop, admin, ring guru (2003) 'Remake versus Original debate', *Ringworld's Ring Forum*, http://ringworld.somrux.com. Posted 15 March.
41. See Morley and Robins.

13. CASE STUDY: CINEMATIC HYBRIDITY IN SHIMIZU TAKASHI'S *JU-ON: THE GRUDGE*

Jay McRoy

FILMMAKING WITH A VENGEANCE

Long a staple within Japanese literary and dramatic arts, the *onryou*, or 'avenging ghost' motif, remains an exceedingly popular and vital component of contemporary Japanese horror cinema. Drawing on a plurality of religious traditions, including Shintoism and Christianity, as well as plot devices from traditional theatre (for instance Noh theatre's *shunen-* [revenge-] and *shura-mono* [ghost-plays], and Kabuki theatre's tales of the supernatural [or *kaidan*]), these narratives of incursion by the spectral into the realm of the ordinary for the purposes of exacting revenge continue to find new articulations, as well as new audiences, courtesy of visually arresting and internationally acclaimed works by directors such as Nakata Hideo (*Ringu*, 1998 and *Dark Water*, 2002). Like the myriad of cultural texts from which Nakata draws his inspiration, including now 'classic' films such as Shindô Kaneto's *Onibaba* (1964) and Kobayashi Masaki's *Kwaidan* (1965), these recent revisions of the 'avenging spirit' trope continue to relate tales of 'wronged', primarily female entities who return to avenge themselves upon those who harmed them. The targets of these angry spirits' rage, however, are often multiple, and careful analyses of the focus of the spirits' wrath, as well as the motivations behind their actions, provide valuable insights into the historical, political and economic logics informing current socio-cultural tensions between nostalgic imaginings of a 'traditional Japanese' past and the equally illusory threat and/or promise of an ever-emerging technological, global and postmodern Japan. Furthermore, although exorcising, or even temporarily placating, the 'avenging ghosts' may prove nearly impossible, containment is frequently depicted as achievable, if only – as in Nakata's *Ringu* – through a process of eternal deferment.

Shimizu Takashi's *Ju-on: The Grudge* (2002) extends the *onryou* motif in important new directions. The initial 'big screen' re-imaging of Shimizu's two 1998 straight-to-video precursors, *Ju-on 1* (*The Curse*) and *Ju-on 2* (*Curse 2*), *Ju-on: The Grudge* is a curious filmic hybrid, combining carefully chosen aesthetic trappings of western – particularly US – horror films with visual and narrative tropes long familiar to fans of Japanese horror cinema. Such a combination of filmmaking approaches seems appropriate when one considers that Shimizu Takashi is, by his own admission, largely influenced by US 'splatter' movie icons like *A Nightmare on Elm Street*'s Freddy Kruger and *Friday the 13th*'s Jason,[1] as well as 'an alumnus of the Film School of Tokyo' where he flourished under the tutelage of 'horror maestro' Kurosawa Kiyoshi and *Ringu*'s scriptwriter Takahashi Hiroshi.[2] This meshing of US and Japanese influences is crucial to understanding not only the film's significant appeal in western markets, but also Shimizu's aesthetic as a director of cinematic horror. Additionally, this visual mélange is important since physiological, social and narratological hybridity, as well as the interstitial spaces from which such hybrids emerge, inform not only *Ju-on*'s content, but also how the film posits changes in the institution of the family as at once the result of, and a barometer for, larger socio-cultural transformations.

Of course, tales of horror and monstrosity have long concerned themselves with the notion of hybridity in their exploration of those regions where categories fail to maintain their integrity. Ghosts, for example, are by their very definition liminal entities negotiating the supposedly unbridgeable gulf between the world of the living and the realm of the dead; likewise, monsters are perpetual scramblers of social codes, often troubling the nebulous, perhaps oxymoronic distinction between the 'human' and the 'animal', or the 'human' and the 'non-human'. By combining, in his own words, 'an American and Japanese style'[3] of horror cinema, Shimizu creates a hybrid of the US slasher film and the Japanese *kaidan*. Rather than a single, individual ghost returning to seek revenge, *Ju-on: The Grudge*, through a web of primarily non-linear, episodic narratives, confronts viewers with a mother and 'housewife', Kayako, and son, Toshio, one (or possibly both) of whom was slaughtered by their patriarch, Takeo. Restless, they haunt both the house in which they died – a location that can be understood as a microcosm of a Japanese culture in transformation – and the lives of those mortals unlucky enough to enter their abode. The murdered mother and child are at once ethereal and corporeal; they are not merely ghosts, but not fully monsters in the term's most conventional sense. As liminal, hybrid entities demanding the attention of those they encounter, they are perhaps the most appropriate models for exploring a radically transforming Japanese culture in which tensions between an undead past and the unborn future find articulation in the transforming family of a haunted, interstitial present.

HYBRID MOMENTS

The symbiotic relationship between US and Japanese cinema is perhaps the most creative and consistent in the history of motion pictures. Of course, at the epicentre of any discussion of this topic looms the presence of legendary director Kurosawa Akira, whose *Stray Dog* (1949) and *High and Low* (1963) remain vital experiments with the primarily US style known as 'film noir', and whose more canonical works, such as *The Seven Samurai* (1951) and *The Hidden Fortress* (1958), have been famously remade in the US as *The Magnificent Seven* (John Sturges, 1960) and *Star Wars* (George Lucas, 1977) respectively. When one factors in such epic co-productions as *Tora! Tora! Tora!* (Richard Fleischer and Fukasaku Kinji, 1970) and *Gojira 2000* (Okawara Takao, 1999), as well as the increasingly prevalent interconnections between Japanese anime and western science fiction texts, one soon discovers that even a cursory investigation of this phenomenon could fill an entire volume of film scholarship and, most certainly, exceeds the scope of this essay.

Recognising the debts that these two crucial film industries owe to one another, however, is critical to this essay's project. At the very least, it allows us to advance some preliminary theories as to why *Ju-on: The Grudge* has so quickly garnered a modest cult following in the US and other western markets – as evidenced by the impending Hollywood remake, starring *Buffy the Vampire Slayer*'s Sarah Michelle Gellar and helmed by Shimizu Takashi himself. If, as Shimizu claims, US horror film series like *Friday the 13th* and *A Nightmare on Elm Street* have impacted his conceptualisation of cinematic horror, then might *Ju-on: The Grudge*'s international success be a result of Shimizu's skilful weaving of the visual logics behind what Vera Dika and Carol Clover call the 'stalker cycle'[4] with filmic sequences and narrative motifs often associated with Japanese cinema? By acknowledging the hybridity informing Shimizu's technical approach to cinematic horror, including his manipulation of *mise-en-scène*, we gain critical insight into a larger socio-cultural economy of fear predicated upon anxieties over the illusory integrity of the Japanese social body. As Marilyn Ivy notes, this imagined wholeness is fundamental to modern, and pre-modern, perceptions of cultural and national identity. The Japanese social body, for Ivy, is a hybrid entity that often attempts to deny the complex amalgamations that have, and continue to, constitute it:

> The hybrid realities of Japan today – of multiple border crossings and transnational interchanges in the worlds of trade, aesthetics, and sciences – are contained within dominant discourses on cultural purity and nondifference, and in nostalgic appeals to premodernity: what makes the Japanese so different from everybody else makes them identical to each other; what threatens the self-sameness is often marked temporally as the intrusively modern, spatially as foreign. Although those discourses are being altered by the effects of advanced capitalism . . . they have proved remarkably resilient as they haunt the possibilities of a postnationalist consciousness in contemporary Japan.[5]

Ivy's overarching motif of 'haunt'ing, both in the above quote and throughout her book, *Discourses of the Vanishing: Modernity, Phantasm, Japan*, is instructive in that it represents, and contributes to, a discourse of a returning repressed. Moreover, whether that which is sublimated and/or temporarily contained takes the form of a potentially nation-effacing globalism, or the increasingly important role of women who 'manage the home (even when they labor outside)',[6] horror cinema marks the ideal forum for the metaphoric expression of concerns over an indiscrete (or hybrid) national, social or corporeal body.

The grainy opening montage of Shimizu Takashi's *Ju-on: The Grudge* reveals this latter concern over the shifting role of women in the home, a location which serves as the epicentre of the *onryou*'s unquenchable rage. Beginning with establishing shots of a seemingly anonymous residential street, followed by low-angle exterior shots of a vine-clad house, Shimizu then cuts to a rapid, disorienting montage. The images that flash across the screen range from extreme close-ups of a mouth gnawing bloody fingertips, the blade of a box-cutter clicking slowly out of its plastic casing and Kayako's lifeless eyes framed by streaks of blood, to medium and full shots of a crazed Takeo turning about slowly, the young Toshio drawing pictures of a long-haired woman on a sheet of paper before scampering away to hide in a closet, and a black cat screeching as it is grabbed roughly by the back of its neck. Intentionally disorienting and confusing, these images allow the audience a privileged, if ultimately incomprehensible, glimpse into the violent act that has most likely resulted in the eponymous grudge, a 'curse' that, as the film's title sequence tells us, originates when one 'dies in the grip of a powerful rage' and then spreads virally, killing all those with whom the spirits come into contact and, in the process, birthing new curses. It also anticipates the film's larger organisational logic, a tangled and non-linear narrative that, in its episodic construction, resembles the horror manga of Ito Junji, particularly the vignettes that comprise his anthology *The Flesh-Colored Horror* (2001) or that punctuate his larger collected series, *Tomie* (2001) and *Uzumaki* (2002–3).

The motivation behind Takeo's murderous assault, we eventually learn, is his psychotic anger over Kayako's suspected adultery; while the film's narrative makes it clear that the wife died at her husband's hands, exactly how Toshio met his fate is left vague. Toshio is described only as having 'disappeared', but from the film's first extended vignette, it is clear that both mother and son haunt the site of the carnage presented in the film's opening sequence, as well as the lives of those who move into, or even temporarily visit, the home. This premise reveals a palpable masculine anxiety associated with a rapidly transforming social landscape and its impact upon long established gender roles, a dread exacerbated by the culture's 'strong patrilinear emphasis', as well as women's paradoxical role as 'both a source of danger to the norm and the very means of perpetuating that norm'.[7] If, as Susan Napier argues, Japanese men '[c]onfronted with more powerful and independent women . . . have suffered their own form of identity crises',[8] then the core of Shimizu's film is the ultimate nightmare for a phallocentric culture: the patriarchal paradigm assaulted at its very foundations. Central to *Ju-on: The Grudge*, then, are those social transformations linked with the radical changes in the socio-cultural landscape that followed the bursting of the nation's 'bubble economy' in the early 1990s – an implosion that has resulted in not only transforming notions of gender roles, but also what cultural theorists like Hayao Kawai identify as the collapse of the 'Japanese-style extended family'[9] and the rise of domestic violence.[10] One can read the fragmented, impressionistic opening montage as illustrative of a profound social disorientation, but one can also comprehend the sequence's implied violence as emblematic of a larger compulsion to re-establish and/or maintain a regime of masculine dominance.

Of course, similar 'gender trouble' has long informed western horror cinema, and so Shimizu's occasional appropriation of visual tropes from US slasher films of the late 1970s and early 1980s seems apposite, particularly given both the often neoconservative agendas of such texts[11] and the shifting alignment of the spectator's gaze. This is not to suggest that apparently ideologically recuperative productions lack the potential, in spite of themselves, to advance progressive political perspectives. As Douglas Kellner notes, even the most 'conservative' horror films not only 'put on display both the significant dreams and nightmares of a culture and the ways that the culture is attempting to channel them to maintain its present relations of power and domination', but also expose the 'hopes and fears that contest dominant hegemonic and hierarchical relations of power'.[12] Nevertheless, the US horror film icons Shimizu cites as inspirational (*A Nightmare on Elm Street*'s Freddie Kruger and *Friday the 13th*'s Jason), as well as the slasher film/'stalker cycle' subgenre from which they arise, are veritable repositories of 'repressed body anxiet[ies] . . . erupting with a vengeance'.[13] In this sense, even if these films from which Shimizu borrows seemingly promote a certain political or ideological agenda by 'punishing' certain behaviours (for instance, sexual promiscuity or drug use) while 'rewarding' others (chastity, self-reliance, the willingness to resort to violence when necessary),[14] it remains possible also to view these texts as engaging in 'an unprecedented assault on all that Bourgeois culture is supposed to cherish – like ideological apparatuses of the family and the school'.[15]

As with the US horror tradition that influenced Shimizu, it is possible to interpret *Ju-on: The Grudge* as both conservative and progressive; in this way, Shimizu's film exposes many of the socio-cultural anxieties that permeate Japan's increasingly hydrid, transitional culture. At times, the film's articulation of an apparent nostalgia for disappearing 'traditions' in the face of an emerging 'modern' socio-economic climate resonates with a conservative ideology that borders on the reactionary. A sombre, Ozu-like meditation on generational differences and the collapse of the extended family finds expression in the disquieting image of a neglected elderly woman sitting passively near her own faeces-soiled bedding, while in other scenes, shirking social workers and inept law enforcement officers suffer the demonic Kayako and Toshio's wrath. But Shimizu's film also advances a critique of a Japan still very much steeped in patriarchal conventions. While their return to haunt the realm of the living evokes the 'avenging spirit' motif familiar to viewers of Japanese horror cinema, Kayako and Toshio's ultimately uncontainable wrath suggests an irrepressible hostility towards an abusive and antiquated 'official culture, specifically . . . the norms and values of patriarch[y]'.[16] This latter gesture, as Barbara Creed notes, recurs consistently in western horror cinema, often revealing a 'symbolic', anti-authoritarian hostility towards an inflexible 'social body'.[17]

What sets *Ju-on: The Grudge* apart from other works of Japanese horror cinema, and what might be most responsible for the film's international appeal, is the filmic and transcultural hybridity embodied by the figures of Kayako and Toshio. Not quite ghosts in the strictest sense of the *onryou* or *kaidan* tradition, but not quite conventional biological monsters either, this other-worldly, mother-centred family merges a dangerous corporeality (they can physically attack and manipulate their victim's bodies) with an eerie spectral quality without adhering absolutely to one convention or the other. Furthermore, this uncanny mother and son become even more disturbing, as well as less exclusively linked to traditional Japanese horror cinema, when one factors in Shimizu's masterful camera work and brilliant control of the film's *mise-en-scène*.

In keeping with 'classic' and contemporary works of Japanese horror, Shimizu allows tension to build slowly, almost contemplatively, throughout *Ju-on: The Grudge*'s numerous, non-linear episodes. Many of the expected, culturally specific trappings of filmic terror are present: long black tresses framing wide staring eyes, ominous *tatami* shots of sliding closet doors, shadowy apparitions that render their victims virtually paralyzed with fear. However, true to his roots as 'an eighties splatter movie kid',[18] Shimizu also incorporates a slasher/'stalker' film aesthetic throughout *Ju-on: The Grudge*, most obviously via the occasional alignment of the viewer's gaze with not only the central protagonist's perspective, but that of Kakayo and Toshio as well. Such compositions and camera movements allow us, by turns, to 'stalk' and 'be stalked', a visual motif almost exclusively applied to what Shimizu refers to as 'splatter movies' or 'monster stories'.[19] This collision of 'an American and Japanese style'[20] creates a cinematic hybrid that appeals to viewers familiar with the visual iconography and cinematography of both Japanese and US horror cinema. This is not to suggest that *Ju-on: The Grudge* would meet with success if released widely in the US. Shimizu's film is very much a product of contemporary Japanese culture and, as I shall discuss in this chapter's final section, the commercial success or failure of the forthcoming US adaptation will rest in Shimizu Takashi's ability to retain the lessons he learned from viewing works of US horror cinema and to translate his tale for a culture that, informed by different expectations, nevertheless possess a similar desire to be scared.

Lastly, by vacillating between limiting what we see and revealing the objects of our fear in groundbreaking ways that separate him aesthetically from other directors, Shimizu creates a text that may very well alter forever the way that some viewers process cinematic horror. By frequently relegating frightening images to the extreme edges of the frame, thereby investing them with the power of a fleeting, yet troubling figure glimpsed peripherally but never completely, Shimizu artfully manipulates the audience's gaze, creating the impression that we may have just witnessed a flash of something disquieting – as if from the corner of our collective eye. During other moments, most particularly the climactic sequences that inevitably bring each of the film's episodes to a sudden close, Shimizu culminates our rising dread by propelling us face to face with Kayako and Toshio in all their monstrous alterity. Finally, *Ju-on: The Grudge* is a film that disallows its characters and, by extension, its audience, access to those conventional 'safe spaces' to which people most commonly retreat when the tension escalates or becomes too much to take. Peering through the fingers covering one's face does not distance the imperilled spectator from that which is frightening; rather, it forces immediate confrontation with the horrific. Likewise, pulling the covers up over one's head does not provide a buffer zone but, instead, reveals that the monster you most fear has been in the bed with you the whole time.

JAPANESE HORROR CINEMA AND THE POLITICS OF ADAPTATION

The increasing popularity of Japanese horror cinema outside Japan is a testament not only to the unique and compelling vision of directors like Shimizu Takashi, Nakata Hideo, Kurosawa Kiyoshi and Miike Takashi, but also to the stale redundancy that has become an all too familiar trait in horror films produced within major 'western' studio systems, especially Hollywood. With the success of Gore Verbinski's remake of Nakata's *Ringu*, North America and Europe seem primed for an influx of horror titles that find their inspiration in, or are themselves direct remakes of, popular Japanese horror films. Such productions, however, risk alienating audiences through the application of visual and narrative tropes most frequently associated with Japanese cinema; additionally, in an attempt to reduce the Japanese films' perceived 'difference', filmmakers can imperil, through heavy-handed direction, the very aesthetic and narrative content that render the original texts effectively unsettling or terrifying. Consequently, directors (including Japanese filmmakers) drawn by the allure of bringing Asian horror films to western markets must account for the cultural specificity of certain themes and motifs and *adapt* or, perhaps more accurately, *translate* (rather than literally *remake*) the original film for their audiences. This process, however, is a risky one, for if directors attempt to overcompensate for these cultural particularities, they may end up reproducing the very stagnant and repetitious motifs that have led to the current deluge of unimaginative sequels and bland, formulaic narratives.

Successful transnational adaptations, then, must be translations in the literal sense of the term, yet avoid spiralling irrevocably into the realm of 'western' cinema cliché that resulted in George Sluizer's clumsy 'Hollywoodised' rehashing of his brilliant *Spoorloos* (or *The Vanishing*, 1988), or John Badham's uninspired *Point of No Return* (1993), a tamer, less morally ambiguous revisioning of Luc Besson's international hit, *La Femme Nikita* (1990). At the time of this writing, how Shimizu Takashi reworks *Ju-on: The Grudge* for an expansive western audience remains to be seen. The modest international success of the film's current incarnation bodes well for the remake, as does Shimizu's obvious understanding of US and Japanese horror film conventions, as well as how these traditions' aesthetic practices can be variably combined for dramatic effect.

Ideally, however, the best way to experience the distinctive tension and visceral thrills contemporary Japanese horror cinema offers is to view the films as their directors intended, experiencing the increasingly wide variety of inventive narratives and striking images with, at the very least, an introductory understanding of the genre's major aesthetic and thematic trends as they relate to Japanese culture and its various cinematic traditions.

NOTES

1. Macias, Patrick (2003) 'The Scariest Horror Ever? "Juon" Director Takashi Shimizu Interview', *Japattack*, http://japattack.com/japattack/film/juon_itv.html.
2. Sharp, Jasper (2002) 'Juon', *Midnighteye: The Latest and Best in Japanese Cinema*, 12:23, http://www.midnighteye.com/reviews/juon.shtml.
3. Macias.
4. See Dika, Vera (1987) 'The Stalker Film, 1978–81', in Gregory A. Waller (ed.), *American Horrors: Essays on the Modern American Horror Film*. Urbana and Chicago, IL: University of Illinois Press, and Clover, Carol J. (1992) *Men, Women, and Chainsaws: Gender in the Modern Horror Film*. London: BFI; Princeton, NJ: Princeton University Press.
5. Ivy, Marilyn (1995) *Discourses of the Vanishing: Modernity, Phantasm, Japan*, Chicago: University of Chicago Press, p. 9.
6. Allison, Ann (2000) *Permitted and Prohibited Desires: Mothers, Comics, and Censorship in Japan*, Berkeley and Los Angeles, CA: University of California Press, p. 174.
7. Martinez, D. P. (1998) 'Introduction: Gender, Shifting Boundaries and Global Culture', in D. P. Martinez (ed.), *The Worlds of Japanese Popular Culture: Gender, Shifting Boundaries and Global Cultures*, Cambridge: Cambridge University Press, p. 7.
8. Napier, Susan J. (2001b) *Anime from* Akira *to* Princess Mononoke, New York: Palgrave, p. 80.
9. Kawai Hayao (1986) 'Violence in the Home: Conflict between Two Principles: Maternal and Paternal', in T. S. Lebra and W. P. Lebra (eds), *Japanese Culture and Behavior*, Honolulu, HI: University of Hawaii Press, p. 303.
10. Ibid., p. 306.
11. See Sharrett, Christopher (1993) 'The Horror Film in Neoconservative Culture', *Journal of Popular Film and Television*, 21:3, pp. 100–10.
12. Kellner, Douglas (1995) *Media Culture: Cultural Studies, Identity and the Politics Between the Modern and the Postmodern*, London and New York: Routledge, p. 111.
13. Dery, Marc (1997) *Escape Velocity: Cyberculture at the End of the Century*, New York: Grove Press, p. 233.
14. For a more advanced and specific expansion of this premise, see Dika (1987) and Clover (1992).
15. Modleski, Tania (1986) 'The Terror of Pleasure: The Contemporary Horror Film and Postmodern Theory', in Tania Modleski (ed.), *Studies in Entertainment: Critical Approaches to Mass Culture*, Bloomington and Indianapolis, IN: Indiana University Press, p. 158.
16. Creed, Barbara (1995) 'Horror and the Carnivalesque: The Body Monstrous', in Leslie Devereaux and Roger Hillman (eds), *Fields of Vision: Essays in Film Studies, Visual Anthropology, and Photography*, Berkeley, CA: University of California Press.

17. Ibid., p. 146.
18. Macias.
19. Ibid.
20. Ibid.

FILMOGRAPHY: JAPANESE HORROR FILMS AND THEIR DVD AVAILABILITY IN THE UK AND US

Gareth Evans and Jay McRoy

Note: This filmography lists several crucial contemporary Japanese horror films that have yet to find distribution through either US- or UK-based companies. Happily, many of these titles are available, complete with English subtitles, through the following highly reputable on-line companies: Asian Cult Cinema (www.asiancult.com), HK Flix (www.hkflix.com) and Poker Industries (www.pokerindustries.com).

A

Title: *All Night Long 1*
Director: Matsumura Katsuya
Starring: Kadota Eisuke, Suzuki Ryosuke, Hino Toshiki, Takagi Mio, Tagushi Tomoroh
Studio distribution: Japan Shock DVD Entertainment (UK and US)
Running time: 90 minutes
Year of DVD release: 2001

Title: *All Night Long 2: Atrocity*
Director: Matsumura Katsuya
Starring: Endo Masa, Kadomatsu Kanori, Hino Toshiki, Takagi Mio, Tagushi Tomoroh

Studio distribution: Japan Shock DVD Entertainment (UK and US)
Running time: 78 minutes
Year of DVD release: 2001

Title: *All Night Long 3: The Final Chapter*
Director: Matsumura Katsuya
Starring: Kitagawa Yuji, Kadomatsu Kanori, Taguchi Tomoroh
Studio distribution: Japan Shock DVD Entertainment (UK and US)
Running time: 83 minutes
Year of DVD release: 2001

Title: *An Actor's Revenge*
Director: Ichikawa Kon
Starring: Hasegawa Kazuo, Yamamoto Fujiko
Studio distribution: BFI (UK)
Running time: 108 minutes
Year of DVD release: 2003

Title: *Angel Dust*
Director: Ishii Sogo
Starring: Minani Kaho, Kamatsu Takeshi, Toyokawa Etsushi
Studio distribution: Panorama Entertainment (UK)
Running time: 116 minutes
Year of DVD release: 2001

Title: *Angel of Darkness Collection*: vol. 1 to vol. 4 (a.k.a. *Sex Beast Teacher* [*Injukyoushi*])
Vol. 1 director: Mitsunori Hattori
Starring: Akira Seo, Ayu Shinoharu
Vol. 2 director: Atsushi Shimizu
Starring: Rika Mizutani, Mayu Nakata
Vol. 3 director: Mitsunori Hattori
Starring: Kanori Kadomatsu, Rika Mizutani
Vol. 4 director: Mitsunori Hattori
Starring: Chiyuri Matsuda, Marina Yabuki
Studio distribution: ADV Films (US)
Running time: vol. 1 70 minutes; vol. 2 70 minutes; vol. 3 72 minutes; vol. 4 76 minutes
Year of DVD release: 1994–6

Title: *Another Heaven*
Director: Iida Jôji
Starring: Eguchi Yousuke, Harada Yoshio

Studio Distribution: Artsmagic Ltd (UK); MTI Home Video (US)
Running Time: 132 minutes
Year of DVD Release: 2003

Title: *Audition*
Director: Miike Takashi
Starring: Ishibashi Ryo, Eihi Shiina
Studio distribution: Metro Tartan (UK); Chimera Entertainment (US)
Running time: 111 minutes (UK); 115 minutes (US)
Year of DVD release: 2001

B

Title: *Babycart at the River Styx*
Director: Misumi Kenji
Starring: Wakyama Tomisaburo, Tomikawa Akihiro
Studio distribution: Artsmagic Ltd (UK); Koch Vision Entertainment (US)
Running time: 85 minutes
Year of DVD release: 2000

Title: *Babycart in Peril*
Director: Buiichi Saito
Starring: Wakayama Tomisaburo, Tomikawa Akihiro
Studio distribution: Artsmagic Ltd (UK); Koch Vision Entertainment (US)
Running time: 82 minutes
Year of DVD release: 2000

Title: *Babycart in the Land of Demons*
Director: Misumi Kenji
Starring: Wakayama Tomisaburo, Tomikawa Akihiro
Studio distribution: Artsmagic Ltd (UK); Koch Vision Entertainment (US)
Running time: 89 minutes
Year of DVD release: 2001

Title: *Babycart to Hades*
Director: Misumi Kenji
Starring: Wakayama Tomisaburo, Tomikawa Akihiro
Studio distribution: Artsmagic Ltd (UK); Koch Vision Entertainment (US)
Running time: 89 minutes
Year of DVD release: 2000

Title: *Babycart White Heaven in Hell*
Director: Kuroda Yoshiyuki
Starring: Wakyama Tomisaburo, Tomikawa Akihiro

Studio distribution: Artsmagic Ltd (UK); Koch Vision Entertainment (US)
Running time: 84 minutes
Year of DVD release: 2001

Title: *Battle Heater*
Director: Iida Jôji
Starring: Kawai Pappara, Enomoto Akira
Studio distribution: Artsmagic Ltd (UK)
Running time: 93 minutes
Year of DVD release: 2004

Title: *Battle Royale*
Director: Fukasaku Kinji
Starring: Fujiwara Tetsuya, Maeda Aki
Studio distribution: Metro Tartan (UK)
Running time: 109 minutes
Year of DVD release: 2001

Title: *Battle Royale* (Special Edition Director's Cut)
Director: Fukasaku Kinji
Starring: Fujiwara Tetsuya, Maeda Aki
Studio distribution: Metro Tartan (UK)
Running time: 117 minutes
Year of DVD release: 2002

Title: *Battle Royale II: Requiem*
Director: Fukasaku Kenji and Fukasaku Kenta
Starring: Kitano Takeshi, Fujiwara Tatsuya, Maeda Ai, Oshinari Shugo,
    Sakai Ayana, Takeuchi Riki, Maeda Aki
Studio distribution: Not yet released in UK or US
Running time: 133 minutes
Year of DVD release: 2003

Title: *Beautiful Girl Hunter*
Director: Suzuki Norifumi
Starring: Namino Hiromi, Asagiri Yuko, Hyuga Akiko
Studio distribution: Japan Shock Video (UK)
Running time: 100 minutes
Year of DVD release: 2000

Title: *Black Angel 2, The*
Director: Ishii Takashi
Starring: Amami Yuki, Terajima Susumu
Studio distribution: Tokyo Bullet [MIA] (UK); Media Blaster Inc (US)

Running time: 105 minutes
Year of DVD release: 2002

Title: *Black Angel, The*
Director: Ishii Takashi
Starring: Hazuki Riona, Takashima Reiko
Studio distribution: Tokyo Bullet [MIA] (UK)
Running time: 95 minutes
Year of DVD release: 2002

Title: *Blackjack*
Director: Dezaki Osamu Dezaki
Starring: N/A
Studio distribution: Manga Video (UK); Palm Pictures (US)
Running time: 90 minutes
Year of DVD release: 2003

Title: *Blind Beast*
Director: Masumura Yasuzo
Starring: Funakoshi Eiji, Sengoku Noriko
Studio distribution: Manga Video (UK); Image Entertainment (US)
Running time: 86 minutes
Year of DVD release: 2001

Title: *Blood: The Last Vampire*
Director: Kitakubo Hiroyuki
Starring: Kudoh Youki (voice), Nakamura Saemi (voice)
Studio distribution: Manga Video (UK); Palm Pictures (US)
Running time: 48 minutes
Year of DVD release: 2001

Title: *Blue Remains*
Director: Takizawa Toshifumi, Takabayashi Hisaya
Starring: Fukiishi Kazue, Koyasu Takehitu
Studio distribution: Artsmagic Ltd (UK)
Running time: 77 minutes
Year of DVD release: 2003

C

Title: *Chaos* [*Kaosu*]
Director: Nakata Hideo
Starring: Nakatani Miki, Hagiwara Masato, Mitsuishi Ken
Studio distribution: Kino International (US)

Running time: 104 minutes
Year of DVD release: 2003

Title: *Charisma*
Director: Kurosawa Kiyoshi
Starring: Koji Yakusho, Hiroyuki Ikeuchi, Ren Ohsugi, Yoriko Doguchi, Jun Fubuki
Studio distribution: Not yet released in UK or US
Running time: 104 minutes
Year of DVD release: 2003

Title: *Cops vs. Thugs*
Director: Fukasaku Kinji
Starring: Bunta Sugawara, Hiroki Matsukata
Studio distribution: Eureka (UK)
Running time: 101 minutes
Year of DVD release: 2003

Title: *Cure*
Director: Kurosawa Kiyoshi
Starring: Hagiwara Masato, Yakusho Koji
Studio distribution: Home Vision Entertainment (US)
Running time: 75 minutes
Year of DVD release: 2004

D

Title: *Dark Water*
Director: Nakata Hideo
Starring: Kuroki Hitomi, Kanno Rio
Studio distribution: Metro Tartan (UK)
Running time: 99 minutes
Year of DVD release: 2003

Title: *Death Powder*
Director: Izumiya Shigeru
Starring: Izumiya Shigeru, Inukai Takichi
Studio distribution: Not yet released in UK or US
Running time: 90 minutes
Year of DVD release: N/A

Title: *Demon*
Director: Furuhata Yasuo
Starring: Kitano Takeshi, Takakura Ken

Studio distribution: Artsmagic Ltd (UK)
Running time: 118 minutes
Year of DVD release: 2002

Title: *Down to Hell*
Director: Kitamura Ryuhei
Starring: Miyata Masami, Goto Koji, Okamoto Yoshihiro, Kitamura Ryuhei, Morino Nobuhiki
Studio distribution: Not yet released in the UK or US
Running time: N/A
Year of DVD release: N/A

Title: *Dream of Garuda, The*
Director: Zeke Takahisa
Starring: Zeke Takahisa
Studio distribution: Screen Edge (UK); MVD (US)
Running time: 55 minutes
Year of DVD release: 2002

E

Title: *Eko Eko Azarak: Wizard of Darkness*
Director: Sato Shimako
Starring: Yoshino Kimika, Kanno Miho, Tamura Miho, Kadomatsu Kanori
Studio distribution: Media Blasters Inc. (US)
Running time: 82 minutes
Year of DVD release: 2003

Title: *Eko Eko Azarak II: Birth of the Wizard*
Director: Sato Shimako
Starring: Yoshino Kimika, Shiratori Chieko, Ohtani Akira
Studio distribution: Media Blasters Inc. (US)
Running time: 83 minutes
Year of DVD release: 2003

Title: *Eko Eko Azarak III: Misa the Dark Angel*
Director: Katsuhito Ueno
Starring: Hinako Saeki
Studio distribution: Media Blasters Inc. (US)
Running time: 95 minutes
Year of DVD release: 2001

Title: *Entrails of a Beautiful Woman* [*Bijo No Harawata*; a.k.a. *Guts of a Beauty*]
Director: Gaira (Komizu Kazuo)
Starring: Ozawa Megumi, Ishii Junko, Kitagawa Seira
Studio distribution: WEA Corp. (UK and US)
Running time: 68 minutes
Year of DVD release: 2004

Title: *Entrails of a Virgin* [*Shojo No Harawata*; a.k.a. *Entrails of a Whore*]
Director: Gaira (Komizu Kazuo)
Starring: Kizuki Saeko, Hagio Naomi, Kawashima Megumi
Studio distribution: WEA Corp. (UK and US)
Running time: 73 minutes
Year of DVD release: 2004

Title: *Evil Dead Trap*
Director: Ikeda Toshiharu
Starring: Ono Miyuki, Katsuragi Fumi
Studio distribution: Artsmagic Ltd (UK); Image (US)
Running time: 100 minutes
Year of DVD release: 2003

Title: *Evil Dead Trap 2*
Director: Hashimoto Izo
Starring: Nakajima Akiko, Kondo Rie
Studio distribution: Artsmagic Ltd (UK); Music Video Distribution (US)
Running time: 97 minutes
Year of DVD release: 2003

Title: *Evil of Dracula*
Director: Yamamoto Michio
Starring: Kurosawa Toshio, Tanaka Kunie
Studio distribution: Artsmagic Ltd (UK)
Running time: 85 minutes
Year of DVD release: 2002

F

Title: *Freeze Me* (a.k.a. *Freezer*)
Director: Ishii Takashi
Starring: Inoue Harumi, Takenaka Naoto
Studio distribution: Metro Tartan (UK); Media Blasters, Inc. (US)

Running time: 103 minutes
Year of DVD release: 2002

G

Title: *Gemini*
Director: Tsukamoto Shinya
Starring: Motoki Masahiro, Ryo, Tsutsui Yasutaka, Takenaka Naoto, Taguchi Tomorou, Akaji Maro, Ishibashi Renji
Studio distribution: Not yet released in UK or US
Running time: N/A
Year of DVD release: N/A

Title: *Ghost Story of Kasane Swamp* [*Kaidan Kasanegafuchi*]
Director: Nakagawa Nobuo
Starring: Wakasugi Katsuko, Tanba Tetsuro, Kitazawa Noriko, Wada Takashi
Studio distribution: Not yet released in UK or US
Running time: N/A
Year of DVD release: N/A

Title: *The Ghosts of Yotsuya* [*Yotsuya Kaidan*; a.k.a. *The Ghost Story of Yotsuya*]
Director: Mouri Masaki
Starring: Wakayama Tomisaburo, Souma Chieko, Tanaka Haruo, Iida Chouko, Ogura Shigeru, Ozawa Michiko
Studio distribution: Not yet released in UK or US
Running time: 85 minutes
Year of DVD release: N/A

Title: *Godzilla: King of Monsters*
Director: Honda Ishirô
Starring: Hirata Akihiko, Shimura Takashi
Studio distribution: Simitar Video
Running Time: 79 minutes
Year of DVD release: 1998

Title: *Guinea Pig* (series) Part 1
1. *Devil's Experiment*
Director: Satoru Ogura
2. *Android of Notre Dame*
Director: Kuramoto Kazuhito
Starring: Hino Toshiki, Takagi Mio, Iori Yumi, Taguchi Tomoroh
Studio distribution: Unearthed Films (US)

Running time: 100 minutes
Year of DVD release: 2002

Title: *Guinea Pig* (series) Part 2
1. *Mermaid in a Manhole*
Director: Hino Hideshi
Starring: Saiki Shigeru, Rijyu Go, Hisamoto Masami, Somei Mari
2. *He Never Dies*
Director: Kuzumi Masayuki
Starring: Sato Masahiro
Studio distribution: Music Video Distribution (US)
Running time: 103 minutes
Year of DVD release: 2002

Title: *Guinea Pig* (series) Part 3
1. *Flower of Flesh & Blood*
Director: Hino Hideshi
Starring: Tamura Hiroshi, Yugao Kirara
2. *Making of Guinea Pig*
Interviewer: Iwanami Miwa
Starring: Hino Toshiki, Takagi Mio, Taguchi Tomoroh, Iori Yumi
Studio distribution: Unearthed Films (US)
Running time: 89 minutes
Year of DVD release: 2002

H

Title: *Happiness of the Katakuris, The*
Director: Miike Takashi
Starring: Sawada Kenji, Nishida Naomi
Studio distribution: Metro Tartan (UK); Ventura Distribution (US)
Running time: 112 minutes
Year of DVD release: 2003

Title: *Hiruko the Goblin*
Director: Tsukamoto Shinya
Starring: Sawada Kenji, Takenaka Naoto
Studio distribution: Artsmagic Ltd (UK)
Running time: 89 minutes
Year of DVD release: 2003

Title: *Hypnosis*
Director: Masayuki Ochiai

Starring: Inagaki Goro, Kanno Miho
Studio distribution: Artsmagic Ltd (UK)
Running time: 109 minutes
Year of DVD release: 2002

I

Title: *Illusion of Blood*
Director: Toyoda Shiro
Starring: Nakadai Tatsuya, Okada Mariko
Studio distribution: Artsmagic Ltd (UK)
Running time: 105 minutes
Year of DVD release: 2002

Title: *In The Realm of the Senses*
Director: Oshima Nagisa
Starring: Fuji Tatsuya, Matsuda Eiko
Studio distribution: Nouveau Entertainment (UK); Fox Lorber (US)
Running time: 97 minutes
Year of DVD release: 2001

J

Title: *Jigoku* [a.k.a. *Hell*]
Director: Nakagawa Nobuo
Starring: Amachi Shigeru, Numata Yoichi, Mitsuya Utako, Ohtomo Jun,
    Miyata Fumiko
Studio distribution: Eclipse Film (UK)
Running time: 101 minutes
Year of DVD release: 2003

Title: *Jin-Roh: The Wolf Brigade*
Director: Oshii Mamoru
Starring: N/A
Studio distribution: Bandai Entertainment (UK and US)
Running time: 105 minutes
Year of DVD release: 2001

Title: *Junk*
Director: Muroga Atsushi
Starring: Shimamura Kaori, Kishimoto Yuji
Studio distribution: Artsmagic Ltd (UK); Ventura Distribution (US)

Running time: 83 minutes
Year of DVD release: 2002

Title: *Ju-on* [a.k.a. *The Curse*]
Director: Shimizu Takashi
Starring: Yanagi Yuurei, Kuriyama Chiaki, Miwa Hitomi, Suwa Taro, Yoshiyuko Yumi
Studio distribution: Not yet released in the UK or US
Running time: 70 minutes
Year of DVD release: N/A

Title: *Ju-on 2* [a.k.a. *Curse 2*]
Director: Shimizu Takashi
Starring: Daike Yuko, Ashikawa Makoto, Fujii Kahori, Saito Mayuko, Iizuka Minoru
Studio distribution: Not yet released in the UK or US
Running time: 76 minutes
Year of DVD release: N/A

Title: *Ju-on: The Grudge*
Director: Shimizu Takashi
Starring: Okina Megumi, Ito Misaki, Uehara Misa, Ichikawa Yui
Studio distribution: Lionsgate (UK and US)
Running time: 92 minutes
Year of DVD release: N/A

Title: *Ju-on 2: The Grudge* (2002)
Director: Shimizu Takashi
Starring: Sakai Noriko, Niyama Chiharu, Horie Kei, Ichikawa Yui, Katsurayama Shingo
Studio distribution: Not yet released in the UK or US
Running time: 95 minutes
Year of DVD release: N/A

K

Title: *Kaïro* [a.k.a. *Pulse*]
Director: Kurosawa Kiyoshi
Starring: Kato Haruhiko, Aso Kumiko, Koyuki, Arisaka Kurume, Aikawa Sho
Studio distribution: Not yet released in the UK or US
Running time: 118 minutes
Year of DVD release: N/A

Title: *Kakashi* {a.k.a. *Scarecrow*]
Director: Tsuruta Norio
Starring: Nonami Maho, Sibasaki Kou, Ip Grace, Matsuoka Shunsuke
Studio distribution: Not yet released in the US or UK
Running time: N/A
Year of DVD release: N/A

Title: *Kokkuri*
Director: Zeze Takahisa
Starring: Yamatsu Ayumi, Shimada Hiroko, Ishikawa Moe, Nakae Hitoshi
Studio distribution: Not yet released in the US or UK
Running time: 88 minutes
Year of DVD release: N/A

Title: *Kwaidan*
Director: Masaki Kobayashi
Starring: Rentaro Mikuni, Michiyo Aratama
Studio distribution: Criterion Collection (US)
Running time: 161 minutes
Year of DVD release: 2000

L

Title: *Lady Snowblood 1: Blizzard from the Netherworld*
Director: Toshiya Fujita
Starring: Kaji Meiko, Kurosawa Toshio
Studio distribution: Artsmagic Ltd (UK); Koch Vision Entertainment (US)
Running time: 97 minutes
Year of DVD release: 2001 (UK); 2004 (US)

Title: *Lady Snowblood 2: Love Song of Vengeance*
Director: Toshiya Fujita
Starring: Kaji Meiko, Harada Yoshio
Studio distribution: Artsmagic Ltd (UK); Koch Vision Entertainment (US)
Running time: 97 minutes
Year of DVD release: 2001 (UK); 2004 (US)

Title: *Lake of Dracula* [a.k.a. *The Bloodthirsty Eyes*]
Director: Yamamoto Michio
Starring: Kishida Shin (Mori), Fujita Midori, Takahashi Choei, Emi Sanae,
    Ohtaki Shuji, Takashina Kaku
Studio distribution: Warrior (UK)

Running time: 83 minutes
Year of DVD release: 2002

Title: *Legacy of Dracula* [a.k.a. *The Bloodthirsty Doll*]
Director: Yamamoto Michio
Starring: Matsuo Kayo, Nakao Akira, Kobayashi Yukiko, Takashina
  Kaku, Minakaze Yoko
Studio distribution: Warrior (UK)
Running time: 71 minutes
Year of DVD release: 2003

Title: *Long Dream*
Director: Higuchinsky
Starring: Horiuchi Masami, Tsugumi, Tsuda Kenjiro, Hatsune Eriko
Studio distribution: Bigimaster (UK)
Running time: 79 minutes
Year of DVD release: 2003

M

Title: *Malice@Doll*
Director: Motonaga Keitaro
Starring: Yamada Yukie
Studio distribution: Artsmagic Ltd (UK)
Running time: 74 minutes
Year of DVD release: 2003

N

Title: *N-Girls vs. Vampire* [a.k.a. *Pop Chicks vs. Monster*]
Director: Miike Takashi
Starring: Ayana Sakai, Takashi Nagayama, Chiaki Ichiba
Studio distribution: Storm Limited (UK)
Running time: 202 minutes
Year of DVD release: 2003

Title: *Naked Blood* (a.k.a. *Splatter*)
Director: Sato Hisayasu
Starring: Aika Misa, Abe Sadao, Kirihara Mika, Hayashi Yumika
Studio distribution: Not yet released in UK or US
Running time: 76 minutes
Year of DVD release: N/A

Title: *Ninja Scroll*
Director: Kawajiri Yoshiaki
Starring: Yamadera Koichi, Shinohara Emi
Studio distribution: Manga Video (UK); Palm Pictures/Manga Video (US)
Running time: 94 minutes
Year of DVD release: 2000

O

Title: *Onibaba*
Director: Shindô Kaneto
Starring: Otowa Nobuko, Yoshimura Jitsuko
Studio distribution: Public Media Inc.; Criterion Collection (UK); Criterion
    Collection (US)
Running time: 103 minutes
Year of DVD release: 2004

Title: *Organ*
Directed by Fujiwara Kei
Starring: Fujiwara Kei, Hasegawa Kimihiko, Nasa Kenjin, Hirota Reona
Studio distribution: Synapse Films (UK); Image (US)
Running time: 105 minutes
Year of DVD release: 2000

P

Title: *Parasite Eve*
Director: Masayuki Ochiai
Starring: Mikami Hiroshi, Hazuki Reona
Studio distribution: ADV Films (UK and US)
Running time: 120 minutes
Year of DVD release: 2001

Title: *Perfect Blue*
Director: Kon Satoshi
Starring: Iwao Junko, Okura Masaaki
Studio distribution: Manga Entertainment Ltd. (UK); Palm Pictures/Manga
    Video (US)
Running time: 75 minutes
Year of DVD release: 2000

Title: *Perfect Blue* [*Perfect Blue: Yumenaraba Samete*]
Director: Sato Toshiki
Starring: Maeda Ayaka, Ohmori Nao, Toda Masahiro, Watanabe Makiko
Studio distribution: Not yet released in UK or US
Running time: 103 minutes
Year of DVD release: N/A

Title: *Pinnochio 964*
Director: Fukui Shozin
Starring: Suzuki Hage, Chan Onn
Studio distribution: Ventura Distribution (US)
Running time: 93 minutes
Year of DVD release: 2004

Title: *Portrait of Hell*
Director: Toyoda Shiro
Starring: Nakadai Tatsuya, Nakamura Kinnosuke
Studio distribution: Artsmagic Ltd (UK)
Running time: 91 minutes
Year of DVD release: 2002

Title: *Princess Blade*
Director: Sato Shinsuke
Starring: Ito Hideaki, Shaku Yumiko
Studio distribution: Metro Tartan (UK); AD Vision (US)
Running time: 91 minutes
Year of DVD release: 2002

Title: *Pyrokinesis* [a.k.a. *Crossfire*]
Director: Kaneko Shusuke
Starring: Yada Akiko, Ito Hideaki
Studio distribution: Artsmagic Ltd (UK); Media Blasters, Inc.
Running time: 115 minutes
Year of DVD release: 2002

R

Title: *Read or Die*
Director: Masunari Kouji
Starring: Miura Reiko, Neya Michiko
Studio distribution: Manga Video (UK); WEA Corp. (US)
Running time: 90 minutes
Year of DVD release: 2003

Title: *Ringu* [*Ring*]
Director: Nakata Hideo
Starring: Matsushima Nanako, Sanada Hiroyuki
Studio distribution: Metro Tartan (UK); Universal Studios (US)
Running time: 91 minutes
Year of DVD release: 2001 (UK); 2003 (US)

Title: *Ringu 0: The Birthday* [*Ring 0*]
Director: Tsurata Norio
Starring: Nakama Yukie, Aso Kumiko
Studio distribution: Metro Tartan (UK)
Running time: 99 minutes
Year of DVD release: 2002

Title: *Ringu 2* [*Ring 2*]
Director: Nakata Hideo
Starring: Ban Daisuke, Fukada Kyoko
Studio distribution: Metro Tartan (UK)
Running time: 95 minutes
Year of DVD release: 2001

Title: *Ring: Spiral* [*Rasen*; a.k.a. *The Vortex*]
Director: Iida Jouji
Starring: Sato Koichi, Nakatani Miki, Sanada Hiroyuki Henry, Tsurumi
    Shingo
Studio distribution: Warrior (UK)
Running time: 97 minutes
Year of DVD release: 2003

Title: *Ring: The Final Chapter* (The complete twelve-episode TV series)
Director: Fukumoto Yoshihito and Matsuda Hidetomo
Starring: Yanagiba Toshiro, Nagase Tomoya, Kuroki Hitomi, Kyono
    Kotomi, Yada Akiko, Yamamoto Kei, Kato Takayuki, Fukayama Yuta
Studio distribution: Not yet released in the UK or US
Running time: N/A
Year of DVD release: N/A

Title: *Rodan*
Director: Honda Ishirô
Starring: Sahara Kenji, Shirakawa Yumi, Hirata Akihiko, Kobori Akio
Studio distribution: Sony Music/Video (US)
Running time: 72 minutes
Year of DVD release: 2002 (US)

Title: *Rubber's Lover*
Director: Fukui Shozin
Starring: Kawase Yota, Nao, Saito Sosuke, Kunihiro Mika
Studio distribution: Ventura Distribution (US)
Running time: 90 minutes
Year of DVD release: 2004

Title: *Rusted Body: Guts of a Virgin 3*
Director: Komizu Kazuo
Starring: Asano Keiko, Kizuki Saeko, Kiyokawa Ayu
Studio distribution: Japan Shock DVD Entertainment (UK and US)
Running time: 70 minutes
Year of DVD release: 2001

S

Title: *Séance* [*Kourei*]
Director: Kurosawa Kiyoshi
Starring: Yakusho Koji, Fubuki Jun, Kusanagi Go, Aikawa Sho, Ishida
  Hikari
Studio distribution: Not yet released in UK or US
Running time: 118 minutes
Year of DVD release: N/A

Title: *Security Guard from Hell*
Director: Kurosawa Kiyoshi
Starring: Kuno Makiko, Matsushige Yutaka, Hasegawa Hatsunori, Ohsugi
  Ren
Studio distribution: Not yet released in UK or US
Running time: N/A
Year of DVD release: N/A

Title: *Shikoku* [*Dead Land*]
Director: Nagasaki Shunichi
Starring: Kuriyama Chiaki, Natsukawa Yui, Tsutsuo Michitaka, Ren
  Ohsugi
Studio distribution: Ventura Distribution (UK and US)
Running time: 101 minutes
Year of DVD release: 2004

Title: *Snake of June, A*
Director: Tsukamoto Shinya

Starring: Kurosawa Asuka, Kohtari Yoji
Studio distribution: Metro Tartan (UK); Fejui Media Corporation (US)
Running time: 76 minutes
Year of DVD release: 2004

Title: *Stacy*
Director: Tomomatsu Naoyuki
Starring: Kato Natsuki, Omi Toshinori, Hayashi Chika, Uchida Shungiku
Studio distribution: Synapse Films (UK); WEA Corp. (US)
Running time: 80 minutes
Year of DVD release: 2003

Title: *St John's Wort*
Director: Ten Shimoyama
Starring: Okina Megumi, Saito Yoichiro
Studio distribution: Artsmagic Ltd (UK); The Asylum Home Entertainment
   (US)
Running time: 84 minutes
Year of DVD release: 2004

Title: *Suicide Circle* [*Jisatsu Circle*; a.k.a. *Suicide Club*]
Director: Sono Shion
Starring: Ishibashi Ryo, Nagase Masatoshi, Hagiwara Akira, Kamon
   Yoko, Rolly
Studio distribution: TLA Releasing (US)
Running time: 85 minutes
Year of DVD release: 2003

Title: *Sword of Doom*
Director: Okamoto Kihachi
Starring: Mifune Toshiro, Nakadai Tatsuya
Studio distribution: Artsmagic Ltd (UK)
Running time: 115 minutes
Year of DVD release: 2002

T

Title: *Teruo Ishii's Hell* [a.k.a. *Teruo Ishii's Jigoku*]
Director: Ishii Teruo
Starring: Sato Miki, Maeda Michiko, Satsuma Kenpachiro, Tanba
   Tetsuro, Saito Nozomi
Studio distribution: Not yet released in UK or US

Running time: 100 minutes
Year of DVD release: N/A

Title: *Tetsuo: The Iron Man*
Director: Tsukamoto Shinya
Starring: Taguchi Tomorowo, Tsukamoto Shinya
Studio distribution: Metro Tartan (UK); Image Entertainment (US)
Running time: 65 minutes
Year of DVD release: 2002

Title: *Tetsuo 2: Bodyhammer*
Director: Tsukamoto Shinya
Starring: Taguchi Tomorowo, Tsukamoto Shinya
Studio distribution: Metro Tartan (UK); Ryko Distribution (US)
Running time: 81 minutes
Year of DVD release: 2002

Title: *Throne of Blood*
Director: Kurosawa Akira
Starring: Mifune Toshiro
Studio distribution: BFI Video Publishing (UK); Criterion Collection (US)
Running time: 105 minutes
Year of DVD release: 2001 (UK); 2003 (US)

Title: *Tokyo – The Last Megalopolis*
Director: Akio Jissoji
Starring: Katsu Shintaro, Shimada Kyusaku
Studio distribution: Artsmagic Ltd (UK); A. D. Vision (US)
Running time: 135 minutes
Year of DVD release: 2002 (UK); 2004 (US)

Title: *Tomie*
Director: Oikawa Ataru
Starring: Kanno Miho, Nakamura Mami, Douguchi Yoriko, Taguchi
  Tomoroh
Studio distribution: Adness (US)
Running time: 95 minutes
Year of DVD release: 2004

Title: *Tomie: Rebirth*
Director: Oikawa Ataru
Starring: Miki Sakai

Studio distribution: Ventura Distribution (US)
Running time: 95 minutes
Year of DVD release: 2004

Title: *Tomie: Replay*
Director: Mitsuishi Fujiro
Starring: Kanno Miho
Studio distribution: Ventura Distribution (US)
Running time: 92 minutes
Year of DVD release: 2004

U

Title: *Ugetsu*
Director: Mizoguchi Kenji
Starring: Masayuki Mori, Machiko Kyô
Studio distribution: Not yet released in UK or US
Running time: 94 minutes
Year of DVD release: N/A

Title: *Urotsukidoji – Legend of the Overfiend*
Director: Takayama Hideki
Starring: Takada Yumi, Nishimura Tomohiro
Studio distribution: Manga Video
Running time: 185 minutes
Year of DVD release: 2001

Title: *Uzumaki*
Director: Higuchinsky
Starring: Hatsune Eriko, Osugi Ren
Studio distribution: Artsmagic Ltd (UK)
Running time: 90 minutes
Year of DVD release: 2003

V

Title: *Versus*
Director: Kitamura Ryuhei
Starring: Sakaguchi Tak, Sakaki Hideo
Studio distribution: Metro Tartan (UK); Media Blasters, Inc. (US)
Running time: 120 minutes
Year of DVD release: 2003

W

Title: *Wild Zero*
Director: Tetsuro Takeuchi
Starring: Wolf Guitar, Endo Masashi
Studio distribution: Artsmagic Ltd (UK); WEA Corp. (US)
Running time: 95 minutes
Year of DVD release: 2003

Title: *Woman Called Abe Sada, A*
Director: Tanaka Noboru
Starring: Miyashita Junko, Hideaki Ezumi
Studio distribution: Pagan Films (UK); Image Entertainment (US)
Running time: 77 minutes
Year of DVD release: 2001

Y

Title: *A Yakuza Horror Story: Gozu* [*Gokudô Kyôfu Dai-gekijô: Gozu*]
Director: Miike Takashi
Starring: Sone Hideki, Aikawa Sho, Yoshino Kimika, Hino Shohei, Tomita
  Keiko, Ishibashi Reinji, Kato Masaya, Tanba Tetsuro
Studio distribution: Klock Worx (UK)
Running time: 129 minutes
Year of DVD release: 2003

Z

Title: *Zipang*
Director: Hayashi Kazio
Starring: Takashima Masahiro, Yasuda Narumi
Studio distribution: Pagan Films (UK)
Running time: 95 minutes
Year of DVD release: 2000

BIBLIOGRAPHY

Alexander, James R. (2001) 'Obscenity, Pornography, and Violence: Rethinking Oshima's *In the Realm of the Senses*', July, http://www.pitt.edu/~zander/ Obscenity&Oshima.html.

Allison, Ann (2000) *Permitted and Prohibited Desires: Mothers, Comics, and Censorship in Japan*. Berkeley and Los Angeles, CA: University of California Press.

Allon, Yoram (2002) 'Review', of *Audition*, *Kamera*, kamera.co.uk, kamera.co.uk/ reviews_ extra/audition.php.

An Jinsoo (2001) '*The Killer*: Cult Film and Transcultural (Mis)Reading', in Esther C. M. Yau (ed.), *At Full Speed: Hong Kong Cinema in a Borderless World*. Minneapolis, MN: University of Minnesota Press, pp. 95–113.

Andrew, Geoff (1991) *Time Out*, 4 September, p. 58.

Barr, Charles (1972) '*Straw Dogs, A Clockwork Orange*, and the Critics', *Screen*, 13: 2, pp. 17–32.

Barrett, Gregory (1989) *Archetypes in Japanese Film: The Sociopolitical and Religious Significance of the Principal Heroes and Heroines*. Selinsgrove, PA: Susquehanna University Press.

Bartok, Dennis (2000) 'Interview with Takashi Miike'. DVD *Audition*, Ventura Distributors, 4 June.

Barzaghi, Subhana (1993) *Red Thread Zen: The Tao of Love, Passion, and Sex*. Spring Sesshin 1993, Gorricks Run Zendo, NSW, Australia. 14 April at http://www.buddhistinformation.com/red_thread_zen.htm.

Bassnett-McGuire, Susan (1991) *Translation Studies*. London: Routledge.

Bataille, Georges [1929–30] (1994) 'The Use Value of D. A. F. de Sade', in Allan Stoekl (ed.), *Visions of Excess: Selected Writings, 1927–1939*. Minneapolis, MN: University of Minnesota Press.

Baudrillard, Jean (1988) 'Simulacra and Simulations', in *Selected Writings*, ed. Mark Poster. Stanford, CA: Stanford University Press.

Baudrillard, Jean (1990) *The Transparency of Evil: Essays on Extreme Phenomena*. London and New York: Verso.

Baym, Nancy K (2000) *Tune In, Log On: Soaps, Fandom and Online Community*. London: Sage.

Bird, S. Elizabeth (2003) *The Audience in Everyday Life: Living in a Media World*. New York and London: Routledge.

Biro, Stephen (2003) *The Guinea Pig History Page*, http://www.guineapigfilms.com/History.html.

Bolton, Cristopher (2002) 'From Wooden Cyborgs to Celluloid Souls: Mechanical Bodies in Anime and Japanese Puppet Theater', *Positions: East Asia Cultures Critique*, 10:3, Winter, pp. 729–71.

Bornoff, Nicholas (1992) *Pink Samurai: The Pursuit and Politics of Sex in Japan*. London: Grafton.

Bourdieu, Pierre (1984) *Distinction*. London and New York: Routledge.

Bradshaw, Peter (2001 'Audition', *Guardian*, 16 March, film.guardian.co.uk/News_Story/Critic_Review/Guardian_Film_of_the_week/ 0,4267,452311,00.htm.

Britton, Andrew (1978) '*Mandingo*', *Movie*, 22, pp. 1–22.

Brooker, Will (2003) 'Rescuing *Strange Days*: Fan Reaction to a Critical and Commercial Failure', in Deborah Jermyn and Sean Redmond (eds), *The Cinema of Kathryn Bigelow: Hollywood Transgressor*. London and New York: Wallflower Press, pp. 198–219.

Brophy, Philip (1994) 'Introduction', *Kaboom! Explosive Animation from America and Japan*. Sydney: Museum of Contemporary Art, p. 9.

Brophy, Philip (2000) 'How Sound Floats on Land: The Suppression and Release of Indigenous Musics on the Cinematic Terrain', in Philip Brophy (ed.), *Cinesonic: Cinema and the Sound of Music*. Sydney: Australian Film TV & Radio School, pp. 191– 215.

Brottman, Mikita (1997) *Offensive Films: Towards an Anthropology of* Cinema Vomitif. Westport, CT: Greenwood.

Brown, Norman O. (1959) *Life Against Death*. Middletown, CT: Wesleyan University Press.

Bukatman, Scott (1990) *Terminal Identity: The Virtual Subject in Post-Modern Science Fiction*. Durham, NC: and London: Duke University Press.

Caputi, Jane (1992) 'Advertising Femicide: Lethal Violence against Women in Pornography and Gorenography', in Jill Radford and Diana E. H. Russell (eds), *Femicide: The Politics of Killing Women*. New York: Twayne, pp. 203–17.

Catton, John Paul (2002) 'Japan's Dark Lanterns', *The Third Alternative*, 31, p. 31.

Cerf, Christopher (1983) 'Foreword', in Michael Weldon (ed.), *The Psychotronic Encyclopedia of Film*. New York: Ballantine.

Chang, Iris (1997) *The Rape of Nanking*. New York: Basic Books.

Chun, Gary C. W. (2001) 'Competition Taken to a Dark Extreme', *Honolulu Star Bulletin*, 20 April, http://starbulletin.com/2001/04/20/features/story5.html.

Clover, Carol J. (1992) *Men, Women and Chainsaws: Gender in the Modern Horror Film*. London: BFI; Princeton, NJ: Princeton University Press.

Cohen, Jeffrey J. (1996) 'Monster Culture (Seven Theses)', in Jeffrey Jerome Cohen (ed.), *Monster Theory: Reading Culture*. Minneapolis, MN: University of Minnesota Press.

Conrich, Ian (1999) 'Trashing London: The British Colossal Creature Film and Fantasies of Mass Destruction', in I. Q. Hunter (ed.), *British Science Fiction Cinema*. London and New York: Routledge, pp. 88–98.

Craig, Tim (2000) 'Introduction', in Timothy J. Craig (ed.), *Japan Pop!: Inside the World of Japanese Popular Culture*. New York and London: M. E. Sharpe, pp. 3–26.

Crawford, Travis (2003) 'The Urban Techno-Alienation of Sion Sono's *Suicide Club*', in Steven Jay Schneider (ed.), *Fear Without Frontiers: Horror Cinema Across the Globe*. Guildford: FAB Press, pp. 305–11.

Creed, Barbara (1993) *The Monstrous-Feminine: Film, Feminism, Psychoanalysis*. London and New York: Routledge.

Creed, Barbara (1995) 'Horror and the Carnivalesque: The Body Monstrous', in Leslie Devereaux and Roger Hillman (eds), *Fields of Vision: Essays in Film Studies, Visual Anthropology and Photography*. Berkeley, CA and London: University of California Press.

Daniel, Rob and Dave Wood (2003) 'Pain Threshold: The Cinema of Takashi Miike', in Steven Jay Schneider (ed.), *Fear Without Frontiers: Horror Cinema Across the Globe*. Guildford: FAB Press, pp. 285–91.

Davenport, Hugo (1991) '*Tetsuo II: Body Hammer*', *The Daily Telegraph*, 5 September, p. 14.

Davis, Darrell William (2001) 'Reigniting Japanese Tradition within *Hana-Bi*', *Cinema Journal*, 40:4, Summer, pp. 55–80.

Deleuze, Gilles (1990) 'Plato and the Simulacrum', in *The Logic of Sense*. New York: Columbia University Press.

Deleuze, Gilles and Félix Guattari (1987) *A Thousand Plateaus: Capitalism and Schizophrenia*. Minneapolis, MN: University of Minnesota Press.

Dery, Marc (1997) *Escape Velocity: Cyberculture at the End of the Century*. New York: Grove Press.

Desser, David (1988) *Eros Plus Massacre: An Introduction to the Japanese New Wave Cinema*, Bloomington and Indianapolis, IN: Indiana University Press.

Dick, Philip K. (1995) 'How to Build a Universe That Doesn't Fall Apart Two Days Later', in Lawrence Sutin (ed.), *The Shifting Realities of Philip K. Dick: Selected Literary and Philosophical Writings*. New York: Pantheon Books.

Dika, Vera (1987) 'The Stalker Film, 1978–81', in Gregory A. Waller (ed.), *American Horrors: Essays on the Modern American Horror Film*. Urbana and Chicago, IL: University of Illinois Press

Eisner, Ken (1999) '*Audition*'. *Variety*, 1 November, at findarticles.com/cf_0/ m1312/ 11_376/57608502/p1/article.jhtml?term=audition.

Ellis, Sara (2001) 'Teenage Wasteland: Battling the Royale Mess of Japanese Education', 31 December, http://www.authorsden.com/visit/ viewarticle.asp?AuthorID=6139.

Faure, Bernard (1998) *The Red Thread: Buddhist Approaches to Sexuality*. Princeton, NJ: Princeton University Press.

Felix-Didier, Paula (2000) '*Cine y sexo en Japón*', in *Film: On Line*, 15 April, http://www.filmonline.com.ar/40/dossier/40dossier3.htm.

For Men (2002) 'Audition: Takeshi Miike's Twisted Take on Modern Dating Is a Warped Hitchcockian Slice of Paranoia', *Eastern Connection*, 39, 14 Sepbember, formen.ign.com/ articles/098/098316p1.html?fromint=1.

Foucault, Michel (1979) *Discipline and Punish: The Birth of the Prison*, trans. Alan Sheridan. New York: Random House.

Freud, Sigmund [1915] (1984) 'Instincts and Their Vicissitudes: On Metapsychology', *The Penguin Freud Library, Volume 11*. London: Penguin, pp. 105–38.

Freud, Sigmund [1919] (1990) 'A Child is Being Beaten', *A Contribution to the Study of the Origin of Sexual Perversion. The Penguin Freud Library, Volume 10*. London: Penguin, pp. 159–93.

Freud, Sigmund [1925] (1958) 'The Uncanny', *On Creativity and the Unconscious: Papers on the Psychology of Art, Literature, Love, Religion*. New York: Harper.

Freud, Sigmund [1930] (1985) 'Civilization and Its Discontents', *Civilization, Society and Religion. The Penguin Freud Library, Volume 12*. London: Penguin, pp. 235–340.

Fukurai Tomokichi (1931) *Clairvoyance and Thoughtography*. London: Rider.

Gardner, William (2002) 'Attack of the Phallic Girls', *Science Fiction Studies*, 29:3, p. 273–4.

Gauntlett, David (2000) 'The Web Goes to the Pictures', in David Gauntlett (ed.), *web.studies*. London: Arnold, pp. 82–7.

Gibson, William (1984) *Neuromancer*. New York: Berkeley.

Gill, Tom (1999) 'Transformational Magic: Some Japanese Super-heroes and Monsters', in D. P. Martinez (ed.), *The Worlds of Japanese Popular Culture: Gender, Shifting Boundaries and Global Cultures*. Cambridge: Cambridge University Press, pp. 33–55.

Graham, Elaine L. (2002) *Representations of the Post/Human: Monsters, Aliens and Others in Popular Culture*. New Brunswick, NJ: Rutgers University Press.

Grindon, Leger (2001) 'In the Realm of the Censors: Cultural Boundaries and the Poetics of the Forbidden', in Dennis Washburn and Carole Cavanaugh (eds), *Word and Image in Japanese Cinema*. Cambridge: Cambridge University Press, pp. 293– 317.

Gruenberger, Harald (2002) '*Naked Blood/Splatter*', 5 July, at http://www.metamovie.de/.

Hamamoto, Maki (1998) 'Naomi Tani: An Interview with Nikkatsu Queen of SM', *Asian Cult Cinema*, 19 (April), pp. 39–48.

Harootunian, H. D. (1989) 'Visible Discourses/Invisible Ideologies', in Masao Miyoshi and H. D. Harootunian (eds), *Postmodernism and Japan*. Durham, NC and London: Duke University Press, pp. 63–92.

Hawkins, Joan (2000) *Cutting Edge: Art-Horror and the Horrific Avant-Garde*. Minneapolis, MN: University of Minnesota Press.

Hayles, N. Katherine (1999) *How We Became Post Human: Virtual Bodies in Cybernetics, Literature, and Informatics*. Chicago: University Of Chicago Press.

Heal, Sue (1992) '*Tetsuo II: Body Hammer*', *Today*, 13 November, p. 38.

Hills, Matt (2002) *Fan Cultures*. London and New York: Routledge.

Hills, Matt (2003) '*Star Wars* in Fandom, Film Theory, and the Museum: The Cultural Status of the Cult Blockbuster', in Julian Stringer (ed.), *Movie Blockbusters*. New York and London: Routledge, pp. 178–89.

Hodkinson, Paul (2003) ' "Net.Goth": Internet Communication and (Sub)Cultural Boundaries', in David Muggleton and Rupert Weinzierl (eds), *The Post-Subcultures Reader*. Oxford and New York: Berg, pp. 285–98.

Hollows, Joanne (2003) 'The Masculinity of Cult', in Mark Jancovich, Antonio Lázaro Reboll, Julian Stringer and Andy Willis (eds), *Defining Cult Movies: The Cultural Politics of Oppositional Taste*. Manchester: Manchester University Press, pp. 35–53.

Hoxter, Julian (2000) 'Taking Possession: Cult Learning in *The Exorcist*', in Graeme Harper and Xavier Mendik (eds), *Unruly Pleasures: The Cult Film and Its Critics*. Guildford: FAB Press, pp. 173–85.

Hull, Elizabeth Ann and Mark Siegel (1989) 'Science Fiction', in Richard Gid Powers and Hidetoshi Kato (eds), *Handbook of JapanesePopular Culture*. New York and London: Greenwood Press, pp. 243–75.

Hunt, Nathan (2003) 'The Importance of Trivia: Ownership, Exclusion and Authority in Science Fiction Fandom', in Mark Jancovich, Antonio Lázaro Reboll, Julian Stringer and Andy Willis (eds), *Defining Cult Movies: The Cultural Politics of Oppositional Taste*. Manchester: Manchester University Press, pp. 185–201.

Hunter, Jack (1998) *Eros in Hell: Sex, Blood and Madness in Japanese Cinema*. London: Creation Books International.

Hurley, Kelly (1995) 'Reading Like an Alien: PostHuman Identity in Ridley Scott's *Alien* and David Cronenberg's *Rabid*', in Judith Halberstam and Ira Livingston (eds), *PostHuman Bodies*. Bloomington and Indianapolis, IN: Indiana University Press.

Hutchings, Peter (2003) 'The Argento Effect', in Mark Jancovich, Antonio Lázaro Reboll, Julian Stringer and Andy Willis (eds), *Defining Cult Movies: The Cultural Politics of Oppositional Taste*. Manchester: Manchester University Press, pp. 127–41.

Igarashi Yoshikuni (2000) *Bodies of Memory*. Princeton, NJ: Princeton University Press.

Ivy, Marilyn (1995) *Discourses of the Vanishing: Modernity, Phantasm, Japan*. Chicago: University of Chicago Press.

Iwamura, Dean R. (1994) 'Letter from Japan: From Girls Who Dress Up Like Boys to Trussed-Up Porn Stars – Some Contemporary Heroines on the Japanese Screen', *Continuum: The Australian Journal of Media and Culture*, 7:2, pp. 109–30.

Jancovich, Mark (1996) *Rational Fears: American Horror in the 1950s*. Manchester and New York: Manchester University Press.

Jancovich, Mark (2000) ' "A Real Shocker": Authenticity, Genre and the Struggle for Distinction', *Continuum*, 14:1, pp. 23–35.

Jancovich Mark (2002) 'Cult Fictions: Cult Movies, Subcultural Capital and the Production of Cultural Distinction', *Cultural Studies*, 16:2, pp. 306–22.

Jenkins, Henry (2002) 'Interactive Audiences?', in Dan Harries (ed.), *The New Media Book*. London: BFI Publishing, pp. 157–70.

Johnston, Sheila (1991) *'Tetsuo II: Body Hammer'*, *The Independent*, 6 September, p. 16.

Kakinouchi Narumi (1989–98), *Vanpaia Miyu*, vols 1–3, Tokyo: Akita Shoten, translated as *Vampire Princess Miyu* (2001–2). Fredericksburg: Studio Ironcat/I. C. Entertainment.

Karola (2003) 'Italian Cinema Goes to the Drive-In: The Intercultural Horrors of Mario Bava', in Gary D. Rhodes (ed.), *Horror at the Drive-In: Essays in Popular Americana*. Jefferson, NC and London: McFarland, pp. 211–37.

Kawai, Hayao (1986) 'Violence in the home: Conflict between Two Principles: Maternal and Paternal', in T. S. Lebra and W. P. Lebra (eds), *Japanese Culture and Behavior*. Honolulu, HI: University of Hawaii Press.

Kellner, Douglas (1995) *Media Culture: Cultural Studies, Identity and the Politics Between the Modern and the Postmodern*. London and New York: Routledge.

Kellner, Douglas and Michael Ryan (1990) 'Technophobia', in Annette Kuhn (ed.), *Alien Zone: Cultural Theory and Contemporary Science Fiction Cinema*. London and New York: Verso.

Kominz, Laurence R. (2002) 'Origins of *Kabuki* Acting in Medieval Japanese Drama', in Samuel L. Leiter (ed.), *A Kabuki Reader: History and Performance*. New York: Sharpe.

La Bare, Joshua (2000) 'The Future: "Wrapped . . . in that Mysterious Japanese Way" ', *Science Fiction Studies*, 80: 27, Part 1, March, pp. 22–48.

Lachize, Sylvie (2001) 'Interview: Takashi Ishii', *Radio Canada*, http://radio- canada.ca/culture/evenements/fantasia/ishii.html.

Lehman, Peter (1993) ' "Don't Blame This on a Girl': Female Rape-Revenge Films', in Steven Cohan and Ina Rae Hark (eds), *Screening the Male: Exploring Masculinities in Hollywood Cinema*. London and New York: Routledge, pp. 103–17.

Leiter, Samuel L. (2002a) 'From Gay to *Gei*: The *Onnagata* and the Creation of *Kabuki*'s Female Characters', in Samuel L. Leiter (ed.), *A Kabuki Reader: History and Performance*. New York: Sharpe.

Leiter, Samuel L. (2002b), 'Introduction', in Samuel L. Leiter (ed.), *A Kabuki Reader: History and Performance*. New York: Sharpe.

Leong, Anthony (2001) 'Those Who Are About to Die: *Battle Royale*', *Asian Cult Cinema*, 33, pp. 35–40.

Loori, John Daido (1996) *The Heart of Being: Moral and Ethical Teachings of Zen Buddhism*. Rutland, VT: Charles E. Tuttle.

Lu, Alvin (2002) 'Horror: Japanese-Style', *Film Comment*, January/February, p. 38.

Macias, Patrick (2003) 'The Scariest Horror Ever? "Juon" Director Takashi Shimizu Interview', *Japattack*, http://japattack.com/japattack/film/juon_itv.html.

McDonald, Keiko L. (1994) *Japanese Classical Theater in Films*. Cranbury, NJ: Associated University Presses.

Malcolm, Derek (1992) *'Tetsuo II: Body Hammer'*, *Guardian*, 19 November, p. 6.

Martinez, D. P. (1998) 'Introduction: Gender, Shifting Boundaries and Global Cultures', in D. P. Martinez (ed.), *The Worlds of Japanese Popular Culture: Gender, Shifting Boundaries and Global Cultures*. Cambridge: Cambridge University Press.

Maruoka Daiji and Yoshikoshi Tatsuo (1969) *Noh*. Osaka: Hoikusha.

Mendik, Xavier (2002) 'Scream Theory #5', *Kamera*, kamera.co.uk, kamera.co.uk/columns/scream_ theory_27_08_2002.html.

Mesure, Tom (2000) '*Battle Royale*', *Midnight Eye: The Latest and Best in Japanese Cinema*, www.midnighteye.com.

Miike Takashi (2002) 'Commentary Track', *Audition*, DVD. Ventura Distributors.

Miyake Shutaro (1948) *Kabuki Drama*. Tokyo: JTB.

Miyoshi Masao (1989) 'Against the Native Grain: The Japanese Novel and the "Postmodern" West', in Masao Miyoshi and H. D. Harootunian (eds), *Postmodernism and Japan*. Durham, NC and London: Duke University Press, pp. 143–69.

Modleski, Tania (1986) 'The Terror of Pleasure: The Contemporary Horror Film and Postmodern Theory', in Tania Modleski (ed.), *Studies in Entertainment: Critical Approaches to Mass Culture*. Bloomington and Indianapolis, IN: Indiana University Press.

Morgan, Jack (2002) *The Biology of Horror: Gothic Literature and Film*. Carbondale/Edwardsville, IL: Southern Illinois University Press.

Morley, David and Kevin Robins (1995) *Spaces of Identity: Global Media, Electronic Landscapes and Cultural Boundaries*. London and New York: Routledge.

Morris, Gary (2001) 'Gore Galore: Takeshi Miike's *Audition*', *Bright Lights Film Journal*, 34, October, http://www.brightlightsfilm.com/34/audition.html.

Musetto, V. A. (2002) 'An Interview with Takeshi Miike', *Asian Cult Cinema*, 37, Winter, pp. 57–61.

Napier, Susan J. (1996), *The Fantastic in Modern Japanese Literature: The Subversion of Modernity*. London and New York: Routledge.

Napier, Susan J. (1998) 'Vampires, Psychic Girls, Flying Women and Sailor Scouts: Four Faces of the Young Female in Japanese Popular Culture', in D. P. Martinez (ed.), *The Worlds of Japanese Popular Culture: Gender, Shifting Boundaries and Global Cultures*. Cambridge: Cambridge University Press, pp. 91–109.

Napier, Susan J. (2001a) 'The Frenzy of Metamorphosis: The Body in Japanese Pornographic Animation', in Dennis Washburn and Carole Cavanaugh (eds), *Word and Image in Japanese Cinema*. Cambridge: Cambridge University Press, pp. 342–66.

Napier, Susan J. (2001b) *Anime from Akira to Princess Mononoke: Experiencing Contemporary Japanese Animation*. New York: Palgrave.

Napier, Susan J. (2002) 'When the Machines Stop: Fantasy, Reality, and Terminal Identity in *Neon Genesis Evangelion* and *Serial Experiments Lain*', *Science Fiction Studies*, 88, Vol. 29, Part 3, November, pp. 418–35.

Newitz, Annalee (1995) 'Magical Girls and Atomic Bomb Sperm: Japanese Animation in America', *Film Quarterly*, 49:1, Fall, pp. 2–15.

Noriega, Chon A. (1996) 'Godzilla and the Japanese Nightmare: When Them! Is U.S.', in Mick Broderick (ed.), *Hibakusha Cinema: Hiroshima, Nagasaki and the Nuclear Image in Japanese Film*. London and New York: Kegan Paul International, pp. 54–74.

Okada Toshio (2000) '*Otaku gaku nyûmon*', Introduction to *Otakuology*. Tokyo: Shinchôsha OH! bunko, pp. 10–13.

Orbaugh, Sharalyn (2002) 'Sex and the Single Cyborg: Japanese Popular Culture Experiments in Subjectivity', *Science Fiction Studies*, 88, Vol. 29, Part 3, November, pp. 436–52.

Osmond, Andrew (2003) 'Ringing the Changes', *Shivers*, 102, pp. 17–20.

Perry, David (2001) '*Audition*', *Xiibaro Newsletter*, 4.01 cinema-scene.com/archive/volume-4number-01.html#Audition.

Pointon, Susan (1997) 'Transcultural Orgasm as Apocalypse: *Urotsukidoji: The Legend of the Overfiend*', *Wide Angle*, 19.3, July, pp. 41–63.

Prince, Stephen (1998) *Savage Cinema: Sam Peckinpah and the Rise of Ultraviolent Movies*. Austin, TX: University of Texas Press.

Prince, Stephen (2000) *Screening Violence*. New Brunswick, NJ: Rutgers University Press.

Rayns, Tony (1984) 'Nikkatsu's "Roman Porno" Films', in Tony Rayns (ed.), *Eiga: 25 Years of Japanese Cinema*. Edinburgh: Edinburgh International Film Festival, pp. 14–15.

Rayns, Tony (1991a) '*Tetsuo*', *Sight and Sound*, 1:5 (September), p. 52.

Rayns, Tony (1991b) 'Tokyo Stories', *Sight and Sound*, 1:8 (December), pp. 12–15.

Rayns, Tony (1992) 'Sodom and Tomorrow', *Time Out*, 8 November, pp. 22–3.

Read, Jacinda (2000) *The New Avengers: Feminism, Femininity and the Rape-Revenge Cycle*. Manchester and New York: Manchester University Press.

Richie, Donald (1999) *Tokyo: A View of the City*. London: Reaktion Books.

Rodley, Chris (ed.) (1992) *Cronenberg on Cronenberg*. London and Boston: Faber & Faber.

Romney, Jonathan (1992) '*Tetsuo II: Body Hammer*', *New Statesman*, 20 November, p. 33.

Rose, Margaret A. (1992) *The Post-Modern and the Post-Industrial*. Cambridge: Cambridge University Press.

Rose, Steve (2002) 'Nightmare Scenario: Hollywood Horror Is Creatively Dead, but Asian Films are Reviving the Genre', *Guardian*, Friday, 20 September, at http://www.guardian.co.uk/arts/fridayreview/story/0,12102,794834,00.html.

Ross, Karen and Virginia Nightingale (2003) *Media and Audiences: New Perspectives*. Maidenhead: Open University Press.

Saitô Tamaki (2000) *Sentô bishôjo no seishin bunseki* [*Fighting Beauties: A Psychoanalysis*], Tokyo: Ôta Shuppan.

Scarry, Elaine (1985) *The Body in Pain: The Making and Unmaking of the World*. New York and Oxford: Oxford University Press.

Sconce, Jeffrey (1995) ' "Trashing the Academy": Taste, Excess, and an Emerging Politics of Cinematic Style', *Screen*, 36:4, Winter, pp. 371–93.

Sharp, Jasper (2001a), 'Moju Review', *Midnight Eye: The Latest and Best in Japanese Cinema*, 20 March, at http://www.midnighteye.com/reviews/moju.shtml

Sharp, Jasper (2001b) 'Jigoku Review', *Midnight Eye: The Latest and Best in Japanese Cinema*, 25 June, at http://www.midnighteye.com/reviews/jigoku.shtml.

Sharp, Jasper (2002) 'Juon', *Midnighteye: The Latest and Best in Japanese Cinema*, 12:23, http://www.midnighteye.com/reviews/juon.shtml

Sharrett, Christopher (1993) 'The Horror Film in Neoconservative Culture', *Journal of Popular Film and Television*, 21:3, pp. 100–10.

Sharrett, Christopher (1999) 'Afterword: Sacrificial Violence and Postmodern Ideology', in Christopher Sharrett and Barry Keith Grant (eds), *Mythologies of Violence in Postmodern Media*. Detroit, MI: Wayne State University Press, pp. 413–34.

Shaviro, Steven (1993) *The Cinematic Body*. Minneapolis, MN and London: University of Minnesota Press.

Simpson, Philip L. (2000) *Psycho Paths: Tracking the Serial Killer through Contemporary American Film and Fiction*. Carbondale, IL: Southern Illinois University Press.

Skipp, John and Craig Spector (1989) 'On Going Too Far, or Flesh-Eating Fiction: New Hope for the Future', in John Skipp and Craig Spector (eds), *Book of the Dead*. New York: Bantam Books.

Springer, Claudia (1988) 'Antiwar Film as Spectacle: Contradictions of the Combat Sequence', *Genre*, 21, pp. 479–86.

Springer, Claudia (1996) *Electronic Eros: Bodies and Desire in the Postindustrial Age*. London: Athlone Press.

Stephens, Chuck (2002) 'High and Low Japanese Cinema Now: A User's Guide', *Film Comment*, January/February, pp. 35–6.

Stephens, Chuck (2003) 'What's in a Nami?: Takashi Ishii's Brief History of Women', *Pulp*, 4.09, http://www.pulp-mag.com/archives/4.09/reviews_film.shtml.

Stevens, John (1990) *Lust for Enlightenment: Buddhism and Sex*. Boston: Shambala Press.

Stokes, Lisa Odham and Michael Hoover (1999) *City on Fire: Hong Kong Cinema*. London: Verso.

Suzuki Koji [1991] (2003), *Ring*, trans. Robert B. Rohmer and Glynne Walley. New York: Vertical.

Takada Yûzô (1988–9) *3x3 Eyes*, vols 1–3, Tokyo: Kôdansha; translated as *3x3 Eyes*. Milwaukie, OR: Dark Horse Comics, 2001–3.

Tateishi Ramie (2003) 'The Contemporary Japanese Horror Film Series: *Ring* and *Eko Eko Azarak*', in Steven Jay Schneider (ed.), *Fear Without Frontiers: Horror Cinema Across the Globe*. Guildford: FAB Press, pp. 295–304.

Tatsumi Takayumi (2000) 'Generations and Controversies: An Overview of Japanese Science Fiction', *Science Fiction Studies*, 80, 27:1 (March), pp. 105–14.

Tatsumi Takayuki (2002) 'The Japanoid Manifesto: Toward a New Poetics of Invisible Culture', *Review of Contemporary Fiction*, XXII.2, Summer, pp. 12–28.

Thacker, Eugene (2002) 'Biohorror/Biotech', *Paradoxa: Studies in World Literary Genres*, 17, pp. 109–29.

Thornton, Sarah (1995) *Club Cultures*. Cambridge: Polity Press.

Tombs, Pete (2000) 'Oh, Noh . . . Japan Has the Horrors Again', *Guardian Unlimited*, 18 August, film.guardian.co.uk/features/featurepages/0,4120,356916,00.html.

Tookey, Christopher (1991) '*Tetsuo II: Body Hammer*', *Sunday Telegraph*, 18 September, p. 44.

Tudor, Andrew [1997] (2002) 'Why Horror?', in Mark Jancovich (ed.), *Horror: The Film Reader*. London and New York: Routledge, pp. 33–55.

Turner, Bryan (1992) *Regulating Bodies: Essays in Medical Sociology*. London: Routledge.

Weisser, Thomas and Yuko Mihara Weisser (1998a), 'The Violent Pink Films of Yasuharu Hasebe', *Asian Cult Cinema*, 20 (June), pp. 32–6, 38.

Weisser, Thomas and Yuko Mihara Weisser (1998b), *Japanese Cinema: The Essential Handbook*. Miami, FL: Vital Books Inc.

Weisser, Thomas and Yuko Mihara Weisser (1998c), *Japanese Cinema Encyclopedia: Horror, Fantasy, Science Fiction*. Miami, FL: Vital Books.

white pongo (2000) 'Essential Viewing' posted on the Internet Movie Database (User Comments), 3 October, http://us.imdb.com/Title?0217679#comment.

Willemen, Paul (1994) *Looks and Frictions: Essays in Cultural Studies and Film Theory*. Bloomington, IN and London: Indiana University Press and British Film Institute.

Wolfe Murray, Angus (1991) '*Tetsuo II: Body Hammer*', *The Scotsman*, 21 September, p. 22.

Wood, Robin (1998) *Sexual Politics and Narrative Film: Hollywood and Beyond*. New York: Columbia University Press.

Wu, Harmony (2002) 'Tracking the Horrific', *Spectator: The University of Southern California Journal of Film and Television Criticism*, 22:2, Fall, pp. 1–11.

Wu, Harmony (2003) 'Trading in Horror, Cult and Matricide: Peter Jackson's Phenomenal Bad Taste and New Zealand Fantasies of Inter/National Cinematic Success', in Mark Jancovich, Antonio Lázaro Reboll, Julian Stringer and Andy Willis (eds), *Defining Cult Movies: The Cultural Politics of Oppositional Taste*. Manchester: Manchester University Press, pp. 84–108.

Zweekink, Amanda and Sarah N. Gatson (2002) 'www.buffy.com: Cliques, Boundaries and Hierarchies in an Internet Community', in Rhonda V. Wilcox and David Lavery (eds), *Fighting the Forces: What's at Stake in Buffy the Vampire Slayer*. New York and Oxford: Rowman and Littlefield, pp. 239–49.

INDEX